Praise for
liding in the Bathroom

"Introverts will love this practical and moving guide to building a career, network, and life you love." —Susan Cain, author of *Quiet*

"Morra Aarons-Mele has written a great guide for anyone who's feeling the anxiety of introversion and ready to find a way to be true to yourself and feel successful and connected at the same time." —KJ Dell'Antonia, *New York Times* Well Family columnist

"It took me twenty years to understand that I could focus on my strengths as a leader and skip the schmoozing. If you read Morra's book, you won't have to learn the hard way." —Arvind Rajan, former VP international, LinkedIn; cofounder and CEO, Cricket Health

"In this insightful and enjoyable book, Morra Aarons-Mele offers useful guidelines for creating a schedule and work life that you can control, allowing your ambition to shine while taking the space you need." —Leslie Perlow, Konosuke Matsushita Professor of Leadership at Harvard Business School

"Ambitious introverts finally have a career coach! Morra Aarons-Mele knows from personal experience that we shy people have burning desires to build businesses, brands, and careers, too. Her expert playbook shows how to leverage every opportunity, from social media to closing sales to business strategy—including the dreaded networking—without sugarcoating some of the trade-offs we need to make to succeed." —Lisa Stone, cofounder and CEO emeritus, BlogHer Inc.

"*Hiding in the Bathroom* is the book we have been waiting for! It pushes beyond current business messages of leaning in or being brave to reveal that there is no one-size-fits-all—that each of us needs to fashion our own holistic definition of success that includes our work, our personal passions, and our family lives!"
—Ellen Galinsky, president and cofounder of Families and Work Institute and author of *Mind in the Making*

"[A] riveting look at redefining personal approaches to work. . . . Bolstered with helpful tools including quizzes and worksheets. . . . The author's attention-grabbing headlines and subheads . . . keep the pace quick, while her willingness to share illustrative personal experiences, both good and bad, adds vivid color to the strategies she shares." —*Publishers Weekly*

"If your inner-Tracy Flick is constantly at odds with your inner-Batman, Morra Aarons-Mele has a book for you. The recently released *Hiding in the Bathroom* is a guide for maximizing your impact on a public that, if you're honest, you'd rather avoid."
—*Chicago Tribune*

HIDING IN THE BATHROOM

HIDING
IN THE
BATHROOM

How to Get Out There
When You'd Rather Stay Home

Morra Aarons-Mele

DEY ST.
An Imprint of WILLIAM MORROW

"Are You an Introvert?" on page 9 courtesy of QuietRev.com.

Work+Life Fit is trademarked property of FlexStrategy Group/ Work+Life Fit Inc. and used with permission.

"Social Anxiety versus Introversion" in Chapter 1 courtesy of Dr. Ellen Hendriksen.

"Collaborative Negotiation Prep Worksheet" in Chapter 12 reprinted with permission from Tanya Tarr.

"Own Your Expertise" exercise from the Op Ed project reprinted with permission from Katie Orenstein.

HarperCollins books may be purchased for educational, business, or sales promotional use. For information, please e-mail the Special Markets Department at SPsales@harpercollins.com.

A hardcover edition of this book was published in 2017 by Dey Street Books, an imprint of William Morrow.

FIRST DEY STREET BOOKS PAPERBACK EDITION PUBLISHED 2018.

Designed by Paula Russell Szafranski
Title page background by phokin/Shutterstock, Inc.

Library of Congress Cataloging-in-Publication Data has been applied for.

ISBN 978-0-06-266609-3

18 19 20 21 22 LSC 10 9 8 7 6 5 4 3 2 1

To my husband Nicco Mele,
who I love so deeply and learn from every day.

And to Rachel Sklar and Glynnis MacNicol of TheLi.st,
two women who lead fearlessly and give generously.

And finally to my mom, Pamela Aarons,
who taught me how to be strong.

CONTENTS

HIDING IN THE BATHROOM

INTRODUCTION

N etwork your way to the top."
    "Always say yes."
    "Never eat lunch alone."
"Get out there!"

If you're an overachiever like me, you've definitely heard this advice. And, if you're ambitious, you also probably believe that to be successful, you have to be out there 24/7, tirelessly pressing the flesh, doing deals, tweeting, and keynoting conferences. That there's a successful "type"—the intense, sleepless mover and shaker, the person who "leans in" and musters endless amounts of grit. And if you don't fit that type, well, you're out of luck.

I call bullshit.

Much of what we think we must do to succeed is unnecessary and even counterproductive. I've interviewed over one hundred fifty successful entrepreneurs and executives, and I can tell you that most of them aren't the always-on, outgoing superstars we would assume. One new media CEO whose viral videos have garnered over a hundred million views told me that she experiences major anxiety being in a room where she doesn't know anyone. "I go straight into awkward middle schooler mode," she confessed. The founder of a biotech firm who just received Series A financing confessed that she hides in the bathroom at conferences, "usually because I am crying." A former Wall Street banker who now runs a successful tech start-up has to "take beta-blockers for public speaking."

And then there's me. I'm a hermit by nature, an extreme introvert, more comfortable at home, with my kids, my cats, and my kitchen than out there selling to a room. I'll admit it: facilitating meetings and giving speeches intimidate and exhaust me. When I fly to meet a potential client or to give a talk, I take so much anxiety-fighting Xanax that I'm barely conscious. I manage my social media feeds very tightly, doing just enough to keep me in the game. And yet I own and run a successful business in which I am the primary sales driver.

"Hiding in the bathroom" has become my shorthand for hacking and faking my way to appearing like a typical successful business-person. Given my natural inclinations, I would hide almost all the time. I would rarely choose to leave my house. But as extensive as my online network is, I could not sustain a business that way. So I've learned to get out there, building in strategies and tricks that allay my anxieties and introversion while I'm at a professional gathering or client meeting, then creating home time to recharge, be on my own, and do the work.

I used to beat myself up about needing to hide in the bathroom. I would walk into a huge crowd, panic at the number of strangers, and head immediately for the ladies'. But over time I've learned that I often need a moment to reset during a busy workday. Now I know it's okay to take a moment to breathe. Then I put on some lipstick, look in the mirror, and tell myself, *You can do it. Get out there.*

Becoming My Own Kind of Entrepreneur

When I was a kid, I told everyone, "I want to be a media mogul." I had a photo of famed Paramount boss Sherry Lansing on my bedroom wall. I wrote my tenth-grade economics paper on the inside story of Barry Diller's bid to own Universal Studios. And, because I had the good fortune of coming of age during the Clinton years, when jobs were plentiful for precocious twentysomethings, I was well on my way. After graduating from college, I worked a series of high-profile jobs in the marketing world and was even recognized in a prominent national "top 30 under 30" list.

There was one problem: secretly (or perhaps not so secretly), I was miserable. I tried on many different personas, and adopted countless ad hoc coping mechanisms, but nothing helped. I kept torpedoing my success at every turn. I drank too much at office happy hours and acted inappropriately. My weight constantly went up and down as I bounced between bingeing and barely eating at all. I was anxious almost every day, and had frequent panic attacks. Quite often, I was so depressed that I called in sick to work and hid in bed all day.

At my last job, I was asked to start a department from scratch, and I was too prideful, anxious, and shortsighted to secure allies. Eventually the New York office tried to get me fired. Did this girl stand up and fight like a plucky heroine in a novel? No, she did not. She cried in the bathroom and started working from home as often as she could.

But, when she eventually quit and started freelancing, she became an accidental entrepreneur who focuses more on making time for life than making millions.

I run a business called Women Online. We are a social-impact marketing agency with the sole mission of creating campaigns that mobilize women for social good. I like to say we are small but mighty: even though we have fewer than ten people—and are virtual at that!—we help the largest organizations in the world with digital strategy. For example, we helped President Obama's campaign reach mom bloggers and get them to the polls, and we created digital tools that inspired American families to learn about and support the work of Malala Yousafzai and the United Nations, both on a mission to educate girls worldwide.

Over the last decade, I've built a life that allows me to earn enough money and find just enough recognition without driving myself crazy and sacrificing my homebody self. I learned to play to my strengths and nourish my introversion, focusing less on the long-term outcome of "success" and more on the everyday. Today, thanks to the deliberate way I've organized my business, I can literally be at the UN one day and home with the boys digging in the dirt the next. On the days I'm at a client's office, pitching new business or giving a speech, you'll probably find me in the ladies' in between sessions. Every single day I build in lots of breaks and alone time for myself, even if it's just five minutes in a quiet room. Of course, this best-of-both-worlds lifestyle comes at a cost. It has meant sacrifices, less success than some peers, and a slower path. But it's my version of success, and I love it.

The "aha" moment came when I learned to redefine my vision of success. The old vision was media mogul. My new vision was less focused on some far-off notion of success attained. I traded "someday" for "today." For me, it's the choice to be a hermit entrepreneur: a mostly tongue-in-cheek term I use to describe my choice to mostly work at home in my yoga pants.

What if you became the kind of success you wanted to be? What if you could enjoy the everyday of your work life? What if you stopped all that networking? What if you distilled your business development to the bare minimum, and still managed to grow your business or your income? What if instead of getting out there, you could simply stay in?

The good news is that you can learn and practice the skills you need to achieve a version of success that's right for you, and make enough money. And I'll give you strategies and concrete career-development and management tools to get there.

These strategies begin with setting a vision and developing realistic goals that satisfy all of your needs, even if it means accepting a more modest career or slower business growth trajectory. Then, manage around your goals in ways that allow for an enjoyable, "hermit" lifestyle. To maximize your impact with the least amount of face time, you carve out a strong professional niche and digital footprint for yourself. If you own a small business or work freelance, you price your offerings slightly above market rate. You determine the right client, project mix, or type of work that allows you the time you need for yourself. No matter where you work, you create a long-term, professional "franchise" for yourself that assures you of future jobs, freelance gigs, and business opportunities as well as even more free time in the future. You engage in high-impact, smart networking and only attend a few strategically selected conferences. You track your work flow and scope your work more carefully so as to protect your time for family, friends, and self. And finally, you recalibrate expectations with bosses, spouses, family members, and others.

In this book, we're going to talk a lot about emotions, particularly anxiety. As a business owner and entrepreneur with serious mental health challenges, I've often found myself hiding out in the bathroom. We've all been there, but few of us actually talk about it.

But part and parcel of being a successful introvert is allowing those emotions to be an opportunity to gain knowledge, and to make them work for you, instead of driving your work. As my friend Dr. Kim Leary, associate professor at Harvard Medical School says, "Think about what you give up if you aren't attuned to your emotions." Life would indeed be dull and gray, and you can use that anxiety to help you in your career, not harm it.

Now that I've realized my anxiety is part of who I am, and that, rather than fight it all the time, I embrace what it gives me, like excellent people skills, empathy, and drive. I like to think my anxiety and I are business partners, frequently negotiating, sometimes arguing, but often creating great work. Later on, we'll examine what I call the "gift of anxiety"—the secret skills anxiety gives us in our work lives—and we'll detail specific strategies to manage it when it gets unruly.

Ultimately, hiding in the bathroom means relentlessly attending to the care and feeding of your *whole* being. It means vigorously reinforcing your personal boundaries, even when others pressure you to grow faster or make more money. You will not garner accolades for growing your career or business slowly, or for enjoying your life. You won't be featured in magazines, and you probably won't keynote conferences. Even worse, everyone in your life, from your accountant to your graphic designer to maybe even your spouse, will question your strategy. It's not sexy to develop slowly. But hermit professionals know the truth: it's better. Committed to what will make them happy over the long term, they do what it takes to stay home and make each day rich, meaningful, and fulfilling.

All this might sound unrealistic, but in fact the successful professionals I've interviewed for this book and for my *Forbes* podcast all share one thing in common: they have managed to integrate work with personal passion and interest. Some of them, like me, are extreme introverts—they have social anxiety and hate to fly. These men and women don't follow the traditional rules. They have made their own rules and honed their skills accordingly. You can, too.

Leaning in is great, but not everyone can lean in all the time. It makes us too tired. It's also not that fun. More fun is nerding out on your own for hours, just thinking and doing—engaging in what investor Paul Graham terms "rich, solitary, germinative time." It might be picking your kids up from school every day or taking care of your aging parents. It might be tinkering in your garden or cultivating other hobbies. The dirty little secret of success is that you can grow your business, build your career, and do the work you love while still making room for outside interests. You can hang out at home more and keep travel, networking, and extracurriculars to a minimum. I hope *Hiding in the Bathroom* will show you how.

ARE YOU AN INTROVERT?

Susan Cain's excellent book *Quiet* is the bible for the modern introvert. If you haven't read it, I really recommend it. (There's also the excellent sister website, QuietRev.com.) Here are a list of traits common to introverts to help you discover if you're one, too. (Adapted with thanks from *Quiet,* and amended to my own research.)

I do my best work in a quiet environment.

Too much exposure to noise or light leaves me feeling drained, spacey, or headachy. (Fluorescents!)

Being out and about in a social or work setting leaves me feeling drained, even if I have a great time.

In large social gatherings, I need to take frequent breaks to be by myself or with a trusted friend.

Large crowds drain me.

I recharge and draw energy through alone time.

I like to think before I speak, and I like to feel prepared before I speak.

I have an active interior monologue, and I tend to ruminate a lot on events and decisions.

People would describe me as quiet. (Note: No one would describe me as quiet. In fact, I'm extremely talkative, sometimes loud, and I love public speaking. I'm still an introvert and you can be, too.)

I need a lot of alone time.

Working in an open-plan office is very draining, and I seek quiet spaces to hide out.

I work better at home.

(Courtesy QuietRev.com)

1

My Life as an Unhappy Overachiever

The idea for this book began when I gave a speech at my alma mater, Brown University. I was nervous before the speech (as was the Brown Alumni Relations staff!) because I planned to get raw. In front of a room of two hundred successful women, I was going to share the story of how I became happy at work only after I realized that the idea of who I wanted to be was making me anxious, destructive, and depressed.

I was nervous but also elated as I approached the podium. As I began to command the large hall I'd walked by many times as an anxious, and often sad, undergraduate, I felt free. "If you knew me at Brown, I don't think you'd have expected I'd be keynoting the dinner," I opened.

"I have the dubious distinction," I continued, diving in, "of being an ambitious risk taker who also struggles with anxiety and depression. This has forced me to learn some very helpful coping mechanisms, and I want to share some today with you."

But first, I told them, there were the panic attacks. That time sophomore year I couldn't get out of bed for a week. Hiding in my dorm room, and then, when I graduated, in my apartments. How

I sought geographical cures, moving to different cities, like London, and even farther-away continents, like Africa. How I did a fair amount of drugs—the worst of which, ironically, were by prescription. (Okay, I didn't mention that in the speech.)

I talked about how, as a young woman, I wanted so badly to be liked, and to do everything right. I felt it was expected of me. I had been the kid who cried at sleepaway camp and wouldn't let my mother and sister leave my first night at college. I only wanted home, and comfort. Instead I dealt with its absence like many young people do: through eating, drinking, and hookups.

I told them how, because I was very ambitious and driven, I went for every big job and opportunity I could—how I ran marketing for Europe's largest online travel company when I was twenty-five. How I kept getting promoted, and I kept being miserable. The work was easy, but the office politics, the hours, the pace, networking, and rules of getting ahead rubbed up against my very temperament. I was living out someone else's climb up the ladder, and I was fighting a losing battle.

I had quit nine jobs, I wasn't even thirty, and I cried in the bathroom almost every day.

I talked about the day I realized that who I was and what I was doing every day were completely mismatched.

It was during my final corporate job, when, under the ubiquitous fluorescent lights, I realized I was *allergic* to them. They give me migraines. And as long as I had to show up and sit under those lights for ten-plus hours a day simply because I was expected to, I could never be happy.

"I see now," I told the audience, "that I was caught in a cycle of achievement, of working hard for someone else's dreams or expectations, and not my own." It was only when I accepted that I needed a quieter life, needed to reframe success on my own terms, and figure out the tool kit I needed to get there, that I could find joy at work. Becoming "less successful" set me free.

Not exactly your typical go-get-'em women's leadership speech. I looked around the room and was terrified. Would the under-grads and alumnae think I was a nutjob? I had worked so hard on the speech, and it was the first real keynote I had delivered. (It's still one of the few.)

The speech got a standing ovation, and I felt like Oprah.

Many of the women in the room came up to me. Some were cry-ing. Thank you, they said. We're so anxious all the time, and no one tells us the truth.

I'll never forget one young woman, a senior who was an econom-ics major. She said to me: "I'm just so tired of trying to be this per-fect person." Like me, and many in the audience, she was on both antidepressants and antianxiety medication.

I felt her pain. Growing up, I was sent to the best private schools, and it never occurred to me to do anything less than achieve. Those of us fortunate enough to be raised with expectations of academic or financial success learn that when we achieve, we garner praise and positive attention—even if we're faking our own enjoyment. Through childhood, adolescence, and into adulthood, we keep achieving, craving the external validation that comes when we get all As or are chosen to captain the team. I was, and am, extremely ambitious. But the more we achieve in order to win the approval of others, the further we get from our own goals—and happiness.

In the twenty-two years since I entered college, it has only gotten worse. The achievement pressure starts at birth, and snowballs from there. When a good friend, my commiserator in the high-stakes process of applying to private kindergarten in Los Angeles, visited her alma mater, the admissions director told her, "You wouldn't rec-ognize the program. It's much more challenging than it was when you were here."

For similar reasons, even to this day, I don't like to visit college campuses—and my husband is a professor! I can feel the echoes of anxiety and profound loneliness so strongly. And it's not only me. A recent Duke study found that women who graduated in the 1970s were much happier than those graduating now, and had far more self-confidence. The report concluded that the women who graduated in the seventies cared less about what people thought about them, and were able to take risks—such as pursuing a nontraditional career or starting their own business. In fact, women seem to be increasingly less happy, even as they achieve more professionally.

Ambitious and privileged young people on the path to college are raised with a narrative of achievement—a surround-sound, multifaceted version—that no generation has experienced before. Do the most extracurriculars. Have the perfect internship. Get a great first job. Build your personal brand. Run that marathon. Eat organic. Get perfectly hairless and smooth. Fuck perfectly. Navigate dating. Enter your thirties, find a partner, conceive, and give birth (naturally, of course). Make your pregnant body the perfect temple for your perfect newborn, who will become a precociously perfect toddler. With the addition of social media, you're supposed to share it all, too—as you suffer the FOMO of watching everyone else seemingly sail through life.

I've found that it is especially hard to achieve in a traditional career ladder scenario if you are an introvert, and if you need more control over your space, pace, and place of work than others. Let me be clear: this has nothing to do with laziness, or lack of ambition. Your need for a different kind of workday has nothing to do with the level of effort you will put in, or the drive you possess. That's ingrained in who you are just as much as your need for quiet or alone time. When you work differently, it may even mean you work harder than someone who's spending plenty of time at the office surfing Gilt.com. I may be a hermit who rarely eats lunch with anyone, but ask anyone who knows me and they will agree: I work hard and I am driven as hell. (They don't know I'm usually working in bed.)

THE OVERACHIEVER INDEX

Are you addicted to achievement? No score needed here; you know it when you see it.

You regularly get nine hours of sleep, and you feel guilty.

You're really sick. But no one needs to know. (Cough.)

You only got 720 on your GMAT.

You lost five pounds. Time for the next five.

You've actually made up boyfriends for your parents. They'd worry if you were single.

Work isn't enough: you need to join a board or volunteer or start a nonprofit.

You hired a designer for your three-year-old's preschool project.

You don't let anyone over unless the house is perfectly clean.

Nothing store-bought will tarnish your Thanksgiving table.

After your (99 percent glowing) performance review, you can't stop thinking about the one piece of negative feedback you got from your boss.

Reading about your former college roommate's new start-up totally ruins your day, but you obsessively search Google for more news.

THE TWIN PLAGUES:
FOMO AND ACHIEVEMENT PORN

You're sitting in your home office, scanning Facebook. Friends and colleagues are giving TED Talks, being featured in interviews, and posting pictures of fabulous events. You're not even dressed. Another day, another professional conference, keynote, or viral event that's not yours. Why aren't you out there? What's wrong with you?

FOMO is the curse of our social media moment. According to Wikipedia[1] (and who better to define the digital age?) it's a "pervasive apprehension that others might be having rewarding experiences from which one is absent." (As Mindy Kaling succinctly puts it, "Why is everyone hanging out without me?") You always know what colleagues and competitors are up to—as long as it's good.

When I launched my podcast series for *Forbes,* I obsessively tracked how many "likes" other hosts got on their social media. At least once a week I lie on my bed in the dead silence of my workday and scroll through Twitter, just to feel bad about my choice to be a hermit entrepreneur. And even though I'm a middle-aged married lady who's off the dating market, social media FOMO still causes me anxiety, except now it's about my feed's professional accomplishments and political activism ("Such an honor to receive the alumni achievement award!"); amazing exotic vacations with kids who don't seem to whine or bitch on the plane; or marathons run.

I don't know any human being, introverted, extroverted, or in-between, who doesn't fall prey to FOMO on a regular basis. It's the most human thing in the world to compare oneself to others. Not to sound like a thirteen-year-old, but it sucks, no matter what kind of personality you have.

If I'm an Introvert, Why Do I Feel FOMO?

But wait a minute: Didn't you make a choice to be in your home office and not out there socializing? You hate the idea of giving a TED Talk! So why do you feel so left out?

If you're an anxious introvert, in conflict over where you belong in the rat race, an Instagram picture can turn into a dagger. *If only I were different,* you might think, *I, too, would be invited to that party. I'd be getting that award. Instead I'm hiding.*

But remember—actually, this feeling isn't about you at all. It's *the whole point* of social media. The creators of Instagram, Twitter, Facebook, and other FOMO-inducing sites specifically developed a product that would be addictive because it preys on our most human emotions.[2] When you feel different and lesser than the perfect vignettes filling your feed, social media is cruel indeed—and it makes you want to come back for more.

Caterina Fake, who cofounded the groundbreaking Flickr *and* coined the term *FOMO* (she is my hero), explains how social software both "creates and cures FOMO. If you didn't know that party was going on, you'd be home contentedly reading your latest *New Yorker.* But since you do, you hungrily watch each new tweet. It gives you a sense that you're missing out, even when you aren't." Your FOMO isn't about your failure. It's actually the marketing strategy of Instagram, Facebook, Snapchat, and Twitter.

And I'm not innocent. When I have something fabulous to share, what do I do? Show off—the speaking gig, a VIP invite, a great photo where I look awesome, or my adorable baby. I understand the rush of endorphins a really well-received social media post brings. It's almost more fun than the event itself.

But, while posting gourmet meals or a fun night out is one thing, tech writer Brian Solis reminds us that all of us who use social networks and apps channel the "'accidental narcissist'" in us. We act out roles, ignoring our own enjoyment.

I call this syndrome "achievement porn." I know using the term *porn* is controversial, and yet I can think of no other word that quite describes what I'm talking about: airbrushed, glossy images of successful people in made-for-coveting environments. Social media like blogs or Instagram allows fledgling achievers to craft powerful narratives about their potential, and rise. (My least favorite? The "mompreneur" who just happens to whip up a million-dollar business while messing around in the kitchen.) By consuming ever-higher levels of broadcast, digital, and social media, we've come to believe the impossible. And we watch it all unfold, feeling jealous it's not ours.

No one likes to feel jealous—and in a world in which social media has made subtle showing off the default, we now have an opportunity to feel jealous several times a day. In tweets and awards and magazine spreads, achievement is fetishized, and logging onto Facebook can lead to a paralyzing wave of FOMO. By the time you've reached the workplace, chances are you've internalized it so deeply you don't even question it. You're so busy performing so others can validate you, you forget to notice if you're working toward your own goals.

Still, FOMO is a clever tool, and every businessperson cultivates it. In his brilliant podcast series *StartUp*, Alex Blumberg notes that FOMO drives Silicon Valley investing; if a potential investor doesn't feel a sense of FOMO when learning of a new investment opportunity, then the rich guy will find another idea to throw his money at. The object that inspires FOMO is imbued with an aura of success.

Like FOMO, achievement can be an illusion and publicity doesn't pay the bills (nor do TED Talks). Take Theranos founder Elizabeth Holmes. She built a company that promised to simplify blood tests, and she raised at least $750 million in backing. We all wanted to believe the incredible story of the tenacious, glamorous blonde who disrupted an industry and became a billionaire. Too bad it wasn't true.

Bea Arthur's Story

It's crucial to remember that thousands of follows on an Instagram feed or a *Fast Company* feature isn't money in your bank account. Bea Arthur learned that in Silicon Valley, when solid revenue, TV appearances, accolades, and tons of PR still didn't pay the bills for her second start-up, the online therapy company In Your Corner.

The child of entrepreneur immigrants from Ghana, Bea Arthur was brave and confident, and by all appearances, a Silicon Valley success story: the first African American woman invited to Y Combinator, the famous Silicon Valley start-up incubator. She had a TEDx Talk in her pocket, multiple TV appearances, and glowing press. And, unlike most start-ups, her company actually earned money.

But, in real life, as she scaled, her start-up was failing, and she was living on loans. "I'd have to get up and smile and do these talks and go on TV," Bea says, "and it was raining inside my soul."

Here's where the irony gets even deeper: the more Silicon Valley courted her, providing venture capital and media attention, the more she abandoned her original mission and overspent. "I fell for all of the start-up scene's charms," she says. "I loved how they knew the best apps to get analytics, and the best places to get burritos."

She also wanted to look like them: swanky, even when it didn't make sense for the kind of company she was running. "When I got back to New York, I got a super-nice, superexpensive office, even though my team was small and mostly remote, and I worked from home a lot," she says.

As Bea told *Forbes,* she drank the "Start-up Kool-Aid."

Ironically, as her business was failing, her personal visibility hit new heights: no one could imagine a Y Combinator pick failing; after all, Y Combinator had discovered Airbnb and Dropbox. In private, she took out a disastrous loan, stopped paying herself, and let go of her favorite employees. But in public, she put on a brave face, trying to raise more money for the company, and spending money to keep up appearances.

People want to believe the hype, because, she says, "We're in the age of crushing it."

The good news: the pain of closing reconnected Bea to her roots as a therapist, and her company's original mission, which had been to make sure people "don't have to suffer alone." Now Bea is focused on what the future of therapy will be and is founding a think tank to discover just that. Her new nonprofit, The Difference, will be devoted to innovations in mental health research and resources, and based on the belief that the right talk at the right time can make all The Difference.

CONNECTING VERSUS "CURATION"

Dadvertising and Public Parenting

At a low point in our marriage, I accused my husband of being a dad "only for Facebook" because he frequently posted only the cutest images and stories. His social feed portrayed a superdad, and only I knew the truth: at the time, Nicco was actually spending very little time with our kids. But his social media narrative made it seem otherwise. He knew that men who are cute daddies are rewarded by society, and he knew how to play the game. In his own way, he created a narrative of achievement porn that was irresistible: a successful man with a big book coming out, with adorable children he doted on. If I was his publicist, I'd give him an A-plus.

That's right: on social media, people are often faking it. And, when you fake it, suddenly you're all about reaching someone else's goals instead of working toward achieving your own.

Parenting on the Internet didn't start with performing. In 2005, at the first BlogHer conference, blogger Alice Bradley stood up and declared, "Mommy blogging is a radical act." At the time she was right. The very act of giving voice publicly to the everyday struggles of parents was incredibly brave, not least because writing about parenthood—especially motherhood—had always been dismissed. Now social media was giving moms and dads a chance to connect and be heard.

But along the way, something nefarious happened. As online parenting culture evolved, it became less about community and more about curation. Instead of sharing real stories about our lives, we began to curate them in adorable images and anecdotes. Instead of turning to each other for information, support, and expertise, we started to judge and compare. We had been using the Internet to share stressful moments during what can be a lonely, isolating experience. Now public parenting was becoming a competitive sport.

And, as social media emerged as a platform where people could build influence and social currency, parents became strategic about what they posted. Instagrams emphasize the aesthetic, using filters, airbrushing, and retouching, and personal family photo shoots are par for the course. People edit their 140 Twitter characters like each is a novel. And Facebook posts highlight only the best in our lives— down to awesome parenting bloopers that become book deals.

When social media makes us our own personal PR firms, it's only natural that we begin to worry we don't measure up. It also means that the online world becomes less a place for community and more a world of personal advertisements.

For working mothers, online community is a double-edged sword. For me, the mere act of posting a snippet of work-life conflict on Facebook can feel so healing. But the more we share, the more we create a public narrative of what life *should* look like for a working parent—not what it actually *does* look like. My mother frequently served up Cheerios for dinner when I was growing up. Now there are endless blog posts and Instagrams and Pinterest pages featuring perfectly composed organic meals for the perfect working mom to feed her kids. Seeing into the exquisite bento box lunches of the world is a pretty pressure-filled way to spend your morning.

In addition, there's a tremendous taboo about talking about child-care help. When she was doing press for *Lean In,* Facebook COO and wonder woman Sheryl Sandberg barred any reporter from commenting about her nannies (emphasis on the plural). But, as Julia LeStage, a former TV producer who commissioned the very first *Big Brother* and then sold the world's first crowdsourced weather app, says, "If you're working, someone else is taking care of the children." They're not hiding under the table in the conference room! That parents are expected to hide the help they get while humblebragging their adorable kids at the same time, makes it even worse.

Posting parenting now starts as early as conception. (I'm looking at you, "baby bump" watchers and Facebook Gender Reveal All-Stars.) Writer Chimamanda Ngozi Adichie, who quietly had a baby without announcing she was even pregnant, explained why in a recent interview on Jezebel: "I just feel like we live in an age when women are supposed to perform pregnancy."[3]

And that's too bad. Rather than being an opportunity for more achievement posting, the reality of a baby at home can just as easily make the expectations of the rest of our world matter so much less.

We guilty hermits can take a breath and stop searching for the perfect job to make us happy, stop going out every night, stop performing for an external audience. Which is great practice for the hermit at work. Whether it's about parenting, success, or any other kind of achievement, FOMO distracts us from what we really want and need.

The "Belfie" Trap

In 2001, when I was marketing manager at iVillage.co.uk, the Shape Up Challenge was the cutting edge of community weight loss. On message boards, women came together in a six-week program to lose weight and get fit. Every day participants checked in to cheer each other on. I loved the pure support the women showed for each other.

Now my sensible middle-aged friends are more likely to post pictures of their run rather than belfies (look it up). You know the post: "Nancy ran six miles and felt great." Good for Nancy. Except, now I feel a subtle sense of competition. Nancy ran six miles, and I'm sitting here surfing Facebook like a lump, reading about it. I feel FOMO.

Many of the young women I spoke to at my Brown lecture, and at many other talks thereafter, talked about body pressure. When I was in college, my (perfect . . . really, she was my idol) friend Jenny once said to me, "I think I'm addicted to running. It makes me feel in control." Now we can post our fitness and weight-loss milestones online and get even more validation of our achievement. Any overachiever knows that this external validation intensifies the feeling of being in control, and we want more of it. After all, what feels better than being told how great you look, or how hard you must work out?

Body image is one of the most powerful ways we internalize achievement porn. Now amplified by the media, poor body image affects everything from self-esteem to academic performance.[4] But when it comes to the impact of social media, we are living out an experiment in real time. Women (and men) who share their bodies online take two forms: empowered and disturbing. On the one hand, social media is a medium to fight back against fat-shaming and to challenge stereotypical portraits of beauty, including lack of diversity. Think about videos that reveal Photoshop tricks or that have become social media movements to resist these beauty stereotypes. Conversely, on any given day, I'm exposed (and I'm sure I'm not alone) to up to a hundred images of my social-network friends flaunting their hard work on those hot bods. Do I cheer them on? Feel jealous? Or both? I find myself having to take a step back, and consider how all the bodies online make me feel about my own.

The support of online community when you achieve that great body, or you run every day, can feel wonderful. But it can also be a Band-Aid to cover a deeper sense of unease—both for the person doing the posting and the person reading it. That's why I've followed the latest iteration, hashtag-driven community "challenges" and social media stars' diet programs, with great interest.

Among the latter, Kayla Itsines is—no pun intended—perhaps the biggest. Her #BBG, or Bikini Body Guide, brings over three million people united by a hashtag and a regimen to get—yes—beach-body ready. Participants regularly thank Kayla for inspiring them to find their best selves (and their hidden six-packs), and the beautiful-by-any-standard Kayla posts inspiring Instagrams like "I'm not beautiful like you. I'm beautiful like me."

How Much Do You Need Validation?

How much do you know about your peers?

a) I have Google alerts set up for all of them.

b) I try to scope out the competition, but I have confidence in my own projects, too.

c) You can't win the race if you're always looking at the other lane. My day is spent on my own product.

How often do you compare yourself to someone else?

a) Do they have five kids and fifty employees? Were they on the radio yesterday? Did they lose the baby weight in three months? I'm always comparing myself to other people.

b) I do feel bad when I see how much other people get done, but I try not to get bogged down in it.

c) I definitely have career idols I try to live up to, but as for professional peers, I know we all go up and down.

When you get good professional news or feedback, is your first call to one of your parents?

a) Yes. I don't feel like an accomplishment is truly mine until someone related to me gives their stamp of approval.

b) I like to share things that make me happy and proud, because the people I share them with will be, too.

c) I'll include it in my holiday letter.

You realize you forgot a big presentation in your office, and your boss and clients are waiting in the conference room. You:

a) Apologize eighteen times and run to your office to get it. Afterwards, you apologize again. And again.

b) Apologize, book it to your stuff, then set up quickly. If all goes well, they'll remember the presentation, not your flub.

c) Who cares? You're there to show them your work. Nobody's perfect.

An e-mail from a new client lands in your in-box. You:

a) Are terrified. You're always afraid someone's going to yell at you.

b) Have no idea what it is, but flag it to make sure you get back to the client that day.

c) Are excited. You really have some good ideas on how to move forward.

You have what you think is a great proposal. Everyone hates it. You:

a) Are devastated. You've failed. Probably you shouldn't have this job. In fact, they're probably coming to fire you this minute.

b) Feel like a failure. But time has shown you that feedback can be very useful, and that it's usually not personal.

c) Still think it's a pretty good idea. Hopefully, you can sell it to someone else at some point.

You're about to meet your significant other's parents. In the past week, you:

a) Dieted, bought a new outfit, and quizzed your partner on his parents' likes and dislikes relentlessly.

b) Are kind of scared, but looking forward. But you Googled them, and got a haircut. You're not crazy.

c) Hope you don't have a big political argument at the table. But you're sure everyone will survive.

Your profits dropped by 50 percent this year. You:

a) Need to find an entirely different field.

b) Will assess what happened. You might need to get a new job, but maybe not.

c) Take a deep breath. That's what savings are for.

Someone asks you what you do at a party. You:

a) Always feel like you're explaining something you messed up.

b) Have a set answer. No one cares THAT much; it's just chitter-chatter.

c) Like to hear what other people do. You have to think about yourself ALL DAY.

You get your work back. It's been marked up with red ink. You:

a) Have failed again. They are coming to yell at you, tell you how much better everyone else is doing, that you are on Google too much, that your partner's parents think you should go on a diet, that the fact that you apologize so much means even you know you should be fired, and that you're fired.

b) Er . . . okay. Did you do something wrong? Or did she just really want something else?

c) Try to put a positive spin on it. After all, edits from someone else actually mean less work for you!

You ran a 5K.

a) Your friends ran a 10K. You'll start training tomorrow.

b) You ran a 5K! And now . . . brunch!

c) You will never understand this whole 5K thing.

Mostly a's

Whoa! You need to take a step back. Not only are you working overtime to please other people, you're terrified what will happen if you don't. News flash: Sometimes you'll make other people unhappy (even as I write this I know I can't take my own advice here). Sometimes you'll fail. But if you don't take that risk, and take it on your own terms, you'll spend your whole life apologizing for decisions you didn't even believe in.

See Chapter 5 for some tools on determining the work you want to do—and learning how to cope with people who disagree. (And they will.) And delete those Google alerts.

Mostly b's

You're the middle child in the validation family—you're capable of suddenly needing the world to love you, but you're pretty sure that's not realistic. (Most of the time.) What's great is that you're open to learning from what the world dishes out. But, because you're open to others' opinions, your task is to always take them for what they are: other people's opinions. That means needing to remind yourself that no one's perfect, but other people can have useful things to say. Life is a collaboration. That sometimes makes you want to hide in the bathroom.

Mostly c's

I'd say you should learn to take other people's opinions to heart, but not only would you ignore me—maybe you don't need to. There will always be people who believe in themselves so thoroughly that they can devote themselves entirely to their own vision. If you become a total despot, that's a problem. But if you can take the hard knocks when no one agrees and go forward anyway, kudos to you.

Browsing the #BBG online commentary, like so much else in social media, provokes a confusing mix of envy, voyeurism, and "you go, girl"-ing. Kayla and her #BBGs present an aspiration of perfection. Anyone can look and feel and act like Kayla, she promises, if you just work hard enough: there are tons of perfect #BBG bikini photos online, posted by ordinary, nonceleb women. And with those abs, it seems, you can get Kayla's magical self-assurance.

No doubt, looking thin and fit creates incredible social feedback. I've been chunky, and I've been thin, and it shocks me how differently I am treated when I am thin. And if there's a great skinny-looking photo of me—I am the FIRST person out there, sharing it. #notproudbuthonest.

Body-image FOMO is tough for everyone, but if you're sensitive to achievement porn because deep down you know traditional "achievement" is not for you, think about exactly what you're feeling the next time you see a photo of a friend looking ripped and feel envious, or when you yourself post that photo, hoping to feel . . . what?

GETTING STARTED

Turning FOMO into a Friend

FOMO is human and universal; it will never go away completely. But you can get it under control. Ultimately, the best cure for FOMO is feeling secure in your own day-to-day life. It won't happen overnight. Every single time I feel left out or a twinge of envy, I have to consciously say to myself, *Stop. Here's why what you're doing is right for you.* (Yes, even if it means I'm lying on the couch and haven't exercised in days.)

It might take years to erase FOMO from your vocabulary, but here are some ways to start tackling the challenge for the long haul:

❏ **Use FOMO as a tool, not a cudgel.** Don't beat yourself up when you feel it. Give yourself the opportunity to take stock of your vision and your career. Are you feeling FOMO because you're not doing what you want in the moment, or because you're fundamentally heading in the wrong direction? Momentary jealousy over a friend's glam Saturday night is far different from a consistent gnawing when keeping up with a colleague who's getting a master's degree, for example. Learn to differentiate FOMO (ego) from a true desire to grow and push yourself.

❏ **Turn objects of envy into role models and mentors.** FOMO sometimes means you really want something *for yourself.* That colleague who's getting a degree or writing a book: How did she do it? What are her tips? Just because someone is a couple years ahead of you doesn't mean her accomplishments are unattainable for you!

❏ **Praise somebody.** When you tell someone how amazing they are, you'll be surprised how often they were impressed by something you did, too. When you know you're not just in competition, you can see that you're both working to make your entire field better.

❏ **Set your own pace.** I felt jealous of friends writing books for years, but I knew it wasn't yet my time. Well, the day I decided I was going to write this book, I worked twelve hours a day for three straight days to get a proposal off the ground. I'd never done that before! I was driven by a force within, and it felt good.

❏ **Turn FOMO into JOMO—Joy of Missing Out.** "Think of it as a lifestyle shift, in which you feel grateful for what you have, instead of resentment of what you're missing." Anil Dash, a tech entrepreneur and the dad who coined the term *JOMO,* says there's a practical angle, too: "Cultivating JOMO came from parenthood. It's pragmatic. I can't do everything I would like to do, so I'd better find some joy in what I have."

❏ **Everyone feels FOMO.** That's why there's a word for it (and a hashtag). We're not insecure, and we're not failures. We're just human.

Use FOMO to Find Yourself

I have a colleague I adore whose Facebook notifications nonetheless generate a cloud of noxious FOMO for me. Every time I read her business has won an award or announced a new hire (which is often), I'm filled with envy, even anger. Why isn't my business doing as well? After all, we're in the same field. We even collaborate. I was plugging along happily, and suddenly I feel like a failure.

We used to be able to live in blissful ignorance of our friends' successes, at least on a daily basis. With social media, we can't. But here's the thing: once you get in touch with your FOMO, it can be a powerful diagnostic tool. Don't judge yourself, don't feel petty. Merely observe.

Everyone has a particular FOMO trigger. Do you feel jealous of how much money other people are making? How often they appear in print? How their achievements stack up against yours? How many social media followers they have, or how often they're checking in from exotic places? If they have kids and a partner—or if they don't? It's true that you may never be on the cover of *Wired,* but maybe you've realized that eventually, you want to do something worth writing home about.

Like a sore muscle or overused tendon, excessive FOMO is also a sign that a behavior has to change. Do you want the boss's praise? Do you want to sell your product to the company? Train people in workplace politics? Design the table in the conference room? Buy the company? Build the company? Or just be the boss? Focus not only on your career, but on the kind of power you want.

Finally, analyze. After my husband heard me bitch about my colleague for the umpteenth time, he asked why I felt so personally affronted by her success. I sat with it for a while and realized: it wasn't about her, it was about me. I was feeling guilty about my firm's earnings, which were lower than I felt they should be. I was feeling guilty that I hadn't given my team a raise in a while, that we hadn't been hiring, and that earnings were stagnant. "But, sweetie," my husband said, "you try to maximize your flexibility."

So I had a tough conversation with myself about my goals both for my personal time and for my company. I came to realize I had made a choice to earn less money and grow more slowly than other firms, and it was a choice I was comfortable with. Ironically, once I wrote publicly about my choice, I was interviewed about choosing flexibility over maximizing earnings for the *Wall Street Journal.* (I bragged so much, it's possible I created some FOMO myself. You can't win.) But once I used the FOMO to find out something about myself instead of beat myself up, I was able to stop feeling that anger, and even to move forward in my own career.

Career-Boosting FOMO

What's amazing is that reframing FOMO into the warm wishes of an acknowledgment or repost is actually a great business development tool for hermits. Plus, it can create community. A single mom of one toddler recently told me she had no idea how, with three kids, I managed to work so much—and I told her I had just been thinking I couldn't believe how much she worked as a single mom! We both felt better—instead of less than. Here are some healthy and advantageous ways to deal with those FOMO moments:

- ❏ **Break the cycle of bragging.** Use online community for what it was invented for: advice! You have really smart friends (and clearly they are perfect parents or amazing social activists), so why not gain counsel and conversation? Facebook can be annoying, but it's also an incredible place to engage both strong and weak ties on your silly and tough questions alike.

- ❏ **Use Shine Theory.** Ann Friedman, who, along with Aminatou Sow, the two brilliant writers, entrepreneurs, and podcasters who coined the term *Shine Theory,* suggests befriending the girl who intimidates you most, because it doesn't make you look worse by comparison—it actually makes you look better.[5] As Ann says, "I don't shine if you don't shine." It's a fantastic cure for your own jealousy—and also a way of quashing the damaging stereotype of the "mean girl."

- ❏ **Do what privileged white men do.** Use the achievement of those you associate with as a symptom of your own greatness. (My husband is a master of this technique.) Name-dropping builds credibility for you by doing nothing.

❑ **You are who you hang out with.** I use this technique a lot in my work in mobilizing online audiences for social good. It's called social proofing—a theory that people gain social capital and credibility when they are have special access or are privy to special information. For example, I'm part of an online community of women called The List. And one of the rules is that we cheer (publicly, on social media) for any Lister who does something good. It's success by association, but it's also loving, kind, and creates a great community.

❑ **Share FOMO with a friend.** That friend who triggers your FOMO? Chances are if you asked her, she would list off similar characteristics in you that trigger her. When you constantly feel you don't do enough, share that with a friend. I promise you, it's hilarious.

❑ **Get out of your head.** Flip the script. If you are prone to rumination about how little you do, do some good for someone. As ABC News reporter Claire Shipman, a ruminator, too, says, "I think that's a real confidence boost for women." The simple act of getting outside yourself to acknowledge the needs or good work— even with a quick tweet—of someone else can literally shift your whole day.

BEFORE WE DIVE IN

When I say "entrepreneur," chances are you think two words: Mark Cuban. A billionaire tech founder, Cuban is also a prolific speaker who provides stirring advice about how to become a successful entrepreneur. He is smart and charismatic, and embodies the macho, always closing, "sleep when I'm dead" (and seemingly extroverted) business persona so popular today. He's a classic extrovert—exactly the kind of person who would make an anxious introvert think they could never succeed.

And then there's Gary Vaynerchuk. Already a legend in the social media world for having transformed a family wine store into a multimillion-dollar business, Gary was on fire and my client's editor had just published his bestseller *Crush It*. As one of the first social media celebrities to break through, he was everywhere, all the time. I admired what he had accomplished. He seemed to embody what a digital-age entrepreneur *should* be: an energetic, larger-than-life, frenetic personality who was simultaneously a master salesman and a people pleaser.

When first starting my business, I was in a planning meeting with a client and her publisher. It was a big, well-respected house on Avenue of the Americas. And guess who was involved in the planning, as a favor to my client's editor?

Gary Vaynerchuk.

We tried to schedule a meeting to talk about ideas, and Gary put us on speakerphone with his assistant. "Well, I can offer you three A.M. on Wednesday," she said. We all laughed. "Yes," she continued, "that's literally the only free space on Gary's calendar."

Curious about how Gary had built a massive social media following and a big business, I pulled up one of his YouTube instructional videos a few days later. In the video, he was sitting on the toilet. With his laptop. Yes, he told viewers, "I do e-mail when I poop."

My heart sank. And you know what? That was when I knew I was never going to be like Gary Vaynerchuk—or Mark Cuban, for that matter. Nor would I be like all those fabulous women leaders I saw onstage at conferences like Women in the World or TED Women. I wouldn't be like Kara Goldin, who grew the healthy soda-alternative Hint Water into a $90 million company while raising four children. I wouldn't be like my colleague Cheryl Contee, who helped build a consulting firm and a tech platform that has helped so many progressive organizations. (Oh, and she's also a single mom.)

I love a good *Shark Tank* episode as much as anyone, and I have tremendous respect for Sheryl Sandberg. But we have to lose the idea that there's one, unique blueprint for success. Think of all the amazing potential business owners out there who never take the plunge because they believe they're not "the type." Think of all the unhappy executives who put relentless pressure on themselves to build a vast network and achieve boundless growth and sales, but who too soon burn out and leave their professions (I've talked to more than a few). Think of the many successful professionals everywhere who suffer in silence, performing work that consumes their lives and smothers their souls.

I wouldn't be like all those friends and colleagues who have rocketed past me in their careers, getting big promotions, making lots of money, winning awards, and getting interviewed in *Fast Company*. I could feel envious—and I did—but I had to accept that being on and out there all the time just wasn't right for me, and that it was making me unhappy. Yes, I wanted to work hard and make an impact in the world, but I also wanted to stay close to my natural equilibrium, which involves being at home, where I feel content, surrounded by my family, animals, and kitchen.

As I joked to the audience at Brown, if you spend enough time on the American Airlines shuttle between New York, Boston, and Washington, D.C., you'll learn all about successful people's anxieties. During delays or jumbled boarding calls, I'm often sharing flying anxiety and other stories with fellow road warriors. All of us look ambitious, together, and successful on the outside. And we are! But on the inside we may struggle with anxiety every time we "get out there." We may be introverts who have to learn how to work a room. We may be hermits by choice, heading home for some quality time working in a home office. These intricacies don't stop you, but they do force you to work differently, to learn strategies and coping skills. Most of all, they force you to ask, is this the best life for me? I hope the techniques, stories, and tips that follow will be as helpful to you as they are to me.

2

Lean in Less

L ike almost every female entrepreneur, I have a huge amount of respect for Sheryl Sandberg, author of *Lean In* and *Option B*. She's everything I admire: accomplished, groundbreaking, successful, and generous. She's turned the story of the endless juggling of the working mom's life into a bestseller, and made it critical for alpha-dog men to sit up and listen.

And, until *Lean In* came out, I felt pretty smug. At thirty-six, I was doing work that I loved, occasionally dipping into the spotlight, then returning home to chill with my precious family. I could handle a demanding business trip, and get through difficult situations with my head held high. I could congratulate friends on their rise and not feel jealous (mostly), because I liked the formula I'd figured out for my life. I was so much happier than when I was conventionally successful. And I didn't cry every day at work.

But when *Lean In* was published, accompanied by a barrage of media stories and think pieces, I felt disheartened, even angry. I was thrilled that the book tackled the very real barriers women face in the workplace. But most of the women I knew could not work any harder. They simply could not lean in more.

And suddenly I was forced to reckon with a choice that now had a name: Was I leaning *out*?

The Sandberg Freak-Out

I began to worry about my own career trajectory. I had left corporate America at twenty-nine and had worked from home ever since. I only networked when I absolutely needed to, and made sure I schmoozed in very small doses. All that hiding in the bathroom meant that what had started out like a rocket seemed to be flattening out. Although I ran a fairly successful business, I wasn't getting rich by any measure. Sure, I'd feel "in the game" when I was invited to give a big speech, or won an important new contract. But that would pass, and I'd lose the burst of adrenaline. I had my yoga pants, but while friends got big jobs, I stayed status quo.

Had I given up? Let the sisterhood down? Would I be a disappointment to Sheryl?

I'd like to say I resolved my self-doubt quickly, but in truth it stayed with me for several years after *Lean In*'s publication. And the questions were occupying not only me, but so many women who had read Sheryl's significant book.

Leaning Out: Sara Critchfield and Jessica Jackley's Stories

As the founding Editorial Director of Upworthy, the fastest-growing media company of all time, Sara Critchfield achieved social-media-legend status through her team's ability to make almost anything go viral. But four months into maternity leave with her first baby, Sara realized she wanted to spend more time with her daughter.

When we first met, her anxiety was palpable. Like me, she was convinced she would be eclipsed in the marketplace by up-and-comers, become irrelevant, and no one would hire her six months from now. She didn't want to lean into her career in digital media and it scared her to death.

Jessica Jackley, who cofounded the revolutionary online micro-lender Kiva while still in her twenties, had a similar story. When the incredible superconnector Susan McPherson (more on her later) introduced us, I was both nervous and thrilled. I was nervous because Jessica intimidated me, and also because I had recently moved to Los Angeles, a city where it seems everyone is vegan, skinny, and gorgeous.

Susan suggested we meet for lunch with several other women who worked in social impact. Over our vegan lunch, Jessica and I bonded: we were both nursing new babies (neither of us felt very skinny or gorgeous), and we both have sons named Asa. But as we got to talking, I learned something about Jessica few would ever guess: she was *leaning out*.

"When we were launching Kiva, my work pace was unhealthy, unsustainable, and ruined my first marriage," she told me. In her new work life, she says, "I put on grown-up clothes twice a week."

What I immediately loved about Jessica's story, and what I tell myself now when I feel like I'm working on autopilot, is that it's a gift to do just enough work sometimes, and it doesn't hurt you to change your pace. It doesn't mean your rocket-ship days are over.

After burning out with Kiva, getting divorced, then getting remarried and having three children in the following five years, Jessica used her reputation to cultivate a successful consulting and speaking practice that focuses on her experience with Kiva. Leveraging her core of knowledge with fifteen to twenty lectures a year, "I can sustain myself," she told me. And, particularly important for a parent, she added, "And because speaking comes particularly easy to me, it's actually a low-stress activity. At this point I can give a talk backwards, inside out, standing on my head. Or while nursing, which I've actually done a few times!"

As we know, ambitious women are under constant pressure to produce and achieve, much of it self-inflicted. If you're a size six, get to four! If you get $1 million in sales, go for $1.5!

Life, however, demands adaptation—which means our generation, however ambitious, doesn't always benefit from the *Lean In* message. You're in grad school while working full-time, a toddler needs you at home, you have a sick parent needing your care, and you need to keep your day job, even though you don't like it. Because the concept of leaning in is binary, if you don't keep working harder and doing more, you've failed. This creates a tremendous amount of pressure on a single individual to achieve a whole lot. Lean in too far, and you can fall on your face.

If you've been conditioned to achieve, *compromise* is a dirty word. It's not something they teach in business school, and it's never going to put you on the cover of *Forbes*. But you will get things done, and in doing so you will learn skills and tactics that prepare you for success. My extroverted friend Samantha calls my approach to compromise perfect for those of us "who don't want to lean in, but want to stay in."

No two people have the same ideal mix of work and life. That's why in this book, we'll refer to **Work+Life Fit** (no balance!).[1] Work+Life Fit was developed by Cali Yost, an international workplace strategy expert. It honors the notion that no two people want the exact same integration of work and personal life. (Which is why your boss may be e-mailing you at midnight, not because she thinks you need to work harder, but because she's a night owl.)

Because that's what it's about: what really matters to *you*! Your definition of success. My version of success might very well be the ability to earn a good living while rarely having to leave my home office, while someone else might consider leaning in less the very definition of failing. Both definitions are legitimate.

And as for Sara, she sat with her anxiety for a while, and realized she wanted to go back to where she started out: faith-based organizing. Instead of following the money, she is, as she puts it, "following the energy." She takes on fifteen hours a week of consulting work to pay the bills, and saves the rest of her work time for reengaging in community organizing. A compromise for now, but Sara says, "I feel like I'm playing. The pressure is gone."

LEANING OUT

It's Not Just for Parents

The notion of working less by choice has gotten seriously mommy-tracked. Work-life balance and flexible work arrangements are so strongly correlated with parenthood that we assume a successful childless person prioritizes career advancement over anything else.

But leaning out is not just a mommy issue. Some working parents want to work all the time; some professionals without children want a less draining schedule.

Consider the idea of "holistic success." Twenty-seven-year-old Rhonesha Byng, founder of the media company HerAgenda, who coined the term, is on a mission to promote holistic success. Her ambition is to make sure the professionals she reaches through her community don't ignore their personal lives, even if they are only in their early twenties.

"I didn't understand it at first when my mentors would tell me, 'Take breaks, make sure you make time to go out on dates,'" Rhonesha says. "But I realized that, looking back, they realized what they had given up by spending all their time and energy focused on work."

Integrating work and everything else in your life is not just for moms and dads. After all, some parents may want to work all the time, while some nonparents choose to spend the minimum in the office in favor of other pursuits. Your goal may not be to make room for kids, but for a side hustle or another project such as graduate school or writing. I quit my last full-time job years before I got pregnant, because, as we know, I didn't like showing up for work. It wasn't about parenting for me.

In fact, it's optimal to determine your work+life fit before you have kids, which is why Rhonesha's message is so important. When her mentors encouraged her to go out on dates, to prioritize her stated goal of having a family one day, what they were really telling her was, "Think ahead. Prepare. There's more to life than your day job."

My Managed-Growth Story

My last job was running the digital public affairs division of a large PR firm. Over the years, in tons of political campaigns and start-ups, I had worked twelve-hour (and more) days. Now, if I left before six thirty, I felt that I was letting people down.

I was twenty-nine, and I looked at the women ten years ahead of me, and at the sacrifices they'd made to manage family and work. I knew I didn't want to be in the same position in ten years. Why was being in the office a measure of how effective you were at your job, anyway? There had to be a better way.

That's how I became obsessed with work: not with doing it, but with how to make it better for people like me who love what they do but hate going to the office.

So I went back to school for a degree in clinical social work and a master's in public administration at Harvard, where I immersed myself in the data of work life. The literature confirmed what I'd observed: rich or poor, workers can no longer set ordinary boundaries to protect their time and personal lives—even though it doesn't lead to higher productivity.

My own boundaries were about to take a hit. The plan for my new, flexible career was to continue with a social work degree at Boston College, then specialize in work-life consulting. But I got pregnant with my first son two months before I finished my MPA, and then the economy crashed. My husband's small business hit rocky terrain, and everyone around me, it seemed, had lost much of their life savings. And though I was still struggling with antenatal depression, now I was panicking, too. I had to earn money, quick.

So back I went to digital consulting full-time, but now with an agenda. I wanted to work for myself and have more control over my time while still doing meaningful work. I knew I needed to take care of my physical and mental health. I wanted to optimize my stress-to-income ratio.

Ellen Galinsky, who cofounded the Families and Work Institute, gave me my start. Knowing my interest in workplace flexibility practices, she offered to mentor me in work life while I helped her with social media. Ellen is a legend in the field, and she opened many doors. By 2011, I had turned that freelance consulting into Women Online. By 2012, I had a team of four employees, plus four contractors staffed on individual projects. I worked four days a week, and was pretty disciplined about controlling my time.

When people started to call me an entrepreneur, at first, I drank the Kool-Aid. I began to dream of the kind of growth that was entirely ridiculous for a firm my size. I spent too much money on the business with expensive dinners out, always picking up the tab, not to mention on my own travel. I bought another small firm and invested in a software product. I was "playing start-up," as Bea Arthur calls it, and the result wasn't good.

When the 2012 Obama campaign hired us to do women's outreach online, it was an amazing validation of our work. But the same day I went to the bank. I was an extra (and unaccounted for) $60,000 deep into my line of credit, and I didn't know how I would pay it back.

Everyone says that's a natural feeling for an entrepreneur— you're always on the edge. But the push and pull of my feelings that day sticks with me: excitement at landing such a big client, and fear that I owed so much money. I vowed then I'd stop playing start-up, and control workload and finances as much as possible.

So what did I do? I began to keep the scope of the services we offer very specialized, rather than expanding offerings into a full-service digital marketing or PR firm. I kept the staff small, and even now I try constantly to manage everyone's expectations, including my own.

This was my journey toward accepting growth . . . with compromise.

Sometimes it sucks. It's much sexier in a culture that idealizes the entrepreneur to be always hungry, always wanting to grow faster. You know, to *lean in*. When other firms grow their staffs, I feel tremendous FOMO. Many times we've lost contracts to larger firms with bigger offerings and bigger names. There have been so many smart people I've wanted to hire, or opportunities I had to turn down, because they would place too much pressure on me to earn, earn, earn. And sometimes I end up in that situation anyway, because business is fickle and I have bills to pay.

Growth with compromise requires constant recalibration. If the sales pipeline is slow, or if I have an opportunity to nail down future work, I have to take it. Every new child (I have three) has altered my work+life fit. When my third baby, Josephine, was due, I was grounded. I couldn't fly or attend many new business meetings. I only took one week of maternity leave. But I socked away five months of cash—and I did work from bed!

So, that's my story. People call businesses like Women Online "managed growth." But that's too fancy a term. Because I wanted time, and to have work that meant something to me, I set limits on my goals—and I surprised myself by managing to earn a good living. In fact, my limits actually helped Women Online specialize, and grow.

GETTING STARTED

Think About Compromise as Your Friend, Not Your Enemy

To set limits on the pace of your growth, you have to figure out what you will and won't give up. HelloFlo founder Naama Bloom provides a great example: "Instead of staying in a big corporate job just because it was responsible, I realized I'd rather compromise on savings, exercise and a social life."

Like Naama suggests, first, establish some nonnegotiables in your work life. Be specific! Below is an example list with some typical career goals, but feel free to create your own. Once you know your nonnegotiables, it's much easier to figure out what you can compromise on and manage your growth intentionally.

RENOWN
I want magazine covers!

MONEY
I have a target salary and savings plan, and I won't budge.

EXCITEMENT
I need to be inspired by my work.

TITLE
My goal is to eventually be CTO (sole business owner, management, etc. . . .)

PROMINENCE IN YOUR FIELD
It's important to me that my work is honored by colleagues.

Now write down what you are willing to give up to achieve your goals; be specific. Again, below are some examples.

SOCIAL LIFE
I can miss a few Saturday nights with my friends.

SAVINGS
My work now is important enough to suspend future security.

DISPOSABLE INCOME
Shoes? Starbucks? I can live without it for a while.

WHERE I LIVE
My job is in Cleveland, but my heart is in New York.

THE CAR I DRIVE
Walking is great exercise.

VACATIONS
I'm okay only getting a week off a year.

And some biggies. Do these fit you now, or can you take them or leave them?

FAMILY
I want a healthy family life, and that means being in the office at nine and out by five / I'm not focused on family right now.

PERSONAL SPACE
I can't be on all the time—no texting from the boss at 10 P.M. / I live for Slack.

WORK ENVIRONMENT
I want to be in a supportive, friendly work space / I love competition— work isn't for friends.

STABILITY
I want a job for the long haul/I like to switch it up.

You can also think in terms of ratios. Juliette Kayyem, Harvard professor, national security adviser, and public speaker, talks about her "influence-to-stress ratio." (The minute I heard that, I thought,

I'm stealing it!) After a day of running around in her yoga pants, in the evenings she often goes on CNN to provide spot-on national security analysis. That is high influence to low stress!

You could also think about your ideal *income*-to-stress ratio, or your personal-space-to-work-environment ratio. Would you give up a little of one to have a lot of the other?

Once you have your list, think about your pace. What are your targets? Do you want to be management in the next five years? Start a family by thirty-five? Buy a house next year? You don't necessarily have control over timing, but setting some specifics down will help you assess where you need to add and take away. (For instance, if you want to take a four-month trip around the world, you may need to be frugal for a year—and cultivate a really good relationship with your boss!)

EXPECTATIONS CHART

There's a famous poem by Kenneth Koch about how impossible it is to have a social life, a love life, and a productive work life. ("You Want a Social Life, with Friends.") You *can* have them all, of course—but probably not all at the same time.

A great way to figure out if you're on the right path is to actually write down your expectations for the future, how you're handling them right now, and how life intrudes. What might you have to give up? What do you need to put off? Make a column for each heading, and fill in your answers.

FAMILY

I'd like to spend all Sunday with my kids.

I'd like one night out with my partner a week.

I'd like to start college funds and put [X] in them.

WORK

I'd like to bill [X amount] this year.

I'd like to get closer to a senior position.

I'd like to increase my earnings by [X] percent.

INFRASTRUCTURE

I'd like to buy a house in the next five years.

I'd like to upgrade my apartment next year.

I'd like to move to a larger city.

LIFE

I'd like to save 10 percent of my income for retirement.

I'd like to take a two-week vacation to China.

I'd like to see at least three plays/concerts/movies with friends.

Now make a column called **costs/time**. How much will you have to save for each? How much time for family and friends do you have to give up that you currently spend working, and vice versa? What will each require from you?

COST / TIME ANALYSIS

MY EXPECTATIONS	MY COSTS/TIME	WHAT MIGHT I HAVE TO GIVE UP/TAKE ON
BUY A HOUSE IN 5 YEARS	$30K DOWN PAYMENT	EATING OUT ($300 SAVINGS A MONTH) CABLE ($150 A MONTH) GYM ($60 A MONTH)
TRIP TO CHINA IN 2 YEARS	$3,000	FREELANCE CONSULTING PROJECT

Ideally, use a program like Mint to put your spending in categories. Once you know roughly what you spend your money on ($400 a month on restaurants?!) you can cut it down intentionally.

For instance, can you save for college at the same time you save for a house? Can you see friends as much as you want and grow your business? Do you have the extra money required for an extended vacation, or the extra time to attend every soccer match?

Once you know your goals and desires and what they will cost, you can rejigger them a bit. You won't feel guilty for not meeting your own expectations—and you can't do everything—if you have a realistic plan for your life right now.

Appropriate Effort

Last week, in the midst of a deadline, running two extremely demanding client campaigns, recovering from a bad cold, and managing three children, I cooked beef bourguignon for a Tuesday-night dinner party. Why? Why didn't I just order in Chinese food? Everyone at the dinner was a good friend. No one would have been offended.

I don't know about you, but achievement porn's profound effect means I struggle daily with the idea that I might not do everything perfectly—and I mean *everything*, from my first grader's class project to a pitch deck for a new six-figure client. That's why the concept of "appropriate effort" has been so freeing for me.

Appropriate effort is the opposite of our culture's expectation to always do your best. Instead it's doing something well, but removing any emotional investment. Buddhist teacher Sally Kempton, who has done much to popularize the concept, explains that appropriate effort is any effort that doesn't involve struggle. For Sally, the secret of acting with appropriate effort is to ask herself, *If this were the last act of my life, how would I want to do it?*

It's an incredible tool to cultivate if you're a perfectionist or groomed to overachieving. (Especially if, like me, you've found a way to be a perfectionist even at yoga.) And practicing AE regularly can give you some healthy breathing room to accomplish the goals on your big list. By removing fear of the outcome, you bring your whole self into what you're doing—and savor the process.

For example, when I am writing a blog post, client proposal, or even this book, I often fixate so intensely on the outcome (Will it be any good? Will anyone read it?) that the writing becomes merely a chore to get the damn thing done. I have to tell myself over and over: *You love writing, so enjoy this. You can worry about the statistics later.*

By removing the stress of outcome, I am also better able to really focus on pieces that matter, and try to care less about things I cannot change. For example, I hate my head shot, but after agonizing over it for days, I realized my reaction was well beyond appropriate effort, and I tried to channel my energy back into editing, not stressing over my image (which is the height of achievement porn).

How Can You Bring Appropriate Effort into Your Life?

What if you only gave 89 percent? A work project or a homemade cake for your kid's birthday may not need you to pull out the big guns. The key is to acknowledge the outcome. Will what you do be good enough for them? Will what you achieve be good enough for you? The answer to both is: almost surely.

❑ **Remember that the challenge of being always on is universal.** Forty-three percent of highly skilled women with children leave their jobs voluntarily at some point in their careers. Sheryl Sandberg wrote *Lean In* with the benefits of a staff, and an in-office nursery, something most of us can only dream of.

❑ **Compromise between caregiving and work may be unavoidable.** Your kid is throwing up at school. You have to look into nursing homes. A sister far away is getting chemo. Don't torment yourself about taking time for the other important things in your life. The world won't disappear if you're away for two weeks, and if people in your workplace make you feel you're slacking off, consider the bigger picture.

❑ **Nothing is forever.** Remember Jessica Jackley and Sara Critchfield. Giving yourself room by leaning in a bit less—whether it's to spend more time with a kid or take a trip to Rio—doesn't necessarily mean leaving the work you've mastered forever. You're not out of the game, you're recalibrating.

❑ **Reality bites.** Sometimes, you will need to do less. You get tired. You will say no. You will fuck up. You won't get a promotion or your business might never earn you millions of dollars. You will accept less. If you've been conditioned to achieve, this will make you feel like a failure. Know that it's okay to make your dreams and your career a little smaller in order to have the complete life you want.

CAN WE ALL JUST SLEEP?

The cult of achievement porn says that the successful person relentlessly drives forward, with little time to rest, recharge, or unplug. We expect successful people to be like presidents: on 24/7/365.

Achievement porn articles contribute to the illusion that successful people don't sleep. But, as CEO coach Meredith Fineman puts it, we must get rid of all the articles titled "Twelve things eight of the most productive people (you won't believe how productive they are!) in the world do before 6 A.M." or "You'll never believe how the most productive people go to bed (they hang upside down like fruit bats)." "Here are sixteen reasons why getting up before 4 A.M. increases your productivity, and also some oatmeal recipes." I'm waiting for the moment a hugely successful leader (besides Arianna Huffington, and I don't even believe her) admits that they get enough sleep.

Sleep is like work+life fit: everyone's is different. My husband, bless him, usually doesn't need more than six hours a night. (Just like Barack Obama.) He gets up at five to work out and goes all day. He always naps on the weekend. On my perfect day, I wake around six thirty, nap at four, and then work again until about nine thirty. I need nine hours of sleep.

I used to be embarrassed about this, and I lied to everyone I knew because if they didn't sleep, why should I? But it's important to understand your sleep needs and be honest about them. Arianna Huffington (of course) reviewed the book *Rest* by Alex Soojung-Kim Pang in the *New York Times,* and pointed out something valuable: it was actually the industrial revolution that created a drastic separation of work and leisure, which are now perpetually in conflict with each other.

Before the industrial revolution, when most people worked where they lived, work and rest patterns were very different from our own. Many people went to sleep when the sun went down, only to rise in the middle of the night for a few hours to work, have sex, or talk with their partner—even visit with neighbors. And then they would wake again with the sun.

If you ask around, you might find this to be the preferred sleep pattern of some of the most productive people you know. Others nap. When I called Wharton's Stew Friedman to interview him for this book, he proudly stated, "I've just woken up from my nap." It was a Tuesday. But indeed, a nap is part of his work routine, because it energizes him, and tons of data back him up: a nap on the job can increase productivity and reduce workplace accidents.

Not all of us can nap at work, but we can try to get in touch with our natural sleep rhythms and determine how to better meet our rest needs. We can also resist the pressure to conform to an ideal of success that equates lack of sleep with ambition. I like to laugh at profiles of successful women who share that they often get up at four thirty or 5 A.M. for some "me time." To me, that sounds like torture, but it may for work them (apparently it works for Michelle Obama).

In *Rest*, Pang points out that rest and work aren't opposites, like "black and white or good and evil. They're more like different points on life's wave." I love this notion of a life in motion, with gentle breaks for rest in between crashes and peaks. Imagine if you had a work life where you could sleep the hours you need to, and also work the hours you prefer to. When we work to our natural sleep schedules, and don't feel like we need to lie about them to maintain our professional credibility, everyone is better off.

WELCOME TO YOUR IMPERFECT LIFE

The very nature of success—perhaps an old remnant from the Calvinist heritage that informed the good old Protestant work ethic and ensuing industrial revolution—is to think about reaching a goal: "When I achieve X, I can finally live a life I enjoy." But growing your career is merely one element of your existence. And ironically, focusing solely on growing your career can blind you to other equally generative opportunities.

In *Composing a Life,* author Mary Catherine Bateson emphasizes that women's lives so often veer from the paths we may intend them to take. This is a wonderful thing, but sadly we're not taught to think of it that way. Bateson writes of the huge creative potential of a life that twists and turns, and is not "pointed towards a single ambition."

If you fear leaning out (and really, how could you not), consider Bateson's wise nudge about how the huge creative potential of the twists and valleys in your work life.

Dreams and great success can get sparked unexpectedly, if you give yourself the space and time. The seed for Kiva was planted in Jessica Jackley's head when she was working in administration at the Stanford Graduate School of Business. This wasn't her dream job, but it was way to pay the bills while she figured things out.

One night she decided to stay late and watch Nobel laureate Muhammad Yunus give a lecture on microfinance. Yunus's speech jolted her thinking. "It seemed like magic," Jackley said, "that a tiny amount of capital could fast-forward the businesses of people living in extreme poverty, through the work they were already doing."[2]

Over the next few years, Jackley explored this new thinking, traveling to Africa, enrolling in business school, learning Swahili. She took the time she needed to create work that would answer her questions about poverty and entrepreneurship. That curiosity helped create Kiva.

When I last caught up with Sara Critchfield, she was in her car heading to the Lake Shrine near Malibu, a famous spot for practitioners of self-realization meditation. "I don't know how helpful I'm going to be for your interview," she said with a laugh. "Why?" I asked; what was she doing? "Piloting a new program for Airbnb," she told me. The lodging giant created special programs to hang out in a city with someone with shared interests, so Sara volunteered to curate a spiritual journey around Los Angeles, including visits to special mosques, synagogues, churches, and meditation fellowships

(Gandhi's ashes are buried at the Lake Shrine). "I've been having a lot of energy for what I started out doing, which is faith-based work. At some point I'll have to do what gives me money, but for now I'm playing," she said. I could hear the joy in her voice.

Sara gave herself permission to play and learn what she might want to do next. We don't get many chances as adults to unleash the joy and curiosity we had as children. Sometimes, being taken off course and getting a moment to breathe can open up new and deeply generative twists in our lives. This could be phoning in a job in order to focus on a side hustle, taking time when you have small children at home, or finding a safe space to land when you know you need a change but still have bills to pay. Some call it leaning out, but I think it's growing something new.

3

The Gift of Anxiety

B e fearless." I listened as Warren Buffett exhorted the crowd
of five thousand women at the first United State of Women
Summit. Everyone cheered. I felt left out.

You've heard this before; it transcends cultures and gender.
Fearlessness, it seems, is the ticket to success. But what about the
rest of us?

In our society, we conflate leadership with fearlessness, and we
are quick to ignore or reject anxiety as a sign of weakness. But I
think fear is a powerful clue, and anxiety can be a gift.

Jesus, Morra, Why Would You Ever Say Anxiety Is a Gift?!

Almost everyone experiences anxiety at some point. Life is stressful.
And often anxiety will pass, or therapy and medication can help.

But there are those of us for whom anxiety is a constant com-
panion. Whether you are tightly wound, sensitive by nature, or
experiencing anxiety caused by a specific circumstance, anxiety is
constantly with you. Over the years I've tried everything for mine:

benzodiazepines, meditation, hypnotherapy, Freudian analysis. And even when I find myself happy and relaxed, after ten minutes I think, *Wait, aren't I supposed to be anxious about something?*

I've come to think my anxiety and I are actually in successful negotiation, and we're trying to make this relationship work. Yes, anxiety can be a gift—if you make it a tool to guide you. After all, if anxiety is going to be with you anyway, you might as well make it useful. And when you are attuned to the clues your psyche is giving you, you can use them to propel yourself forward.

When I asked Christina Wallace if she ever considered her anxiety a gift, she didn't waste a second answering: "Absolutely." Wallace is a graduate of Harvard Business School, two-time start-up founder, accomplished executive, and creator of an innovative STEM education program. She is extremely intimidating on paper and in person, because, like me, she's really tall.

Christina had severe childhood trauma, and has done a lot of work to manage the aftereffects. Even so, she says, "Situations where I feel like I can't trust the other person or the rug has been pulled out from under me throw me into fight-or-flight mode." She will have panic attacks and crippling anxiety. She's learned that she needs to work with her managers and her colleagues to find a way that allows her to see feedback ahead of time, for example, so she processes it and prepares instead of feeling blindsided and anxious.

Anxiety has been a gift, says Christina, because "it's made me an incredible manager (according to the dozen or so employees I've managed across my last three start-ups) because I am much more aware of how [my employees] like feedback and how to help them show their best selves." Christina is incredibly attuned to people around her, and she can navigate almost any situation.

Anxiety is never a simple gift, though. Christina notes that being an "achiever on steroids" has propelled her career far, and fast. But, she adds, "I have to make sure I don't just do things for medals or résumé bullets, but things that make me happy and fill me emotionally and spiritually."

Like any special gift, anxiety must be managed. But as you can see from Christina, modulating your work life to better suit your emotional needs doesn't mean hiding in an ashram. Work is demanding, and there will always be times when you have to suck it up, put on your big-girl panties, and walk into that room. But work also demands a healthy scaffolding of support and self-care. With practice and intention, you can minimize the scary stuff and play to your strengths.

Finding Her Voice: Alicia Lutes's Story

Sometimes, a trait that comes up at work for a hermit or an introvert can be key toward helping with management. Writer and editor Alicia Lutes calls her anxiety the "base for [her] creativity," and it makes her a terrific boss. At just thirty, Alicia is Managing Editor of Nerdist and host of Fangirling!, and was previously the Associate Editor at Legendary Digital Networks, which includes Nerdist, Geek and Sundry, and Amy Poehler's Smart Girls.

Like Christina Wallace, Morgan Shanahan, and me (and you?), Alicia is "crazy ambitious," and uses the anxiety that goes along with it to her benefit. "If I want something," she says, "I try and work at it, because I can't deal with the what-ifs and the regrets." This trait has also allowed her to be a better, more empathetic boss. "I think that because of my anxiety and depression, I am better at managing other people than I might be at managing myself. I don't want my staff to get stressed out."

Her own boss returns the favor to Alicia. "If there are moments where I'm being too self-deprecating, she'll say, 'Please don't talk about my friend that way.'" I love that, and I wish sometimes I had a boss like Alicia's!

As a writer, Alicia finds that allowing herself to show her own personality is key to her appeal. "The whole reason I am successful is that I have a distinct voice," she says. "And a big piece of it stems from my anxiety, and my neurosis, and the self-deprecation." Obviously, it's found a huge audience with readers, even those who don't have pervasive anxiety. "It's a very human thing, and even if jokes seem especially relevant to someone who has anxiety or depression, there is a kernel there that is universal," she says.

Going for Broke

Since I was a girl, I've had what's usually referred to as generalized anxiety disorder: an ambient and pervasive sense of anxiety. At three, I developed agoraphobia and refused to go outside for a whole summer. I had migraines. At nineteen, a car accident sent me into a crippling and major depression. One psychiatrist diagnosed me with mild bipolar disorder. Now, at forty, I have mild social anxiety and fear of flying. Oh—and I worry everyone I love is going to die.

I am not fearless. I am fearful. I am an entrepreneur who finds the daily tasks of being an entrepreneur scary and hard. I have panic attacks on planes, at large events, and during the meetings required to get out there and sell my business. It's the rare business trip where I don't make an escape plan. I've run for the airport immediately after showing my face at a conference. I always need to call my poor husband for a pep talk. Every day is a tug-of-war between my ambition and my anxiety.

Still, in terms of my work, my anxiety is a love-hate situation. I am literally often scared to leave the house. But like Christina, my anxiety has gotten me where I am today. I hustle. My anxiety also gives me extreme bag-lady syndrome. I always think my bank account will hit zero, that I won't have a job, and that I'll wind up on the streets. So my anxiety forces me to manage my schedule and workload. The anxiety drives my work ethic. It keeps me asking more of myself. It keeps me hungry. It helps make me successful.

Once you've been through clinical depressions and panic attacks, you're never completely free of them. Anticipating the return can be tough. But, in truth, now my anxiety is almost like a friend to me.

It's forced me to build an excellent infrastructure to remain functional when I really feel like hiding under the covers, and part of my achievement comes from keeping it in check.

Making Your Obsession Work for You: Morgan Shanahan's Story

When I started thinking some more about anxiety, I called up a lot of friends and asked, "How does managing anxiety fit into your career trajectory?" Some had no idea what I was talking about. (Lucky them!) But Morgan Shanahan, senior editor at BuzzFeed, gave a great cackling laugh. Then she said, "From what I gather, the world views me as functional. I don't view myself that way at all."

Early in her career, as a twenty-seven-year-old up-and-coming screenwriter in L.A., she found out she was pregnant. That day she also got fired. Her postpartum depression and anxiety made it impossible for her to keep freelance jobs, while the medication she took for the depression made her nonfunctional in meetings.

As an outlet, she began blogging about her struggle at the818. com. Her writing made it become one of the most powerful—and self-supporting—mom blogs. Now she covers parenting at BuzzFeed, where she is supported by a team, and takes on special projects focusing on mental health.

"Now I'm not obsessed with how horrible I am," Shanahan says. "I'm obsessing about something that I can help people with. You can function with high anxiety and obsessive-compulsive disorder, if you find something positive to be obsessed with."

Even better, Morgan is using her creative voice, passion, and drive to create original content about depression for BuzzFeed video. And it's going viral, which makes her bosses happy.

ANXIETY BY THE NUMBERS

According to the National Institutes of Health, the spectrum of anxiety disorders includes generalized anxiety disorder (GAD), panic disorder (PD) and agoraphobia, obsessive-compulsive disorder (OCD), phobic disorder (including social phobia or anxiety), and post-traumatic stress disorder (PTSD). Anxiety and depression are often comorbid conditions (they go together).[1]

Globally, one in thirteen people suffers from anxiety. Clinical anxiety affects around 10 percent of people in North America, Western Europe, and Australia/New Zealand compared to about 8 percent in the Middle East and 6 percent in Asia.[2]

Social anxiety is the third most common psychological disorder, right after the big boys of depression and alcoholism.[3]

Up to 25 percent of American adults will fit the clinical description of anxiety during their lifetimes.[4]

A typical panic attack lasts between fifteen and thirty minutes.[5]

More than a quarter of Americans take SSRIs or benzodiazepines for anxiety, depression, or other mental health disorders.[6]

Women are far more likely to take this medication, with over 25 percent of American women treated vs. 15 percent of men.[7]

Around 15 percent of all new mothers have postpartum depression, anxiety, or OCD (PPD), and it is treatable.[8]

Cognitive behavioral therapy is the most widely used technique in combating anxiety.[9]

Mindfulness is an effective tool to combat anxiety and excessive rumination.[10]

Breaking the Vicious Cycle

Obsessing about failure is a deadly prescription, and it's especially hard because successful people are supposed to be bold and brave. When anxiety makes us question if we deserve what we want, it creates a self-defeating cycle.

Sometimes the obsessing is about what a failed loser you are: FOMO on steroids. Morgan describes it as "thinking about what a fucking failure I am, and how much better every other parent is than me, how much better every person I've ever met is than me. Looking at the cars of people driving by and being like, well, they have a nicer car, they're more successful, they're a better parent, they can provide for their child."

Another feature of anxiety is globalization: one small worry cascades into a giant one. When my husband was an entrepreneur, it was difficult for us to have conversations about the state of his company. A few rough conversations when he was starting out made me convinced he was about to declare bankruptcy . . . every single month for ten years.

But I think the hardest part of the anxiety-depression combination is constant ruminating and obsessing. You obsess about things you'd never want to admit to anyone, and these little worries become constant fears. That can include obsessing about how much you're obsessing. Writer and Editor Alicia Lutes jokes, "I'm, like, none of these things are actually really anything. You're just a nightmare human that is obsessed with yourself."

And when it comes to career, feeling that an obsession with failure is selfish can be very, very challenging when you're trying to become a "success." Duh. But thinking about the positive effects of your anxiety can help break the cycle, and make anxiety into one of your tools.

CRYING IN THE BATHROOM—AM I ALONE?

The answer to that question is no, you're not—and women's bathrooms have a storied history. Jessica Bennett, a *New York Times* journalist and author of the great book *Feminist Fight Club*, says that women's bathrooms often serve as secret feminist bunkers, good for "hiding tears, planning internal revolts, and figuring out how to ask for a raise." *Newsweek* reporters planned the first class-action sexual discrimination lawsuit largely in the ladies' room, and it was depicted in the book and TV series *Good Girls Revolt*.

But if you're not planning any revolts, you might need to figure out what your tears are telling you. Everyone needs an occasional break to cry, but the women's bathroom is fertile ground for so many emotions. Try to use them to figure out what kind of a work space you want when you open the door.

A nonprofit development director told me of a time at her organization when she was aware that several of her staff were frequently crying in the bathroom. Some less enlightened managers would ignore this, or even shame the staff for their bathroom trips. Not this one: she took it as a sign that something was wrong with the organizational culture, spoke to the staff one-on-one, did some sleuthing, and created a plan to address the culprit (a toxic and abusive board chair). All that crying in the bathroom was an important clue for the leadership.

Is your crying a symptom of a situation you can resolve by approaching a manager or making a change? Is it a situational sadness, such as a breakup or dealing with a loved one's illness or trauma? Are you still depressed and crying when you're out of the office, say, for a business trip, or an off-site meeting? If you work at home, how do you feel? I have experienced the sadness of an ambient depression, and I have experienced the need to be in another role, or in another place. Don't think of crying in the bathroom as hiding—think of it as an opportunity to tune into what your crying is telling you.

The Bright Side: Making Anxiety Work for You

I am not sugarcoating anxiety in the least, but at work, your anxious nature can offer secret skills like social attunement, attention to detail, organization, drive, and the biggest: empathy.

According to leadership guru Marcus Buckingham, data show that working on weaknesses is far less effective than working from strengths. I've come to accept my nature, and value its strengths, like the fact that I have strong empathy and interpersonal skills, and I always get a good night's sleep, 'cause I'm never out late partying.

It was the former LinkedIn senior executive and current Silicon Valley tech CEO Arvind Rajan who told me about Buckingham's observation, and he used his own life as an example. Arvind is a skilled practitioner of cultivating leadership without pressing the flesh, and he has coped with his social anxiety through a very successful twenty-year career in Silicon Valley.

"I didn't even realize how much anxiety I had until I started to go to cocktail parties for work," Arvind says. "I'd make an appearance and find a reason to go to the bathroom and sneak out." (See: men hide in the bathroom, too.)

His simple suggestion: reframe your expectations of yourself as a leader. "Networking is a skill we learn just like we learn how to do Excel," he says. "At some level you need to master the basics. But you're better off playing to your strengths."

This knowledge leads to more security—and being more comfortable revealing your true self. "If you'd asked me to do this interview in my twenties, I would have worried it would make me seem weak," Arvind says. "Now, I don't mind admitting where I have weaknesses."

Most entrepreneurs in Silicon Valley are, in fact, introverts, and a bit socially awkward, Arvind told me. But they know their stuff. They may worry about how they're perceived on a personal level, but professionally, they are 100 percent assured in what they're pitching. It's ironic to me that the leaders we idolize in Silicon Valley are largely introverted, socially awkward, and probably anxious. They certainly play to their strengths.

I love to watch the fantastic example of Richard, the nerdy tech CEO on HBO's *Silicon Valley*. His usual demeanor is so awkward, and he suffers so much anxiety, that in the moments when he does spring into expressing surprising strength and force, he throws everyone off their game, and wins the moment. What a great tactic. Identify your strengths as a leader who has some anxiety, and play to those.

SOCIAL ANXIETY VERSUS INTROVERSION

Introversion and social anxiety are different, but often conflated. Here are a couple of tells to see if you have some social anxiety:

❑   My fear of social activities can cause tension in my personal and professional relationships.

❑   I feel anxious before picking up the phone or arriving at a meeting.

❑   It can be difficult for me to leave my house when I need to attend a social event or work event.

❑   I fear getting rejected or made fun of if I enter a conversation.

❑   I'm driven to get everything perfect, otherwise I might be harshly judged.

(Courtesy Dr. Ellen Hendriksen)

Social Anxiety. Social anxiety can be a wonderful gift at work, because those of us who have it are exquisitely attuned to other people's needs.[11] I always joke that the reason I am so good at client services is that I am deathly afraid my clients will be unhappy.

But as psychologist Ellen Hendriksen writes,[12] for anxious introverts, "the social antennae are too sensitive." Ironically, we can read a room, even if we can't walk into it with confidence. We may imagine people judging us, or pick up negative judgments that aren't there. People like me with social anxiety think there is something wrong with us, and, as a result, we hide in the bathroom, thus avoiding situations that we might even enjoy.

Dr. Hendriksen notes that social anxiety is a learned behavior, usually stemming from a childhood situation where we learned we did not fit. I know for me, I forever feel like an outcast because until I was about nine, I was one. I had no friends, and no one would have lunch with me because I was weird and my mom never packed me anything good to trade. My height didn't help.

But I'm a grown-up now, and with care and intention, I've learned to make anxiety into a useful tool. I tell myself that people do like me now, and I use those attunement skills for good.

Preparation, Organization, and Attention to Detail. I bet you were never the type to wing it! Anticipatory anxiety means you rehearse before doing, and plan for the big events. You plan your body language and practice your tone of voice, in addition to your facts and figures. Perhaps fear of not being good enough means you prepare for every line of a speech and transition in a slide. People get a lot of flak for being prepared (remember Donald Trump's nasty accusation that Hillary Clinton actually prepared for their debates). This is a healthy adaptation to anxiety, and it means you are in control of your work and yourself when it matters.

And, because you're attuned and you can read a room, if your perfectly prepared remarks fall flat, you can pivot on a dime and meet the tone the audience wants.

Time Management. You have no time for time wasters! You don't procrastinate. You know the best way to quell the fear and anxiety is to tackle something head-on, so you start the day with the scariest thing on your to-do list. Then, you give yourself a little treat.

You also use your avoidance to be more judicious in choosing the times when you actually do press the flesh.

You know the people who spend all their time at conferences or lunches? There's a plus in putting yourself out there, but a lot of it is expensive hype.

Being early for meetings, even if you did so because you were terrified, makes clients happy. Also, hello: if you always arrive at the airport an extra hour early, you're much more likely to get upgraded.

Drive. The drive of anxiety can come from a dark place. Morgan Shanahan notes, "I'm an obsessive, so how do I get it all done? I fucking obsess. It's been a blessing and a curse." This is different from a drive that gets fed by the validation of others, one that yields achievement that isn't truly about what you want. A drive born of anxiety is generative and forces us to create solutions. After all, behind every rags-to-riches or unlikely-origin story of success is a deep anxiety: the threat of poverty, loss, and failure drive something great. Anxiety means that every day you have something to prove. Hard to live with; great in business.

Structure. Putting in place a support system for your anxiety also means you have a support system for setbacks. You've built a network of employees, friends, family, and a kitchen cabinet (more on that one in Chapter 4) to keep you going. You're probably good at managing your personal infrastructure and know how to build the scaffolding: the fact that you need to rehearse a scenario (say a business trip in which your kids will be in others' care) in order to survive it means you have the mechanisms in place for healthy transitions!

My colleague has just been treated for her ADHD as a forty-year-old. The tactics she's recently been taught to manage her daily life sound very much like mine: lots of lists, practice at prioritization, and breaking down the work of the day into bearable chunks. For example, something that feels unbearable comes first, and then is followed by completely bearable tasks (for example, a scary call with a client would be followed by busywork like filing receipts or something enjoyable, like writing). It's all about the structure that works for you.

Empathy. The old chestnut for stage fright is to imagine everyone in the audience in their underwear. When you struggle with social anxiety, you can automatically see everyone in their underwear—

figuratively, at least. You can flip the script from being about your-self ("Does anyone like me? Am I stupid?") to tune into how other people feel. Perhaps they're anxious themselves, faking their ex-troversion or enjoyment, or simply having a bad day. Or perhaps they're really enjoying themselves with you and think you're pretty smart. Can you let go and enjoy with them? Nonverbal cues and mirroring others' signals win friends and influence people. Plus, they help you get out of your head.

Your own struggles with anxiety, and how they affect you at work, can also give you insight into other employees' struggles, whether they're dealing with a new baby or a broken leg. Giving support can lead to getting support, and a healthier, more empathetic office for everyone.

GETTING STARTED

Working with Your Anxiety

Imagine you have a business trip coming up. You know that it's go-ing to be all the things you hate: flying, being separated from your kids, your partner, or your space, lots of schmoozing. You can feel the anticipatory anxiety building up.

Your anxiety is part of you, and it can be a valuable piece. But that doesn't mean you should let it take over. Ignoring anxiety can hurt you, and succumbing to it can quash your dreams. You need an excellent scaffolding to support your ambition.

Structure is an anxious person's best friend. I make a schedule with all the details of the day. *(I will shower. I will call the dentist. I will write six e-mails. I will jog for fifteen minutes.)* Even when I'm on top of the world, I keep them up. They help me feel in control, and prevent me from going global.

Team. I've chosen to give up some income because I know that support is crucial to my functioning. My life changed when I de-cided to hire a full-time assistant, who handles my schedule and even structures "break time," which frees me up to concentrate on our P&L, especially when what Winston Churchill, a major depressive, called "the black dog" hits.

But you don't need to hire help. Colleagues, mentors, e-mail lists, and Facebook groups—any support structure—give you a safe space outside your job that you can use for advice, opinions, grousing, networking, and celebrating. When I feel less alone at work, I feel less anxious. And when I don't trust my own opinion or work, I have colleagues whose opinion I really value and who cover my weaknesses.

Save the environment. If your environment is out of control, you will feel out of control. Left to my own devices, I would putter around all day and clean the house. Since this is not productive— and more than a little obsessive—I allot myself thirty minutes every morning and evening to clean up, usually while I'm on a routine work call. And, if your anxiety makes you leave your house a disaster, try giving a deep clean to one room a week.

Self-care. Building in self-care—exercise, massage, alone time —is not selfish. It's a key part of managing your anxiety. Even a ten-minute walk or a cup of coffee with a friend can calm your nerves. There's a great quote from activist and attorney April Reign: "Everyone is finite"—meaning you won't have anything to give if you never take care of yourself. I wish it was tattooed on my hand.

Pep talks. You can give these to yourself, or you can reach out to a trusted confidant. The key is to find what motivates you to reach past your anxiety.

My husband is my official pep talker. He is really good at it. He knows my most ridiculous and minute fears, and he knows the drill. I blub to him, and he simply listens. He asks me important questions when I'm hiding in a bathroom, waiting to run for the exit and next flight home. He'll ask me if I have important client work and *can't* leave. When I give pep talks to myself, it's most often when I am sitting on a plane, ready for takeoff. I remind myself that my children need money just as much as they need me around. This is not a choice; it's not fun. I'm doing what I need to do.

Pep talks are important, because they keep you in the game when it matters. For instance, when I attended the White House summit on the United State of Women, it was one of the most important days of my life. I cheered and teared up as I watched heroes and role models from President Obama to Cecile Richards take the stage. But my palms were sweating with panic. There could be bombings, or shootings. My children were three thousand miles away. In between Joe Biden and Oprah, I tried to rebook my flight home.

But I called my husband for a pep talk, and went through my day and my goals. Hearing the words out of my own mouth made me feel more in control, more empowered. I told him to tell me to stay. And I stayed.

Label your anxiety. Sometimes, simply noting what's making you anxious and acknowledging it can help you calm down. For example, my psychiatrist Dr. Carol Birnbaum taught me to observe my anxiety:*I'm feeling flooded with anxiety because I'm separated from my kids and I can't see them.* Then I remind myself, *You're just like all these other mothers in the world. They're anxious, too.*

Ask for updates. Worrying takes you out of whatever you're doing at the time—not a great plan at work. So build in reassurances. Away from your kids? Get your babysitter to send you pictures. Meeting going on without you? Ask your colleague to shoot you an e-mail. It's much harder to obsess about what's going wrong when you know what's going on.

You're not alone. Besides us garden-variety anxiety experts, there are a ton of people suffering small- to large-scale anxiety at any given time. People are afraid of bugs, mice, spiders, water, death, sharks, clowns, hospitals, blood, elevators. People in their twenties are panicking because they're trying to figure it all out. People in their middle age are having midlife crises. People in their eighties are wondering why they wasted so much time worrying.

The point is, if you're panicking on the runway, you're only human. A bunch of other people on the plane are panicked about something, too.

Send a substitute. If all else fails, remember that *everyone* on your team is a brand ambassador, and every single appearance doesn't need to be made by you. You probably have a colleague who loves being in the press or pressing the flesh. Shift your thinking from "I need to be out there" to a sense of distributed leadership. Send that person out there and bask in the glow!

FLYING HIGH

For those of us whose work demands a lot of air travel, flying anxiety can be very limiting. And for those of us who are more sensitive or need more control, it can be even more intense.

Captain Tom Bunn, an air-force veteran, an airline captain, and a licensed therapist, was part of the first fear-of-flying program, which was started at Pan Am in 1975. Now he's president and founder of SOAR, Inc., which has helped over five thousand people overcome their fear of flying.

"Being on the ground," Bunn says, "is our most basic way of controlling things. When you get lifted up in the air, you don't have control, and you don't have escape, and these are the ways we usually calm ourselves on the ground."

His method involves simple exercises and a lot of oxytocin, powerful tools you can use to ease your fears without drugs or alcohol. (I'm not judging. I've been there.)

Practice vagal maneuvers. The vagus nerve literally controls our fight-or-flight instincts. Signals that we are physically safe stimulate the vagus nerve—which is in charge of panic attacks and other stress responses in the parasympathetic nervous system—to slow your heart rate and calm you down.

So, before you get on the plane, build in a calming presence and link it directly to the challenges you will face on the plane. Imagine the face of someone who loves you: your lover, your partner, your baby, even your dog.

Flood your oxytocin. When you're flooded with oxytocin, a deep sense of well-being will shut down your anxiety. To find your oxytocin, imagine a triggering moment: amazing sex, nursing your new baby, even something like closing a deal. Try to remember every detail and talk yourself through it. I have to admit, I imagine nursing, where I can even feel a "phantom letdown." Captain Tom notes that men who have flying anxiety do better imagining moments of afterglow after great sex.

For a more advanced exercise, you can try to train your brain to link the oxytocin with the elements of flying. When you hear the announcement for boarding, trigger your oxytocin. When you hear the click of the seat belt or the flight attendant asking for devices to be turned off, trigger your oxytocin. In time, your memories will become automatically linked to the flight ritual, and slow down your stress hormones.

Practice "loving-kindness." Buddhists use a simple meditation in which you picture someone you love in front of you, someone who fills you with a sense of security, and imagine them wishing you well. The words of the meditation are, "May I feel safe. May I feel content. May I feel strong. May I live with ease." You can use any words that are natural to you as well: "You are fine," or, "you are safe," for example.

Meditation for the time-challenged. You don't have to spend an hour on a cushion every day or visit a yogi to use meditation for your flight. YouTube is filled with simple breathing exercises, meditations, and thought exercises, some as short as five minutes, to provide a quick burst of calm, as are several free apps, such as 10% Happier.

Medicate. Anne Parris traveled for years working for a large accounting company. Because medication was frowned upon in her family, it never occurred to her to ask for an antianxiety pill from her doctor. So for literally twenty years, on every flight, she sat there, awake, afraid to have any alcohol because she could not lose control, and feared she would die.

She laughed when she told me, "I took Ativan for the first time on a flight a few months ago and it was literally a joyful experience. I still had to do my preflight ritual but at least I didn't worry I was going to die once I boarded the plane."

I think it's safe to say that I have not really been conscious on a flight since 2008. It doesn't mean I don't fly—I do almost every week. It's not joyous, even with medication. Sometimes it gets hairy.

I was at Washington Reagan Airport, awaiting my flight home after forty-eight hours of a presentation to the Council on Foreign Relations, business development meetings and meals, and a five-hour client retreat I'd run and directed. I'd paid for multiple breakfasts, lunches, and Starbucks with former or prospective colleagues or clients. All I wanted to do was pass out in coach, then wake up in Los Angeles.

I performed my time-tested ritual for the perfect medicated flight. One Xanax fifty minutes before takeoff. Except this time . . . I decided to take two. I was really anxious. Forty-five minutes before takeoff, just about to board, I popped two pills, swigged some water, and pulled out my neck roll. Here we go.

Then, a tarmac delay was announced over the loudspeaker. Panic. Would I fall asleep in the boarding area? Who would make sure I get home? I don't remember anything else. I think some kind stranger woke me up when we finally boarded.

If you take a lot of medication to fly (assuming, like I did, some kind stranger helps you make it to your destination!) you may not be able to drive a rental car when you arrive, and you may need to adjust your schedule. You can say no to a client dinner if you're recovering from catatonia when you arrive. At the end of the day, when it comes to coping with the anxiety of travel with medication, it's way more important that you're prepared for the big meeting the next day.

Be choosy. I feel much safer on a 747 than I do on a regional jet. I always do better in business class. As a result, I have worked hard to build up loyalty points on the airlines I feel most comfortable with. Because I have loyalty points, I get upgraded more often, which also makes my flying experience more palatable. If you have the money and being in first class diminishes your anxiety, allow yourself to upgrade.

Lucky charms. I'm not superstitious, but I do have a lucky charm from each of my children that I have to have in my purse when I get on the plane. Having a concrete object, like a picture or piece of jewelry, can help with triggering oxytocin, or be a visual stimulus for your own pep talk.

What Your Body Is Telling You

I am the queen of psychosomatic illness and injury. I get migraines when I work too much or travel. In a job I hated, I developed horrible wrist tendonitis and had to go on leave to get surgery. I get sick when I'm stressed. Every few months I just have to go to bed for a few days.

Over the years I've finally accepted that a dysfunctional body is a clue that something needs to change at work.

Workstations are not natural places for our bodies, and squinting at our smartphones is even worse. My migraines are caused by muscle tension and resulting musculoskeletal dysfunction, all from hunching over my laptop, peering down at my iPhone, clenching my jaw on a plane, or worrying about traffic in the back of a New York City taxi.

Posture is also a clue. Feeling under attack at work, even unconsciously, elicits a fear response: we crouch down to protect the vital organs. Not only can the fear-response posture cause pain, it can affect the digestive system. Even if it's not caused by posture, many women suffer from irritable or irregular bowels or IBS, which can have its root in persistent, low-level anxiety.

My women's community is chock-full of migraine sufferers, all of us type A overachievers who literally send stress and fear to our jaws, shoulders, and backs. We're hurting ourselves, and most of the time we don't do anything to try to stop it.

I have been on a five-year journey to cure mine. It turns out, clenching my jaw 24/7 for years has created the upper body's version of a system failure. Everything is crunched, and what I think are migraines are actually frozen fascia and muscles. After thousands of dollars and countless appointments with neurologists, ENTs, hormone specialists, chiropractors, Botox-administering dentists, orthodontists, and energy healers, I found a solution in the Center for Craniofacial Pain at Tufts Dental School. A plastic jaw appliance that prevents me from clenching—a fancy version of a retainer—and physical therapy have made it better.

Ultimately, my worst enemy in my pain is myself. When you feel pain, take it seriously. And if it's anxiety and stress causing the pain, take that seriously, too. I've learned to take time to respond to my own pain. And now, if I need to avoid a stressful situation or spend half the day lying prone on a heating pad, it's no one's business but my own.

The Listen-to-Your-Body Scan

This two-part exercise can help you see how stress is affecting your body.

First, sit upright in a chair. Put your feet flat on the floor and your hands on your lap. Keep your chin neutral. Note which part of the body you can immediately feel. Then, with your eyes closed, scan through the following:

Your head	**Your stomach**
Your jaw	**Your hips**
Your neck cords	**Hamstrings and butt**
Your shoulders	**Your calves, ankles, and feet**
Your wrists and forearms	
Your upper back	
Your lower back	

Note which feel tight, and, in order to gain some relief, breathe into the area of tightness or pain.

Next, keep a diary for a week. (Don't choose a week in which you have a huge project due.)

❑ Note how you feel at 9 A.M., noon, three, and 6 P.M. How does your body change over the course of the day?

❑ What part or parts of your body hurt at the end of the workday?

❑ When you think about work, is there a part of the body you immediately feel?

❑ How often during the week do you rely on a drink, muscle relaxant, or over-the-counter pain relief, if at all?

❑ Note how often you exercise, do yoga, dance, or take a walk. (The stairs count!) How do you feel afterward?

❑ Note how your body feels on the weekend. Is it different from how it feels at work?

Now you should have a sense of your level of pain response to your work, as well as what times you feel it, and where it is located in the body. The next step is to link corresponding activities to your feelings. Are the feelings triggered by people? Tasks? What relieves those feelings, and what exacerbates them? Do you dread your ten o'clock meeting, but feel thrilled after each phone call with a client? Use your body's signals to find out how your work is treating you.

Stand up Straight

In a famous study, slumped participants used more negative words, spoke with lower affect, and expressed poorer self-esteem than the ones who sat up straight. If you want a quick fix, you can help change your emotions, as well as your mood, by changing your posture.

Wall angels. Here is my number one trick for helping regain good posture and instantly (I swear) quashing a tension migraine or sore shoulders.

Lean against a wall if you can, or simply stand up straight. Make sure your neck is neutral and your eyes are looking straight ahead, not at the floor. Raise your arms to the side to make a T, your elbows bent at ninety degrees. Bring your shoulders back and retract your shoulder blades, trying to make them touch. Keeping your shoulder blades together, move your arms up and down like a set of angel wings. Do three sets of fifteen (it's hard!).

Belly breath. To gain calm, sit in a chair with your feet flat on the ground, hands at your sides. Breathe in and relax your upper body and legs. Then practice moving the breath down from your neck cords to your abdomen. Swell out your belly so you can see it, and visualize moving the breath down from your throat, your diaphragm, and into your abdomen.

Dance party. Put on your favorite music and dance or move for five minutes. Simply swoop your arms over your head to get your energy moving. Roll your neck and shoulders and shift your weight and energy from your neck, jaw, and shoulders into your legs and feet.

Taking the Leap: Therapy

It's hard for successful people to admit they're struggling; or that they don't know what to do; or what they could be doing better. Therapy can be expensive, and it can be daunting to try to find the right person. But what if therapy was like working out at the gym—a preventive measure? It is a crucial part of your tool kit if you struggle with mental health issues.

Some of us need some privacy in order to open up. Whatever you can't say out loud to your friends, colleagues, parents, you can say to a therapist. Trust me, you don't want to wait until crisis strikes. I'll never forget my very first panic attack, when I was nineteen. I collapsed on the floor of the college library and my wonderful roommate walked me home. For some months after, I thought I'd been stricken with an illness or had a bad reaction to medication, because that's what the psychiatrist treating me quickly surmised (he wasn't much for conversation). It wasn't until several months later that I saw a therapist who suggested I'd had a panic attack. She gave me a definition, a framework for identifying and coping with later attacks, and helped me piece together an important puzzle. Therapy doesn't have to be about lying on a couch discussing your childhood; it can be useful and practical, a sensible part of your life repertoire.

There's no doubt about it, though: therapy is expensive. For those whose insurance doesn't cover it, many therapists offer sliding scales, or can recommend a practitioner who does. Also, there are now online and text-only therapists, who can provide a measure of relief for those who may not have time to go in person. And even if you don't plan to go every week, you can see a therapist a few times, and you will always have someone to call if you need urgent help.

Taking the step of going on medication is a personal choice. Don't listen to the opinions of your friends or your hairstylist or anyone else. It's *your* mental health. For me, antidepressants and antianxiety medication have been crucial to my functioning, and can also be a lifesaver for those having a hard time or in transition.

The most important thing is to find a psychiatrist or prescriber you trust, and to work closely on a plan. Don't simply let your GP prescribe the medication—you need a specialist on the case. Finding the right medication cocktail can take time, so don't get discouraged if you have to try a few. And don't be afraid to speak up about side effects. I've been on almost every antidepressant. Some affect your libido, and some make you gain weight. It doesn't make you petty to worry about this!

Parenthood and Anxiety

In today's world, when bombs go off willy-nilly and basic safety at schools isn't even certain, sometimes even the everyday separation from my kids can be excruciating. When my children are out with their nanny and I'm working at home, I can hear sirens in the distance and freeze up. There is not a single time I get on an airplane without worrying I'll never see my children again.

Forget about the crazy hormones and physical changes: your world will never be the same once it's inhabited by precious little people you created, and this can be extremely anxiety provoking.

It can start as soon as you get pregnant. It's not as well-known, but antenatal depression is postpartum depression's ugly sibling. All three of my children gestated on Prozac, because perhaps the worst depression I ever experienced was during the first trimester of my first pregnancy. I hated everything, especially my poor little fetus. I'll never forget the day my mom suggested that perhaps I shouldn't go through with the pregnancy.

After I went back on meds at three months, I gave birth to my beloved and cherished first son, Asa. All along, I worked with a psychiatrist who specialized in pregnant women (sometimes called a reproductive psychiatrist), and so I felt better about any risk to the fetus.

Like me, Morgan Shanahan became pregnant with her first child during the economic crash of 2008. After vomiting multiple times a day the first three months, she found herself simply too sad to function. "I really truly believed that motherhood was going to put a screeching halt on all of my plans, and my plans were already not going the way I wanted them to," Morgan says. "I was like, 'This is it. This is where life goes off the rails. It's over.'"

For some, postpartum depression (PPD) is their first experience of mental illness. Many of us have experienced episodes of anxiety or depression in the past, and pregnancy brings on an episode in full force.

After PPD, when you finally make it back to work, you may find the formerly mundane aspects of work-life (travel, being out of the home) scary. When you are torn between demands at work and those at home, it's normal to ask yourself, *Am I present enough? Am I giving enough to my children?*

I am a huge proponent of never dismissing these feelings. It's important to use them as a barometer and to trust your instincts. It's also important, though, to differentiate between mild mom-FOMO and your true parenting priorities. For instance, I have a dear friend who is a stay-at-home mom. I crave her beautifully made dinners and long neighborhood playdates. But when I leave her house, I don't chew over it.

When I enter a stage of feeling constantly guilty about being out of touch with my kids, which does happen, I say, *Self, nothing is permanent. You are not ruining your children.* For that very reason, every six months or so I reevaluate my work+life fit. If things feel really skewed in one direction or another (for example, too much work and not enough time with my kids, or too much time with my kids and not enough client work) I try to come up with a plan to shift things.

THE BEARABILITY SPECTRUM

In a world where ambient anxiety reigns, the most important thing you need to decide is that your anxiety is not your boss. My wonderful psychiatrist Dr. Birnbaum stresses, "You can't protect yourself from all the anxiety that's out there. But you can get into such a hyperaroused state that it feels almost impossible to calm down. Something really scary may make you anxious. Then your body gets so hypercharged that you don't sleep well, and you don't get refreshed." Which, of course, makes it harder to deal with your anxiety.

A great way to break the cycle is to chop up tasks that make you extremely anxious into bearable pieces. You can also move something from completely unbearable to slightly bearable. For example, you might nudge along your fear of flying from "I can't get on a plane" to "I'm going to pack." "I'm going to make a plan to keep in touch with my kids." "I'm going to order a Lyft and call my friend while I'm stuck in traffic en route to the airport." And finally, once on the plane: "I'm going to take a Xanax, do a calming meditation, and survive."

I use a bearability practice to manage my anxiety, especially around business travel. I get very anxious when I am working far away from home and I haven't heard from my nanny or husband. I worry something bad has happened, and it distracts me and takes me away from my work. So I set up a system: I ask my husband or the caregiver to text me every three hours. I don't want to have to ask them for updates, because they might be driving with the kids in the car and it might be dangerous to respond. (#anxious.)

How can you build in reassurances you need to get through your day and minimize the anxiety?

CHUNKING

Chunking helps manage any act that paralyzes you or gives you panic attacks. Chunking is a simple way to divide any task or block of time into manageable pieces.

Leave time. Once you've got a hold on what predictably makes you scared, you have to give yourself enough space to chunk it. One of the worst ways to handle something that scares you is to put it off to the last minute. That's what causes you to panic on a plane, or obsess in a meeting, or go off the rails when you have to talk to your boss.

Find the fear. Usually, there's a peak moment in any task that terrifies you. That exact moment is what you have to work toward, but you have to locate it first. Is it when you're packing for the trip or boarding the flight? Is it when the project is due or when you sign up for it in the first place? What's the part that puts your heart in your throat?

How can you make that better? Here's the part where you put some of your bodywork to good use, and try out some practical ideas. Maybe you need to work on the project every other day instead of one big burst (hence the time thing). Maybe you need to work in a pep talk from your friend the night before the trip. Maybe you need to put a list of things you predictably find funny, or find adorable (here's where YouTube videos are really handy) to watch before you go into that meeting. Be creative, and try some things out. You're one step closer to finding what works.

Reconsider brave. So maybe you can't deal with making presentations. What did someone once tell you *they* thought was brave about you? Maybe a best friend can't believe you routinely speak in front of crowds. Maybe someone's amazed at how you're not affected by heights, or that you got a degree in poetry as well as business. The truth is, things we take for granted often seem brave to others, and things we can't do are a breeze for some. Remembering that it's all relative can be very helpful when you're feeling defined by what (you think) you can't do.

When you're in the moment, find that brave thing. Let yourself feel proud and brave (or amused and shaking your head at your friend) instead of nuts.

Always be breathing. You lucked out: the human body, full stop, is always calmed by breathing when brainwork won't make it happen. And let's face it—when things are bad, often nothing seems like it will work. Start by simply taking a few deep breaths. Find a breathing exercise that works for you. You can use Google, YouTube, apps. There are a million. At first, it will seem silly. But anytime, anywhere, it will work.

Make it a practice. Part of paying attention to your feelings is not re-inventing the wheel each time you're upset. You can't control your feelings, but you can control how you respond to them. If watching cat videos helps you fly, do it. If going through high school yearbooks the night before a meeting lets you remember that This Too Shall Pass, do that. If making a pie chart of your past clients lets you see you'll get more clients, do that.

Sometimes shame or denial makes you try to ignore your feelings in the hopes that you'll be able to push past them. You don't need to push past them—these are your feelings. You should honor them, not avoid them.

Lay off yourself. If you have tried everything—and I mean everything—acknowledge that this is something you can't do, and figure out how you can live without it. If your job requires flying and you *really can't fly*, have a talk with your boss (or yourself). If you are better at doing than pitching, be excellent at executing. You're not superwoman; you don't have to master every single task that scares you. Sometimes not being able to is actually a sign that it's time for a change in your circumstances, not in you.

YOU HAVE TO DEAL WITH IT

So many of us walk around with anxiety that we express through destructive behavior: binge eating, drinking, drugs, spending, random sex, you name it.

I wrote this chapter because I want you to understand that a life with anxiety can be productive and great—and yes, stressful—and it can be an essential piece of who you are at work and life. It is a lion that can be tamed, even channeled. But to get there, you must have the courage to take the first step toward a treatment plan, and the willingness to accept yourself as you are.

4

Loving Your Inner Hermit

Once, I broke my little toe and worked at home for a week. My boss was flummoxed: he couldn't comprehend why an employee who could be such a powerhouse would stay home for a wonky toe. A few months later I tried to quit the job, and he asked me to stay. He said, "Do you want to work from home three days a week?"

How did he know?

Here's the truth: I took so many sick days at so many jobs that I'm embarrassed. At some, I barely went to work. But once I started freelancing, I had a revelation: though my actual productivity didn't change, I loved the feeling of coming in and out of clients' offices, working my own hours, and not having to be "on" all the time.

Being a hermit is different from being an introvert. While introverts can go out and build billion-dollar companies, hermits understand and accept what makes them thrive, and that might be giving themselves lots of space and alone time at work. It's fundamentally a lifestyle choice. Introversion is a character trait. You are born with it. Choosing to be a hermit usually happens after several years in the working world, when you say to yourself, *This just isn't working for me*. You make a choice to alter the place, pace, or space of your work to better suit your need for quiet. You're also willing to accept some limitations to growth (for example, that billion dollars) in order to control your everyday. Being a hermit is saying, "I need to manage my time and boundaries, like being able to be at home in my yoga pants three days a week. And I am willing to banish FOMO from my vocabulary to get there."

Often, we hermits suffer through years of stress and anxiety before finding our work+life fit, because we're not paying attention to our "tell." That's the emotional or physical state that lets you know you're penned in and strained by a work environment that's wrong for your temperament.

My tell was anxiety. And as we know, my anxiety has been my gift and my curse. It's made me work harder to get to where I need to go while trying to keep the monsters at bay, and it's also helped me become very good at saying no. Most important, it's made me be creative in designing a life that can support my family without ruining my spirit. I love to be in the big world, but only so much. Now, though I have been doing the same work for two decades, I set the terms of my time, space, and schedule.

You can be a hermit and be tremendously influential and successful (and I'm not just talking about a Salinger-like recluse writer in the woods). And, though you may not be able to be a hermit all the time or for your whole career, you can work toward building the time and space you need.

Claire Shipman's story

A role model of mine is "secret slacker" and former *Good Morning America* correspondent Claire Shipman. She's a Peabody Award–winning journalist and former White House correspondent for NBC, and she covered the fall of the Soviet Union for CNN. Her first book, *Womenomics,* written with the BBC's Katty Kay, was a *New York Times* bestseller, and her new work is about cultivating confidence.

A real slacker, right? Except most days, she works from home.

About ten years ago, Claire realized her adrenaline-filled work life wasn't working for her anymore. She only found a work+life fit when she "tuned into what I like about work," cut out the constant demands to travel, and was extremely judicious about what she took on.

Womenomics, in fact, began as a bond between Katty and Claire, who felt like misfits in their field. "Instead of comparing notes about our TV careers," Claire says, "we would literally talk about how we could get out of work the next day, or how we hoped we weren't going to have to do a story that night, so we could get home early and be with the kids."

That wasn't, Claire explains, what you're supposed to want in television, where the premium is being on as much as possible.

"After my second child, I kept saying no to reporting trips," Claire says. "An executive and mentor of mine told me, 'Everybody else at the company jumps when we say jump. You don't.'"

Once Claire realized she had to be realistic about what demands she placed on herself and decide what she was willing to sacrifice, it was crucial to tune out other people when they asked things like, "Don't you want to be anchoring a show?'"

Going part-time meant sacrificing high-profile opportunities abroad and at home, including the "seven-year adrenaline rush" of covering the White House. But, she realized, "there is life out here, and I don't have to be exhausted and half-brain-dead."

"Sometimes I look at people who seem to have endless energy, who aren't sitting around ruminating, who just move through, and I'm in awe," Claire says. "But you have to recognize who you are as a person. It's taken me a long time to be able to say to myself, *You don't need to do everything.*" Claire is still an incredibly high-achieving person, but she has been able to lessen some of her own internal expectations of achievement.

Are You a Hermit?

When I think of jobs like airline pilot or surgeon, in which you have to be at the top of your game because lives depend on it, I can't understand how people manage. Not wanting to run an ER doesn't make you a hermit. It might be that you just dislike your boss, your team, or your work product. You might just dislike your whole field. Still, take a moment to consider if it is simply that you love your work, but feel chafed by your work life. Is your stress about what you do, or about how you do it?

1. You've finally taken the leap to a new field/role you think fits you better. You . . .

a) Were right. Your new tasks and environment are much more suited to you.

b) Have the same amount of challenges you always have at work, but feel like you've advanced and are on the right track.

c) Are still miserable. And this is your third switch.

2. You have a meeting with a new client, and the whole team will be there. You are . . .

a) Glad to have them see you do your thing!

b) Terrified about what they'll think you're doing wrong, but glad to have them as backup.

c) Who cares about this meeting? Why do you have to go? Argh . . .

3. You get a day off. Finally you can . . .

a) See the movie you've been wanting to see. You guys did a great job on that contract.

b) Do some work! You always feel weird about closing the door.

c) Dream about what life would be like if every day were a day off.

4. The best part of your work is . . .

a) You love your work, but you also love the office. You have great coworkers.

b) It's amazing when you finish a project you are really proud of.

c) Leaving.

5. You have to meet with the CEO. You are . . .

a) Thrilled. This is a big honor.

b) Terrified. There will be a lot of judging.

c) Terrified. Will she see what a fraud you are?

Mostly a's

You love your field AND you love where you work! Lucky you! The best part is that since you've found a great workplace, you'll always be able to judge when somewhere or some role isn't a fit.

Mostly b's

You're into the work you do, but your personality contains characteristics of a hermit—you like to stay at home, you prefer to be your own boss, and you feel pressured by the go-getter elements of the job. It's important for you to think about what parts of your job you dread so you can try to turn your environment into a place where you can be productive without too much strain. There's no way to be in the wrong work environment without its doing some harm to your work AND your life.

Mostly c's

You hate your work! Why on earth are you doing it, and does it pay enough to make it worth it? You need to start thinking about a field that may make you less miserable. The good news is that even though switching is scary, you'll find your work more fulfilling when you hit the right field, and more skills will transfer than you thought. Then, and only then, will you be able to tell if you're ALSO, God forbid, a hermit.

GETTING STARTED

The Digital Challenge

There is a premium placed on social interaction and networking, but the workplace is changing, as are social norms about working from home and networking online. There's good news for the ambitious hermit. Here's the wonderful thing about the digital age: it's hermit-friendly.

I love being able to engage in thoughtful conversations via e-mail or Facebook throughout the day. When it comes to this hermit-friendly digital space, the pleasure of a sustained conversation over text should not be quickly dismissed. As much as I struggle with IRL social stuff, I have an incredible community of friends and acquaintances online who ensure I'm supported, mentally stimulated, and kept au courant, all from my home office.

Best of all, it feels completely low pressure. As psychologist and digital media scholar Yalda Uhls says, "When you don't have the social pressure of having to immediately respond to another person, when you have time to write versus speak, you can be more articulate and thoughtful."

However, that digital revolution is a gift and a curse. I can't remember the last time I worked with a large organization whose team was in the same office. Our conference calls are always a jumble of areas codes and muted cell phones. For jobs that rely on a computer, the workplace doesn't need to be in a specific location, and you can get face time from FaceTime.

In fact, 20 percent of American workers "telework" most of the time. Census data show that 50 percent of workers have jobs that are compatible with working remotely. And, unsurprisingly, 90 percent of workers say they would like to be able to telework[1] two or three days a week, with "on" days for meetings with colleagues and clients.

Sounds like the ideal hermit schedule, right?

But for every hour we gain working remotely, our smartphone overcompensates. Constant contact with our work—via mobile technology—is eroding any sense of separation between home and work. Sometimes the race to respond to a colleague's e-mail overwhelms any rational sense of how urgent that e-mail actually is.

Sadly, this is not something that can be changed by implementing a flexible work policy. It's bigger than any of us. Harvard Business School's Leslie Perlow studies time at work, most notably what happens when teams have more freedom to control their time. Spoiler alert: they are happier, more productive, and more engaged. Teams whose managers create and enforce clear boundaries about when to be "on" reduce burnout, turnover, and mistakes made by stress.

Perlow notes even as managers struggle with being "on," they expect it from those they manage. Über-connectivity, in our minds, still equals performance, and the ideal worker is always on. Workers that resist the ideal pay a price.

What's more, as flexibility quickly evolves, we're working without a map. "A strict separation between work and life requires setting micro-boundaries daily," Perlow explains. "Will I answer e-mail now or not? Can I turn off my phone on weekends? Many people don't know where to draw the line."[2]

For a hermit, the tether is a double-edged sword. When the choice is between being chained to our iPhones in the quiet of our own space or working in an open-plan office, we choose the chains.

I made my peace with my smartphone a while ago. The majority of my day, I'm on conference calls and checking e-mail compulsively, just like the rest of us. But I'm doing it in bed or while making soup. And I don't have to talk to anyone during lunch. I control the space, pace, and place of my work.

The flexible workplace is still in its adolescence. But it may help us finally learn that the world doesn't end if you let an e-mail go unanswered for an hour. As Claire Shipman says, simply breaking the cycle of adrenaline we get into when we work in an always-on environment lends tremendous perspective and, ultimately, freedom.

A Hermit's Challenges: Strong Ties and Loose Ties

I don't like socializing, and even though I love my friends, I get nervous before dates. I like to be alone with my family or with myself. As I have gotten older, I've become even more introverted. Because picking up the phone or making a date feels hard, I'm not great at forming close friendships. It's often easier for me to maintain a large network of casual acquaintances on the Internet than see my very close friends in real life.

But there are two types of relationships we must maintain as a functional adult: strong ties and loose ties. Strong ties are your closest social group, your real friends or intimate colleagues. Loose ties are acquaintances, occasional colleagues, and members of your community, such as other parents at school or your neighbors.

Being a hermit is challenging to both kinds of relationship. If you're an introvert, you may love to be with friends and socialize, but doing so drains you of energy, so you have to limit it. Sprinkle in a little social anxiety, and you've got a lot to overcome, because you may find it tough to be a good friend to strong ties and avoid being seen as rude to loose ones. But forcing yourself to work at strong and loose ties is important, first because having good friends is wonderful and healthy, and second because loose ties are the key to your success, especially if you're a hermit. In my experience, relationships with loose ties, ballasted by online conversations, are the secret strategy for a successful hermit to advance or bring in new business without having to get out there too often.

I used to feel tremendously guilty about this, until I learned a lesson from my minister, Claire Feingold Thoryn, who leads my Unitarian Universalist congregation. Funny and charming, capable of commanding a crowd, Claire seemed like the last person to be a secret hermit.

But, as she told us in one of her sermons, when her friend was about to give birth for the first time, and struggling, Claire kept putting off calling and checking in, even though her friend had specifically asked her to. Instead she sent half-hearted texts about plans that never came to fruition. With two young children and a busy congregation, she had no energy to talk on the phone and engage.

But when Claire's friend, having trouble nursing, texted, "I need your help," Claire cleared her day, got in her car, and drove to see her friend. And, as she told us from the pulpit, "I never did make that call, but I helped her latch the baby. Being there in a pinch made up for my lack of follow-through."

Claire's story is useful to think about if you feel guilty for needing alone time and space, even if it's from your good friends. It doesn't mean you don't love them. So maybe you're not great at staying in touch or remembering birthdays. Concentrate on being a good friend when it really matters.

Maintaining Close Ties

Because I need so much alone time, I have a hard time giving over leisure time to others.

I avoid the phone, and the people I love and respect most. I don't call them back not because I don't love them or I don't care, but because I feel anxious doing it.

How silly is that? You're my friend, I love you, but I feel anxious picking up the phone to dial you. I can't really explain it. So I asked Dr. Ellen Hendriksen, the social anxiety expert. It's called anticipatory anxiety, and it's a common behavior if social settings make you anxious. Dr. Hendriksen says she can even feel this anxiety before she hits send on an e-mail, which I can totally relate to. So what's her advice?

"I tell myself to be brave for ten seconds. You can do anything for ten seconds. That's the amount of time it takes to dial a number. That's the amount of time it takes to hit send. That's the amount of time it takes to walk in the door. So, if you can just get over that initial hump, you'll get into the rhythm of talking to your friend and forget you were anxious."

I also like to give myself guidelines I know I can keep to. For example, perhaps quick check-ins are easier for you than heart-to-hearts. Or you can make space only to call one friend a week. Don't forget that a little goes a long way; leave a voice mail if having a conversation is too time-consuming.

Reverend Claire likens being a friend to prayer: pray as you can, not as you can't. She also notes that it's common to have stronger relationships with people who live nearby. It's easy to lose touch with your friends who live far away, but it's meaningful to build your support network where you are.

I am lucky in that my friends persist. Over the years the people I truly value are those who don't let me hide. They don't let me get away with my own bullshit. If I don't return their calls, they keep calling me and calling me.

But over the years, as I've identified this trait in myself, I have gone from slamming myself as a "bad friend" to calling myself an "atypical" friend. Remember: Facebook, e-mail, and texting have brought out the hermit in all of us. Making time in person, even if it's once a year, is the best of all.

The trick behind dealing with your hermit behaviors while still maintaining those close ties is to be a wonderful friend in batches you can handle. And give yourself a little credit, even when you fail.

Maintaining Loose Ties

I love the listening-and-thinking part of church. I was not raised in a faith community, and it is something I want badly for my children. But I hate the coffee hour that immediately follows.

After we'd attended church for a few months, my husband (who grew up going to church several times a week) delivered some bad news to me: coffee hour is how you build community. It, not the sermon, is the key.

And what happens when you throw community out the window isn't pretty. In her essay "Am I an Introvert, or Just Rude?" self-confessed hermit KJ Dell'Antonia[3] tried embracing her desire to skip out. At first, she writes, saying no "brought with it a keen, almost illicit pleasure." She left meetings and assemblies early, and once sat in the car and read a book while her children attended a family athletic event. "I'd spent so long accommodating the world's demand that I get out there and participate," she writes. "Finally, the world seemed willing to accommodate me."

As it turns out, it wasn't. Her friends took her "tortoiseshell" as rudeness, and her kids were enraged. It also wasn't good for her. Data prove that even a small interaction with another person outside your family unit increases personal and group happiness (yes, even for introverts).[4] Giving in to her own discomfort was ruining her friendships, her family life, and the internal life she was working so hard to protect.

But how to engage when you just want to put in your earbuds and disappear? Smile! A warm expression goes far at school drop-off or a professional association mixer. Smiles also serve a social purpose: a warm, genuine smile puts everyone at ease, signaling altruism and community mindedness.[5] It's the first step in striking up a conversation. Ask the dry cleaner how she's doing. Joke with the barista. You'll be surprised at how quickly even greeting the dad you say hi to on the street as you bring your own kid to school develops into a pleasant ritual. And then, when you see him at church, you'll have someone to talk to over the coffee.

The Loose-Ties Payoff

When you're out in a world of strangers, it can be hard to stay open, especially when your phone and headphones are there to give you a perfectly good excuse to shut off from the world. But loose ties leave you open to chance and serendipity, important in both career and community.

As I've said before, I'm never at my best in airports, especially after a flight from Dubai or some other faraway place my work takes me. But I have to remind myself that you never know who you'll meet if you're open and friendly in public. I met Steve, who runs a big division of a giant technology company, in line at Logan Airport—and literally just as I was outlining this chapter, he e-introduced me to his new colleague, who's in charge of women's leadership programming at the tech company. I e-mailed back about the serendipitous moment: "As it happens, I was just working on including a piece about the need to unplug and be present where you are . . ."

Some breaks are also a great way to meet kindred spirits and establish loose ties. Kenny Lao, who founded Rickshaw Dumpling Company, told me he met his most useful connections in front of his headquarters in Madison Square Park—including his future husband—on one of his many smoke breaks. (Kenny wants you to know he has now quit. Cigarettes are the really unhealthy version of hiding in the bathroom.)

I met one of my dearest colleagues and best hires on a smoke break, back when I was young and stupid and smoked. Mike Krempasky and I bonded outside a dive bar in D.C. after the bitter election of 2004. He is a fierce conservative, I am a fierce liberal, and we'd never have become friends were it not for my needing a lighter. A few months later, when I needed to hire a supersmart conservative strategist, he was my first call, and the introduction was easy.

If you don't smoke (and you shouldn't!), you may just have to pluck up your courage to make the first move when it comes to meeting new loose ties—whether it's starting to say "good morning" to the person you pass every day in the street, chatting with the barista, or leaving your house keys with a neighbor. It almost always pays off. The *New York Times's* KJ Dell'Antonia laughed as she told me a story about meeting Nicholas Kristof, the esteemed journalist and activist, at the copier on one of her rare trips to the *Times* headquarters in Manhattan.

Kristof and Dell'Antonia are colleagues, but KJ was still nervous to talk to him in person, although they had e-mailed. "I wanted to meet him," she said. "I'm a great admirer of his. I took a deep breath, turned around, pulled myself together and said, 'Hi.' That's a lot of harder than sending an e-mail or tagging someone on Facebook." But for KJ, that small moment cemented the bond of two colleagues in a visceral way.

Sometimes, a hi is all it takes.

ADOPT AN EXTROVERT

My husband, Nicco, is not only the love of my life, he is also my greatest teacher and mentor. He's helped me temper my reclusive tendencies; to think more expansively; to take risks. And I have literally stolen my entire playbook from him.

Nicco is naturally an extrovert and superconnector. He loves nothing better than a good cocktail party or community event. He would like to be out every night. (It's actually amazing we're still married.)

An extrovert partner has two great uses: he or she can serve both as a model and as a "pipeline for opportunities," as financial therapist Amanda Clayman says about hers. "When I'm feeling inadequate, I think, what would Greg do in this situation?" He's also a constant source of connections for her. "I don't feel like I need to go out and try to socialize all the time," she says.

Of course, your adopted extrovert doesn't need to be a romantic partner. (Sometimes, it's easier if he isn't!) They can be your colleague, business partner, or friend. Play anthropologist: What are the characteristics or traits in your adopted extrovert you'd most like to borrow, if only for a few hours? Perhaps it's being able to enter a group discussion with ease, or recount your hilarious stories to a captivated audience.

I think often of one of my earliest bosses, Betty Hudson. The only six-foot-two-inch cheerleader in the history of the University of Georgia, I'm sure, she was taller than me, but so elegant and graceful. Betty had Ted Turner and half of the most powerful people in media on speed dial, and made you feel like her best friend within five minutes. She would walk into a room and crack a joke (often at her own expense), and everyone melted. I studied her like a book. And on a good day, I think she'd be proud of how I can work a room—even if I have to force myself to take on those traits I don't instinctively have.

Your Kitchen Cabinet

When I set out to interview people for this book, I didn't have to do much research. Just like Mitt Romney had his "binders full of women," I have a digital sisterhood—my kitchen cabinet—of subject-matter experts and wise confidantes. We might see each other once or twice a year, or even less, but we keep in touch in a meaningful way online. (By the way, did you know Mitt Romney actually did have real binders?)

Your kitchen cabinet is separate from supportive colleagues or senior mentors—those are people to whom you might not want to show your vulnerabilities. A kitchen cabinet is made up of people of different skills and professional backgrounds who will push you in different directions and into different arenas—and, ideally, become true friends. Diversity is key: no pale, male, and stale group-think here!

Time, place, and circumstance can work wonders when it comes to creating kinship, and it need not be in person. My friend Allyson Downey created a fantastic Google group for working moms of children under five in order to research her book *Here's the Plan*. She plumbed us for wisdom, and we plumbed each other. When my daughter was eight months old, that group was the only place I felt I could turn when debating whether to wean.

For now, ask yourself, *Who's in your kitchen cabinet? Who could be?* Here are some people to consider . . .

❑ A financial expert
❑ Your personal-brand guru
❑ Someone who will always tell you the truth
❑ A master negotiator
❑ Your friend with amazing personal style
❑ A friend with a similar parenting philosophy, with older kids

Get Out of Your Head

I would wager that if you're a hermit, you're prone to stewing. Ruminating. Dwelling. But if you're a natural ruminator, you have to practice getting out of your head because when you're too much in your head, little gets done and moods get dark. Stepping outside our own feelings gets us in a better frame of mind than wondering how we are coming up short or what other people are thinking.

Here are three simple tricks to get out of your head and engage in the world.

Link into meaning: If you're feeling stuck in a negative pattern and want to retreat from the world, Claire Shipman recommends consciously giving more thought to how your work ties into a larger mission or movement, or how you can help other people. This is similar to the practice of snapping out of FOMO by recognizing a colleague's great work. Meaning in work is very important; sometimes equal to salary or even happiness in surveys of engaged employees.[6] So if you're feeling like a lowly cog in the wheel compared to a superstar friend, remember that wheel is important, and your cog is a crucial piece of getting it done.

Just say hi, or smile to a stranger. Sometimes a smile is all it takes to snap out of rumination. As KJ Dell'Antonia says, "No one wants to be trapped on a plane for six hours looking at your seat mate's grandchildren, but a simple smile and a 'how are you' really is not a lot to ask." She cites a study showing that even though commuters insist they prefer solitude on their journey, when they briefly connect with another commuter—a smile or a pleasantry—they report greater pleasure and a more positive experience.[7]

Send a thinking-of-you text, leave a kind voice mail, endorse a colleague on LinkedIn, or make a small online donation to your favorite charity. Wharton's Adam Grant has repeatedly shown that small but frequent acts of giving fuel productivity and generativity. Giving gets you out of your head.[8] It's a small and nonthreatening way to snap out of it.

THE WAY OF . . . GOING OUT OF YOUR WAY

Love your hermit self, but remember that it's not your entire self. When you love, love hard, and when you choose to communicate outward, do it with your whole self. Every day you can push yourself to be a healthy hermit, protecting your time and space while still engaging positively with the world.

You are not being selfish; you're saving the best for when it's really needed. No one says it better than this wonderful quote from the Indian teachings of Samkhya: "This stopping of the movement outwards is not self-defense, but rather an effort to have the response come from within, from the deepest part of one's being."

Still, when self-defense feels like disengaging, or when my anxiety or depression or even a bad news cycle gets the better of me, I remember that goodness happens when you're engaged in the world, and the very loosest of ties are often in your corner, too.

In February 2015, I was at my wit's end, a five-week-old baby wrapped around me, two screaming boys behind, in line at the local Ralph's grocery store with a giant cart of pantry staples. We'd moved from Boston to Los Angeles exactly three days before, and were sleeping on air mattresses and eating on the floor, awaiting our furniture from the East Coast. I was disoriented, but I was more than that. I was depressed, anxious, postpartum, and in a fog of rage at my husband for moving us all 2,592 miles and promptly disappearing into his exciting new job.

But I must have looked up from my fog and vaguely smiled (or teared up) at the woman in line ahead of me, because she moved aside to let me go in front of her. Then, giving me a sympathetic smile, she asked, "Can I help you with anything?"

"Yes," I blurted. "I need a preschool for my four-year-old."

She didn't miss a beat: call this one, she said, and wrote the name down on a coupon. Sure enough, I called, and they accepted my son Tom to start the following week.

That small act of kindness welcomed me to California in the best possible way.

5

Vision Quest

I t's not a shock: people who wake up with the sense that their lives are guided by a larger plan feel better. Doctors have even found it increases health. And having a strong vision works. A recent survey of 2,631 successful CEOs who ran companies with at least $1 million in yearly revenue found it was the single trait that rose above all others in importance.[1]

But for sensitive souls who are tormented by achievement porn and a poor work+life fit, "purpose" can feel like just one more unrealistic burden. Just think back to perfect-looking Kayla Itsines and her "motivational" Instagram posts ("I hope you feel beautiful today," she grams, next to a selfie of her concave thighs and stunning abs).

Your vision for your career doesn't need to be grand, and I'm not big on the single, overwhelming goal. (Though I like to think that Taylor Swift, whom my son Tom is obsessed with, knew she was going to be the world's biggest pop star when she was only six.) I am big on the nitty-gritty. After all, my vision includes not getting dressed for work until noon and cooking between meetings.

A vision is your core set of principles, aligning your work to the reasons you live your life the way you do. Vision means executing, growing, and managing your own definition of success. It means imagining a work life you really want. Yes, purpose equals power—but if your purpose isn't right for you, the power will not come. Consider a vision that gives you room to be happy *and* imperfect.

Vision vs. Achievement Porn

For many people, achieving a long-term goal is *more* important than being happy every day. That is a wonderful quality and is, I'm sure, characteristic of many people who are tremendous leaders and who work to change the world. It's okay if you're not one of those people. I certainly am not.

We assume a vision has to mean deciding to win Olympic gold or having a *New York Times* bestseller. But your true vision is probably less dramatic in scope. Visions are small, and particular. A great vision is: I want to wake up happy Monday morning.

In fact, creating your vision is mostly an exercise in self-acceptance, and even a decidedly un-fancy one can make you happy and successful. That means you don't need a shaman or a life coach to find one, but you do need to be honest with yourself.

I might want to be a billionaire or live in a castle, but these are fantasies, not visions. A vision is that castle, downsized: a certain level of financial freedom; meaningful work (in my case, a successful small business that allows me to work at home); and room to accomplish a few personal goals, like having children or writing a book.

It's also not about material things. Sometimes when I close my eyes, my vision seems to involve—cough—luxury cars and expensive handbags. When it does, I say to myself, *That's great, Morra, and you should work hard because you like nice things, but your vision for your life is not about Chanel.* It involves never having to go work in an office that uses fluorescent lights again.

WHAT'S WRONG WITH HAVING PURPOSE?

The "double bottom-line business"—one that is successful and does good—is a great innovation, and it deserves its global visibility. But, like achievement porn, widespread social entrepreneurship has had the unintended consequence of convincing young people they are not doing enough if their work does not have a larger global purpose.

But when "purpose" becomes one more box to tick off on the achievement list, it can lose all meaning. There's even pressure for one's extracurricular life to be socially conscious.

But I say, as someone who earns a large portion of my income from helping organizations advertise their purpose, valuing good business practices doesn't have to mean imbuing everything—from what you buy at Safeway to your business plan—with purpose.

If you have not started an organic tampon business by age twenty-five, do not beat yourself up. Please. Do good work, be kind to people, support the causes that truly move you, and your purpose will evolve naturally.

My Company's Vision Story

Sometimes your vision will come to you in a flash, but more often you must create space to let it emerge.

My vision arrived after a tumultuous time: a crippling depression, the birth of my first child, the Great Recession, a move to a new city, and many fruitless applications to doctoral programs. It came when I realized I'd been pursuing a completely financially unviable dream.

Here's how it came about.

Because I was an experienced blogger and expert in women's online community thanks to years at iVillage.com and BlogHer.com, my freelance clients were particularly intrigued by my expertise. I knew a lot about connecting women through online community—and identifying influential women online for my client organizations to partner with. Word started getting around that there was a good consultant who focused on helping organizations reach women online.

About a year in, I was making good money, spending a lot of time with my son, and enjoying my work. I was blogging about women, work, and leadership, which fulfilled my need to be engaged in civic work and discourse, and got me a tiny bit of visibility, which fulfilled both my ego and business development goals. I worked from home unless I was traveling, which meant I put on makeup and nice clothes. Otherwise I was in yoga pants.

And one morning I woke up and it hit me: this was going to be my business. It was going to be called Women Online. We would be the first digital marketing agency focusing on creating online campaigns that mobilized women for good causes. I registered the domain that morning and began thinking about a logo. My first logo was awful. But I was so excited about the idea I couldn't think of anything else.

One month later I knew that my consulting firm was going to be different. Many online leaders build influencer databases, but mine had a key difference: it was database of women bloggers who cared about social change. I called it the Mission List.

Because my vision was about women's advancement, I was committed to my employees having the kind of flexible, manageable workload I set for myself. We wouldn't have an office, and everyone who worked for me would be able to keep their own hours and plan their own days. It would be small and profitable, meaningful and manageable.

But visions are tricky, and you have to give them time to materialize.

Right when we started, it pretty much came to a halt. I got pregnant with my second son when my first was only thirteen months old, and my father was diagnosed with terminal cancer. Although my sister assumed the major portion of caretaking duties, 2010 and half of 2011 were taken up with my dad's care, death, and estate, as well as my wonderful new son Tom. Growing a company was just not on the agenda; it was all about subsistence, paying the bills, and preserving time for Dad, toddler, and baby.

Still, things slowly picked back up.

Now we have worked for two presidential campaigns, for the world's largest charitable foundation, the nation's largest labor union, the nation's largest not-for-profit organization, and even America's largest bank. We've helped the United Nations and Malala Yousafzai get their messages out. There was even a brief, intoxicating period where I flirted with an acquisition offer for the firm. (I felt like I was in a movie—it was sexy and fun, but completely unrealistic.) We have now grown to eight employees.

There's a wonderful British saying: "Start as you mean to go on." I like to think setting a strong vision creates real strength and intention. Through three children, two cross-country moves, and countless other life changes, Women Online's vision has stayed wonderfully consistent.

And I will say, the vision paid off.

WOMEN ONLINE'S VISION STATEMENT

When I started online, I had a clear mission: to work with influential women's communities online; to work with organizations that genuinely had a mission to improve women's lives; and to help empower them so they could take action—because women vote more, we advocate more, and we dominate social media channels. That was key to crafting our vision statement.

"WE'RE A SMALL SHOP, BUT WE HAVE HUGE CLIENTS."

We aim to be a hugely profitable, high-impact boutique firm.

We deliver the absolute best client service and smart thinking.

We sit at the grown-ups' table. We work with clients who value us.

We work with clients whose values we share.

We have a distinct voice, we advocate for social change and social responsibility, and we manage a community of women with the same goals.

All WO team members get to have a life and build a sustainable business.

We focus on what we can achieve and do well, and don't get upset about what we should be doing or what others are doing.

We define success for us.

GETTING STARTED

Setting Your Vision

There are a million books on setting your vision, but before you get overwhelmed, here are some simple steps to coax your vision from its hiding place.

Put It in Writing. Write down a vision statement for your next five years at work, or for your business. It's about putting on paper (or iPad) what you want to carry through on in your life. There are no rules here. Just try to capture a vision that encompasses not only how you want to feel about your work or business, but what you want to do. Shut off your inner critic!

Ask, what motivates me? It may take you a while to arrive at the answer . . . or at least, to arrive at your honest answer. To get started, look at the categories on the next page. How close are you to each category? What are the specifics of your contribution? Your control? Your salary?

❑ **Passion maximizer:** It's very important to me to love my work and feel like I am making a valuable contribution to something I care about. I'd rather work like crazy at a job I love than earn tons of money (although money is fine, too!).

❑ **Income maximizer:** I am motivated by money. I will sacrifice short-term happiness, time, or flexibility to earn the most money I can.

❑ **Flexibility maximizer:** I am motivated by control over my schedule and work flow. It's most important to me to call my own shots and work at the place, pace, and time I want.

❑ **Prestige maximizer:** I need to feel important. I want to be in the thick of it, and feel like a crucial player.

Ask, do my short-term and long-term goals for career and life match up? Goals are complex, and involve an integration of life, work, and leisure. It's important to make sure your short- and long-term goals can work together.

Take a piece of paper and brainstorm responses to the following statements. Be as detailed as you can.

❑ In the short term, I want to work X way and accomplish X, Y, and Z.

❑ In the next ten or fifteen years, I want to do X and I want to have done X, Y, and Z.

If your short-and long-term goals are at a disconnect, you need to rethink things. For example, if you want to take a year off and travel around the world, but also want to be a millionaire in five years, that might need a rethink. But working hard for five years on your income could open up that year off down the line.

More/less exercise. My friend and colleague Christine Koh is a huge intention-setter, and I've learned from her. I asked Christine about the vision she guides her life by, and she shared this exercise:

Take a piece of paper. Make two columns, "More" and "Less." In each column, make a list: What do I want more of? What do I want less of? Look at the list to see what items elicit a really strong reaction. For the items that elicit the strongest reactions, jot down action items to help move them forward. Then, revisit every six months.

What's my vision for the everyday? It's important to have a long-term plan, but you need to stick to those goals in order to achieve them! If you hate your work in the day-to-day, chances are you won't stick to your goals. You need to be sure the actual work you do is the right fit for your temperament and wishes.

When Christine was preparing to write her dissertation, she saw the academic journal articles stacked around her and she felt despair. She hated academic journals. She still powered through and got her Ph.D., but it took her years to realize it was a terrible fit. She wanted to be with people, and to be creative—she just hadn't paid attention to how her work made her feel in the moment.

Another friend of mine had a similar realization after making a ton of money as a recruiter on Wall Street. After years, it finally hit her: she hated the bulk of her workday, which she spent talking on the phone.

So ask yourself some specific questions. Do you want to be at a computer, writing alone? Never in front of a computer? Running around on sales calls?

Do you like to be with people, constantly working in teams? Or do you need lots of alone time? How much flexibility do you like? Deadlines? Needing to be somewhere at a certain time? This stuff matters. How do you feel about flying? I'm serious. Do you love it? Hate it?

A fundamental misfit might necessitate a new career. But I'd wager that there are elements of your work you love (after all, you chose it) and that you might need to shift time, place, content, or pace in order to make work enjoyable again.

If this is the case, then . . .

Tweak It

Cali Yost coined this term, and it's a fantastic way to find your work+life fit without making a 180-degree shift.

Assuming you like the meat of what you do, think about the tasks that are part of your day job that fill you with dread or make you nervous. What kind of scaffolding do you need to make that dread manageable? If you are a hermit or an introvert, how can you shift your work to make it less stressful?

Once I left the 24/7 nature of political campaigns and the stressful and draining, brightly lit corporate office life, I realized I absolutely loved the substance of my work. I could tweak my skill set, my relationships and network, and my professional credibility to meet a new vision for my work life.

So How Do You Start?

My friend Mitra Kalita is a powerhouse media executive. I asked her how she prepares for a big change in her life, and she said, "Haircut. Buy a house. Get the closets done. New me." Her risk profile is definitely not mine, but, as Mitra said, "I stress more over my hair than real estate."

Everyone has a different definition of risk and different triggers for stress. Everything stresses me out, so I have learned to build in self-care tactics to keep the old cortisol down.

For those of us who are prone to high stress and anxiety, building in a calming or meditative habit is crucial, especially when you're entering a period of change. Stanford brain surgeon Dr. James Doty notes, "People don't appreciate the power of their intention to change everything. Even short periods of time where you are attentive, if you will, or mindful, and have intention to open your heart, have a profound effect."[2]

One of my favorite techniques is guided visualization. I'm too anxious and fidgety to sit still and meditate in silence, but I love to listen to a good guided meditation. (Tara Brach's podcasts are favorites, because she had a good sense of humor.)

KITCHEN CABINET WISDOM

Building in self-care as you contemplate change is key. It can be as simple as a walk alone, or time in quiet. I asked some of my most grounded and wise Facebook friends to imagine they were about to embark on a new chapter. What advice they would give? Here are their favorite tools, tricks, and resources:

"I like the idea of thinking of this kind of time as a 'fertile void.' You don't exactly know what's next, but the possibilities are manifold."

—Cynthia Freeman

"I don't ask my kids to figure out what they want to be when they grow up. I ask them to imagine what a happy day would look like. I try to take that advice, too. The trick is not ever asking yourself what you want to BE, but what you want to DO!"

—Dottie Enrico

"I make sure to book time for myself in a setting I can concentrate in and bring along banner paper, a black Sharpie, some colored Mr. Sketch markers, Tony Buzan's Mind Map technique, and some quality time wringing out my brain to squeeze all the ideas out."

—Stephanie Goodell

"Triangulate with insights from your head, heart, and soul. Head: talk with your most analytical advisers! Heart: ask those who know and love you truly, especially your kids. Soul: tap into your inner wisdom."

—Carolyn Ou

"Ask for coffee or lunch dates with people you admire for advice and counsel. Buy a new nice notebook, and take notes on EVERYTHING."

—Leah Russin

"Follow your curiosity and spend time doing things you enjoy. They often lead directly, or indirectly, to new opportunities."

—Britt Bravo

"A weekend away before or during a transition is the best. Stay at the hotel. Do not leave. Actually be quiet and rest. And, always, eat ice cream."

—Jennie O'Hagan Korneychuk

GET SERIOUS

Just because your vision seems less ambitious than the stereotypical business powerhouse doesn't mean you can take it less seriously. Take the space and time to set intentions, to marinate in them, and to write them down. Give yourself the gift of stillness as you enter a period of transition.

Even more important, try to turn off the achievement supersizer. This is really hard to do! It may take you weeks or even months of writing, talking to trusted friends and counselors, and daydreaming to get to the true kernel of your vision. Every time it feels too small, you'll be tempted to beef it up or reframe it in a more societally acceptable way. For example: you may say your vision is to be an entrepreneur, while in truth your vision is to have more control over your work life. Those are two very different things! One is glamorous and the other feels prosaic. So work hard at being honest with yourself.

6

Setting Boundaries

I t's easy for billionaire geniuses like Steve Jobs to say no. It's not easy for people who hide in bathrooms. Why? Because every cultural message says success means saying yes. And I envy every extroverted go-getter out there because I also think I would be thirty-seven times more successful if I actually liked to go to cocktail parties.

But for a hermit, creating healthy boundaries—meaning, saying no—is key.

After my father died in 2010 and I thought I was done having kids, I felt compelled to say yes to almost everything. Deliver a proposal for a potential client by tomorrow morning? Absolutely! Fly to Texas to join a panel discussion for free? Sure. It's business development! Agree to write an eight-hundred-word, unpaid blog post for a barely read website? Count me in!

But the day before that panel in Texas, I'd suffer a crippling anxiety attack. Not to mention, my Amex bill could top $10,000 a month with all that uncompensated travel in the name of "business development."

Although I had the best of intentions when I said yes, I burned a few bridges with last-minute cancellations. I ducked out during meetings. Once, I canceled an important three-day meeting in D.C. when a giant blizzard was predicted to hit Boston and I wanted to return home to my kids. I had reached my personal limit, but it was awkward for me and for my client.

It wasn't merely that giving too much time to pointless efforts strained essential work hours and time with family. Being an entrepreneurial doormat stripped me of an essential strength: the ability to maintain the healthy boundaries I needed.

After too many years of regretting saying yes or being unable to follow through, I learned my lesson. Saying yes too much wreaks havoc on my mental and physical health, my time, and my finances. I had to respect my personal limits, even if I didn't like them.

Tuning In

My dear friend, psychologist Rebecca Harley, tells me that the people who come to see her often have just one question: "How the hell did I get here?" The answer, she thinks, is that they tuned out a lot of messages.

It's very difficult to give yourself permission to get off a path, especially if getting on that path has been hard. It's difficult to say, after years of work, that you are in a place that you really don't recognize. But every time I suffered an anxiety attack on a trip or felt depressed while standing in the middle of a cocktail party, my personal boundaries were being crossed. I just wasn't tuning in.

That's the challenge: to tune into these messages, and then define your boundaries.

Not tuning into anxiety or depression comes at a cost. In my case, the message was my constant, debilitating migraines and pain in my entire upper body. By 4 P.M., I'd be downing Motrin and lying on an ice pack, in terrible pain. That's to say nothing of that retainer I needed to unclench my jaw. Other "messages" your body might be sending you could be an aching back or neck, irritable bowels, panic attacks, inability to sleep . . . I could go on.

This begs the question, why can crossing boundaries cripple you? Because boundaries are a *big deal*. Your physical boundaries control your safety by establishing your level of comfort with touching and interaction, and your emotional boundaries protect you from being crushed by toxic personalities or enmeshed by codependent ones.

Your boundaries around work are equally important, and they encompass every other kind. As Darlene Lancer, licensed marriage and family therapist puts it, "Boundaries are your bottom line."[1] Limits are the rules you put in place to maintain your boundaries, so to stay successful in your job, you might need to set limits on your personal time or distance yourself from coworkers who get too close. You might need to set limits on clients who are discourteous or even abusive, or work that overstimulates you or creates emotional turmoil.

You need permission to feel when your boundaries are being crossed—and it's not a one-shot deal. I give you permission to say, "That's not going to work for me." Find your boundaries and your limits so you can define the terms of your work and success.

What's the Difference Between a Limit and a Boundary?

Understanding the difference between a limit and a boundary has always been difficult for me. So I turned to my wise therapist friend Rebecca to explain them, and she led me through a helpful exercise. She told me to imagine I was in a swimming pool with a rope dividing the shallow from the deep end. Wherever I was unable to stand securely, the boundary was being crossed. A limit, on the other hand, is a declaration of a boundary—it's the rope itself. Limits are tactical: I will not check e-mail after 5 P.M. on a Friday, because working during the weekend sends me off into the deep end—the boundary.

Once you understand what your boundaries are, you can set limits—although they may not make you the most popular girl on the block. Leah Ginsberg, a former travel editor at Yahoo, has a boundary many of us may relate to. On trips with fellow journalists—which often meant hours of group activity—she was always the one to go back to her room after dinner, skipping drinks and socializing. "I think everyone thought I was a bitch, basically. But I literally can't function if I don't have some time to myself." Even if you're not stuck on a tour bus with colleagues twelve hours a day, you may feel overwhelmed by frequent socializing with coworkers. Once you realize that that's a boundary, you can politely set a limit: "No, I can't go to your happy hour tonight." I will leave you here with something to chew on, courtesy of workplace expert Erica Keswin: "When Gallup found that having a "best friend" (not "close" or "good" but "best") at work was correlated to higher performance, they were pointing to something that introverts excel at—making meaningful connections." Focus on the quality of your connections at work, not the quantity!

Setting and Maintaining Your Boundaries

You can't feel 100 percent comfortable keeping your boundaries and your work life in sync unless you feel you are satisfying the expectations of other people in your life. Your efficacy in maintaining your limits is as much about managing your emotions and anxieties around other people's expectations as it is about you actually getting things done. The magic is realizing you don't just have to fulfill expectations. You can meet your boundaries and make others understand your needs.

Whether managing a team at work or a toddler at home, making peace with others' expectations of you is an important skill. And here's the truth: The people in your life may not respect your boundaries! They may want more time, or for you to climb faster, or to make more money.

Living out your own terms of success requires intense focus and self-regulation, as well as practice, with everyone from your romantic partner, to your family, to your team at work, to your boss, and to your clients—even Facebook. (But sorry in advance, I can't really help with toddlers.)

GETTING STARTED

I'm Ready to Tune In. How Do I Start?

Engaging proactively with your feelings can give you, as Rebecca Harley says, an "early warning system" for your boundaries being crossed. She suggests two emotional cues to tune in on: discomfort and resentment.

Both of these emotions are common signals that your personal boundaries are being threatened, but they are also emotions we are taught to suppress and question. When an interaction or situation triggers either emotion, examine the interaction or expectation, and ask why. When your boss texts you at 9 P.M. for a quick urgent matter, you may feel a moment's twinge of resentment but you can understand it's a reasonable request and quickly move on. When she continually texts you just because she can, your resentment is probably growing strong because your boundaries have been crossed.

Rebecca Harley tells us, "We have our feelings not just to communicate outward but to communicate inward." She suggests a mindfulness exercise to begin to tune in. First, simply observe. What doesn't feel quite right? What is arising? Next, try to put words onto the emotion you're feeling. They don't have to be specific.

Once you're paying attention, you're on the road to knowing what comes next. Rebecca says that by virtue of paying attention, you're getting a closer approximation to what the right decision is for you. Give yourself a baseline permission to recognize that your feelings might mean something, then allow a willingness to observe until they start to resolve themselves into a clearer directional message.

Even though I cried in the bathroom and had migraines, it was my hatred of fluorescent lights that allowed me to tune into my feelings—and it's recognizing those signals in yourself that will allow you to tune into yours so you can set the boundaries you need.

THE BOUNDARY TEST

Before I take on a new task, client engagement, trip, or project, I ask these questions of myself and the team. If the project makes us say yes to enough of them, game on.

Is this something I can do from home or with some autonomy in scheduling? I need to feel autonomy over my time, workplace, and the personal space I can maintain from clients or coworkers.

Is the organization or client representative of Women Online's mission? It's very important to our team to feel motivated by what we're doing, and it's crucial that clients support women's advancement.

Is the organization or client someone I respect and look forward to working with? If a potential client or colleague sets off alarm bells or icky feelings, I step away.

Is the person or organization I am assisting fulfilling an important social good, or is it personally or professionally meaningful to me? Sometimes a project won't expressly fulfill our mission, but will hit my personal sweet spot of advancing better and more equitable workplaces for all.

DOES THIS FULFILL ONE OF THE FOLLOWING OBJECTIVES?

- ❑ Earn meaningful money
- ❑ Create powerful new relationships or business development opportunities
- ❑ Raise my professional visibility among a desirable or new audience
- ❑ Advance the company to a higher level

Is this essential to my bottom line? What am I giving up to take this on? This is a business, so sometimes we take on work that simply supports our bottom line. Conversely, sometimes we need to turn down compelling work that we will lose money on.

Will I learn something new? Even though you run a business, you deserve to satisfy your curiosity and keep learning (at least most of the time). Sometimes the least likely projects have the most to teach, so keep your radar attuned to a new challenge or skill-building opportunity.

Does this advance my vision? Projects advance your vision for many different reasons; some pay the bills for months in advance, while others thrust your company into the spotlight for a much-needed business development boost. I keep it simple: I always love a project where I don't have to travel.

Setting Boundaries with Family

My husband, who should be the national chair of Overcommitters Anonymous, is always pushing me to grow more and try harder. He does it out of love. He knows how much I care about my work and he believes in me. It's unfathomable to him that I would not push myself as hard as he pushes himself.

Years ago, a couples therapist gave us a great gift. She taught us that, in addition to marriage matters (dates, sex, kids), we needed to make time for "the corporation." The corporation involves finances, scheduling, childcare, planning, and reviewing our careers and goals.

I try to be very open with Nicco in these conversations. It's taken years to show him I'm strategic about my work choices. And since I take on more of the child rearing, I'm honest about my work+life fit, and whether I feel in control, or am hurtling into the void. (I like to think that I've taught Nicco something, too, and that's the ability to set boundaries and limits. He proudly comes home and reports back all the times he's said no in a week. And I am proud!)

Being honest helps me see my changing limits, and also helps me to set boundaries. When Nicco and I can discuss the work-life equation and reach an explicit understanding of which value is greater, I can let go of my insecurity, and, thereafter, proudly tell him I spent the day not working. On the flip side, good boundaries for your children are important, too. It's hard not to feel guilty when your kids want your attention and you can't give it to them, but if you're clear about when you're "on" and when you're off as a parent, the guilt will lessen. Years ago, a woman I met randomly at an event told me a simple and excellent method of keeping boundaries as a parent who worked at home. She had two signs for her office door. One sign was a smiley face, and the other had the smiley face with a red strike-though (imagine the *Ghostbusters* logo). She trained her daughter to enter the home office or knock only when the smiley sign was up. Kids love rules.

Pleasing my parents and stepparent is another story. Raised to maximize their opportunities, they were mystified when I quit so many jobs in my twenties, and, as I got older, were mystified by my refusal to maximize my income. Now my mom thinks I work too much and it makes me a lousy mother. (You can't win.)

My expectations for my life rarely align with those my mother has for me, which is fine, because I'm over forty years old. But even though I can write this, I still feel bad when I don't meet her expectations. If that sentence resonates with you, it might be helpful to think about the people in your life who really matter to you. Next, consider the primary expectations you have for yourself. Then think about what expectations other people have. For example, you might expect your partner to be the main breadwinner, leaving you the freedom to earn less. But does she agree? Is it worth discussing with her? Here's a commonly mismatched expectation about boundaries that seems silly but can have deep impact: my partner and I will not use smartphones after 8 P.M. Do you both agree?

You don't need your family to understand your motives, or to justify your workday to them. But it can be helpful to review others' expectations in your mind, and think about where misalignments may occur. When you're making a change, it's really helpful for your nearest and dearest to understand why and how you're making it. As long as you're clear about your boundaries, you have freedom to create limits.

Setting Expectations at Work

Last year I gave an interview about work+life fit for a new book on working mothers. When the author asked me how I manage my mommy guilt, I paused to think, then blurted, "I don't feel guilty about my kids. I feel guilty about my staff!"

I have a wonderful team at Women Online. We have worked together for years, and I feel lucky to have such talented people with me. The team enjoys incredible flexibility, work with wonderful clients, and its members are treated with respect.

But the truth is, they could all find higher-paying and higher-profile jobs. Similar firms grow more quickly. No one has received a raise in the past three years. I bring in all the business, and, while we won't turn down big, exciting new clients, we won't necessarily seek them out either. I try to be clear: this is part of the deal. Sometimes, however, I can feel them itching for a change. But since I tell them my boundaries, they can set limits, and I can, too.

When you work for someone else, setting limits can be challenging. That doesn't mean you shouldn't try, though. Work+life fit expert Cali Yost offers some valuable advice: "Your boss cares about two things: can they reach you if they need you, and if they need you, will you come through." People who look at the big picture, she says, are generally able to set reasonable limits in other ways.

As the boss, I like to keep my boundaries clear with my clients, too. I am direct when I need to put family or personal matters first. But I'm happy to have clients ask me personal questions and call me in the evening, and I accept that I'm attached to my iPhone and will work weekends. Being choosy about my clients and extracurricular responsibilities makes this easier.

I learned about setting boundaries from powerful women who'd figured it all out before me—from pollster and business owner Margie Omero, who took Fridays off with her father when she was well under thirty, to my client who left the office each day at four thirty and expected her staff to be ready with their questions for her well before three so she would not get stuck and miss her train home.

Because I had come from start-ups, politics, and a huge client services firm, for many years I had no idea it was even permissible for anyone below the CEO to state they might be unavailable or unwilling to work at any moment. When I began to pay attention, to study about workplace flexibility, and, most importantly, to ask lots of questions to those leaders who seemed to have good limits, I realized the world wouldn't end if I didn't always answer an e-mail immediately.

Setting Boundaries with Social Media

Shonda Rhimes, the legendary TV producer, has a signature on her e-mail that says, "Please Note: I will not engage in work e-mails after 7 P.M. or on weekends. If I am your boss, may I suggest: PUT DOWN YOUR PHONE."

When leaders are open and clear and unapologetic about the lines they draw, the rest of us have permission to consider our own boundaries. It's a gift to everyone. But, as people whose bosses are not as enlightened as Shonda Rhimes know, your workplace can tank your e-mail boundaries. Harvard's Leslie Perlow, the author of *Sleeping with Your Smartphone,* writes, "When you innocently clear out your inbox on Saturday morning, think about your subordinate who's on the soccer field with their kids."

Perlow calls this the cycle of responsiveness, and has wonderful

suggestions on how to break it—starting with teamwork, like agreeing to not answer phones on Saturday mornings. And bosses and
employees both need to examine the in-box addiction: Is the lack of
boundaries driven by urgency, habit, disorganization, or a lack of
clear limits?

Social media is another minefield, especially now that corporations regularly use platforms like Twitter and Instagram for personal branding. Everyone has different boundaries regarding
self-exposure, which means everyone needs to set different limits.
As Leah Ginsberg says, "You have to put yourself out there and you
have to play a role, and I'm not good at either of those things." For
hermits, just keeping a toe in someplace like LinkedIn may be the
solution.

Phone usage is another source of conflict. The phone is an ever-
present appendage for my husband, Nicco, and though he doesn't
mind if I check mine, the fact that he's always checking his can fill me
with rage. So we've set some boundaries on phone usage. We don't
during family time, or even when he and I are driving together.

Many introverts or people who struggle with social anxiety in
face-to-face situations absolutely love social media. In fact, the best
community managers I have ever worked with are usually introverts who tend to avoid face-to-face socializing. They come alive
online. However, other introverts feel conflicted about our society's
decreasing boundaries between personal and professional space and
time, and how this affects our social media profiles.

Is it even possible these days to maintain, say, a personal Facebook community while having LinkedIn and Twitter profiles that
are explicitly public facing? I don't think you can, to be honest—just
remember Election 2016 and hacked gmails. Nor do I even think it's
advisable if you're planning to be a hermit entrepreneur, because
building your online brand on all platforms is a wonderful way to
develop business when you don't want to physically get out there.
Any sense of privacy you feel online is fake, so by all means try to

keep your Facebook profile among friends, but don't ever assume it won't go public. Be conscious about that, especially when it comes to sharing personal news and information that can make you squirrelly.

Social media for work may have more interpersonal impact than we think. Christine Koh notes that if being active on social media is key to your professional status, boundary issues may, as a result, arise with your partner or family. In her case, a "front-facing" life requires vigilance. "My husband and I came to an explicit agreement about how much the kids will be on social media," she says. "You'll see them from the side. You will see them from the back. You will see them in sunglasses, but you actually never see their faces."

Being Flexible . . . Even with Boundaries

However firmly we set our own boundaries, all of us constantly break our own rules. Sometimes you just need to; for instance, answering e-mail after hours during a busy time at work. But it's also a worthwhile way to see if the limits you've set are really necessary.

If you say you're not going to check Facebook during work, but you still get your work done when you do check it, maybe that's not a limit you need to set. Or, if you realize you're leaving yourself enough time for personal responsibilities at work, maybe you can lighten up on work at home. (I work late every night!) Being comfortable with breaking your own rules is actually really liberating.

That flexibility also leaves room for life changes. Once you are aware of them, your boundaries are likely to stay put, but limits might vary over time. A new mom with an infant may set completely different limits on e-mail hours than an empty nester, who won't feel upset with weekend or evening e-mail. Or maybe a new mom wants the e-mail for distraction, while the empty nester wants to read a book! Either way, use your life changes as an opportunity to switch it up.

SAYING NO WELL

Learning to say no without guilt is the greatest gift you can give yourself, and one of the hardest things to do, especially for women. If you're going to succeed in setting boundaries, you need to learn how to say no. (And think twice about the next time you start a no with "I'm sorry." You don't have to be sorry just because you're saying no.)

That's where a framework comes in. I asked my community on Facebook for their words of wisdom on saying no with grace and strength.

Beth Monaghan, founder of the hundred-person PR agency Inkhouse, learned to say no by writing down her goals for the year, and literally carrying them around. "Every time something comes up, I can ask, 'Does this help me achieve a goal?' If the answer is no, I say no. And if I'm trying to convince myself to say yes, it's still probably a no."

MBA coach Andrea Sparrey envisions some of her fondest mentors in her head and imagines what they would counsel her to do if she explained the yes/no dilemma to them.

Entrepreneur Lauren Bacon's method: "I always respond with a variant of 'Thanks so much for the invitation! Let me sleep on it and get back to you first thing tomorrow.' That allows me time to step back, look at my goal list, and figure out how I really want to answer."

Author Samantha Ettus, the queen of anti-guilt, told me, "Guilt never creates good decisions. I would not want someone to say yes to me out of guilt, so I don't allow guilt to determine my decisions."

Podcast entrepreneur Molly Beck says no as quickly as possible and then suggests another person to take her place, trying especially to offer opportunities to people who might not otherwise get them.

For Elisa Camahort Page *no* can mean *not right now*. I really agree with this. A good, firm no allows you to maintain a relationship with the other person, and you never know where that will lead. Any businessperson will tell you that a no can turn into a yes over time. And, if you're feeling anxious about saying no to someone with whom you'd like to have a long-term business relationship, it's okay to reconsider and say yes to something that will eat up your time without compensation.

Many in my kitchen cabinet suggest practicing your noes, or having a few ready-made responses. I love Deb Roby's script for a graceful no: "Thank you for thinking of me; I am honored. However, this project does not line up with my goals for this (cycle/quarter/season/year), so I will have to decline."

Here's a final note for those of us with anxiety: sometimes you can talk yourself into a no when you really mean yes. Practice tuning into your gut reaction upon hearing an invitation. If you're excited about an opportunity at first, only to let anxiety set in later, let the excitement win over anxiety. For example, you're invited to a wonderful conference in a faraway city, and you're thrilled. You say yes, and immediately feel anxiety: What if your plane crashes on the way? What if you make a fool of yourself? Try to work through this and tune back to your excitement. Anxiety can be negotiated with.

THE BEAUTY OF BOUNDARIES

Steve Jobs famously said, "Innovation is saying no to 1,000 things."

Saying no and setting strong boundaries makes you powerful! I know it feels scary, especially if you're starting out or starting again. In my case, learning to say no meant realizing that my inability to do it stemmed from insecurity. I feared that turning down any opportunity was pure hubris. If I turned down an opportunity, certainly few other chances would come along, right? I'm no Steve Jobs.

It doesn't matter. Every no is time you can put to good use and innovate, or further your own work.

I love to think of Steve Jobs brusquely turning down invitations to focus on creating the devices that would change the world. Maybe he got invited to attend a tech networking hour on Sandhill Road but instead said, "Nah, I've got a little computer I'm working on." Don't waste your "no" time second-guessing your decision or feeling guilty. Use the time well, and you, too, will innovate.

7

Time Is on Your Side

'm obsessed with reading articles about how luminaries use their time. For example, the *New York Times* tells me Italian luxury design magnate Brunello Cucinelli starts his day by swimming laps in his pool for an hour, and finishes it by reading some Socrates. Meanwhile, *Forbes* let me know Alice + Olivia founder Stacey Bendet wakes up at 4:45 A.M. for a bowl of quinoa, then does an hour of ashtanga yoga.

I will never have enough freedom or brain cells to end my day with Socrates, and stealing me time from sleep time, as Stacey does, would make me miserable. For those of us with far more plebeian lives, gaining control of our time usually comes from adjusting work patterns. Study after study shows that the most engaged and productive workers are those who feel a sense of autonomy and control over their work lives.

I always joke that if tomorrow someone promised to pay me over $500,000 a year in salary alone, I would consider going back to full-time work in an office environment. But right now, unless something drastic changes, control over my time is worth more to me than a fat salary.

Because, as with everything else, there's no free lunch. For every chunk of time you take back from work or other people's expectations, you'll probably lose something else: money, prestige, career advancement, or that feeling of being in the thick of it.

Although there are many, there are a few different methods of pacing I regularly consider: building in flexibility; bursting and leapfrogging; chunking your day; and finding the right level of busy.

Your time is yours, and you can be strategic in how you use it. I call it pacing your career, and it means thinking about how can you creatively seize control over your time—both in the minute and over the long term.

The Flexible Worker

Let's say your company has invested a lot in you. Your boss is grooming you. You're grateful, and you've always seen yourself reaching a certain level of success. But now you realize your schedule is actually making you anxious and miserable. You've decided you want to pare down. So how do you have that conversation? And how do you set yourself up for success?

Workplace expert Cali Yost tells us that, first, you need to ask yourself, *What do I need? What does it look like, and how does flexibility help me do that?* while taking into account those who have control over your time, work, and money.

One of Yost's clients, a woman who worked in the financial services industry, was very much on the fast track. But, nine months pregnant with her third child, she burst into tears as she told Cali, "I'm quitting."

Instead of agreeing, Yost told her she needed to propose a different way of working. The woman said her boss would never go for it. Yost replied, "The worst thing that can happen is she says no. And she's likely to listen if you come in with a plan."

They sat down at Starbucks and went over every aspect of the new work paradigm, detailing, as Yost told her, "what parts of your job you're going to let go, what you're going to keep, how you're going to keep contributing, how your compensation's going to change, how you're going to supervise people." Yost encouraged her to present it, but the woman was still dubious.

The next day the woman called Yost and told her, "I'm mad!" Yost began to apologize, and the woman interrupted. "No, I'm mad because my boss said okay. I went through every talking point. I had every argument. And it was just . . .'okay!'"

If Yost's client's experiences resonate with you—whether you are experiencing a life change or acknowledging new boundaries or limits—consider what you would ask your boss, and what your plan would be. Do you want one afternoon a week? How can you stack your business development schedule to accomplish what you need to in four days? What meetings can you move? What responsibilities could you give up, and how can you keep the ones you have?

Here are a few starters:

❑ Reduce your commute by working at home.
❑ Adjust your hours worked during the day.
❑ Change the number of days each week you work.
❑ Lessen business travel.
❑ Cut out some meetings so you can have alone time.
❑ Reshuffle your day to maximize productivity.
❑ Reduce the number of professional events you attend.
❑ Cut down "extracurriculars" like serving on committees or boards or in internal working groups, or writing/doing social media, to a bare minimum.

Having a plan means you're coming from a position of strength not weakness. As Cali says, "Your boss wants to know where you are, and can you get the work done." Bosses also prefer that your flexible schedule doesn't create more work for them or the team. So when you present a case for flexibility, assure your manager you will be reachable, you will copiously communicate with your peers or clients to make sure the transition is seamless, and, of course, you'll get the work done. After all, who doesn't get more work done out of the office and in the quiet of home or their favorite coffee shop?

You have to show you've thought it all through. "It's not enough to just figure out what you do when. You have to go to the how, where, and with whom," Cali says. "Be clear: Where am I going to do it? I'm doing it in my home office in the basement. With whom am I coordinating this? I'm going to let my family know that I'm going to be working for these four hours in the basement office. I'm going to have to tell my team, 'These four hours are meant to be my focus time. If you really need me, I am available. Here's the technology I'd like you to use to get in touch with me.'"

After the baby came, Cali's client in financial services managed her new schedule, working four days a week, with one day a week working from home. But here's the rub: because she was a senior leader in a traditional environment, she had to give something up. "You can't keep all the good things, and then pass off the crap you don't want," Cali told her. "What part of your job is awesome but takes up a lot of time and somebody else could do it?"

Flexibility will always require redefining success for yourself. Which is another way of saying: compromise.

DON'T LET "FLEXIBILITY" RUIN YOUR DAY

Until about three years ago, I was constantly pulling over to the side of the road to dial into conference calls, or balancing a Lego in one hand while answering an e-mail with the other. I thought this was freedom. Instead it made me crazy. And because I didn't have a set work schedule, I was always carving out time for life during the workweek.

I had to have an honest conversation with myself, and say: *You are not delivering the best to your clients, your team, or to your children.*

Those of us who run flexible workplaces share some of the blame for an always-on culture. But companies have begun making changes. Leaders from the president of a hip Hollywood digital studio to the work-life director at accounting giant Ernst & Young suggested creating a basic scaffolding for flexibility, and tweaking from there. For example, as long as there aren't pressing client deadlines, create two or three core business days when people are expected to be in the office for meetings, and let people work flexibly the other days of the week.

Here's how I decided to change how we at Women Online operate during the nine-to-five.

- ❑ Work core business hours four days a week (nine to five). If you have a dedicated day or afternoon off, let the team know, and mark it on the shared company calendar.
- ❑ Schedule personal appointments or time on the calendar, and don't be ashamed (thank you, Cali Yost).
- ❑ Make a concerted effort to do work calls on a landline, or ensure you have a good cell connection so conference calls are doable. If you have to be in transit during a call, let the client or team know beforehand.
- ❑ Don't send external e-mails after business hours. Clients deserve a life, too!
- ❑ Schedule time for a phone call; don't let e-mail chains drag on or get complicated.
- ❑ Here's the hardest one: unless it's to a quick yes or no question, if you are working out of office or on your iPhone, resist the urge to respond quickly or less thoughtfully than you might while sitting at your desk. A good answer is usually better than a quick one.

Forcing myself to be fully present at work actually reduced my anxiety. I could get into "flow" and focus on the work I love, and the team felt more cohesive.

Even in the digital age, structure and boundaries are key. If you're a manager, be honest about your bad habits, and work flexibly—with guidelines.

Strategic Time Use

We develop strategies for career advancement in order to save money, even to find love. But time underpins everything else, and it's finite.

To use the time you gain constructively, it's important to know what you want the time for—and what you're willing to give up for it. Take a minute to jot down some goals, and arrange them in terms of priority.

GOAL

EXAMPLES:

Time with kids when I'm not so exhausted

Time to exercise

Study for my GRE

Time to cook dinner instead of ordering out

Use my vacation time

Have one night out a week

Work from home one day a week

Take a longer maternity leave

NOTES:

_____

_____

_____

_____

SACRIFICE

Will I get promoted if I give less time?

Take it out of work day or sleep time

Sleep

No working around the clock

Will be out of the loop

Sleep

Salary? Advancement?

Salary, advancement, out of the loop

_____

_____

_____

_____

GETTING STARTED

Leapfrogging and Bursting

Early in her career, Sheryl Sandberg received some important advice from Google CEO Eric Schmidt. "When companies are growing quickly and they are having a lot of impact, careers take care of themselves," he said. "If you're offered a seat on a rocket ship, don't ask what seat. Just get on."

That brings us to leapfrogging.

People who leapfrog work in bursts, channeling their skills, energy, and joie de vivre into short periods of time, taking advantage of slow times at work to recover and recharge. Leapfrogging is how I learned that a career doesn't have to be linear, and you can be successful and still get a rest.

Some people do this strategically, as an unconventional way to grow their careers rapidly. I met my first leapfroggers working in politics. D.C.'s staffers work 24/7 on yearlong or eighteen-month campaigns, then, after Election Day, turn to lucrative private-sector consulting work to refill their coffers. The bigger the race they work on (a presidential or major senate race, say), the higher the fees they can command in the private sector, with their pick of plum jobs. Check out the flow of Obama staffers who went to Silicon Valley's hottest companies or to teach at Harvard and Stanford Business Schools, for example. The glow of their high-profile and, frankly, sexy election work meant they could raise their prices and coast on some major laurels for a while.

My first leapfrog came from working on the Kerry-Bush presidential campaign for two years. I wasn't high level, or even very talented, but because I worked on the digital side at a time when politics was going online, I was in demand. Near the end of the campaign, a former staffer for Bill Clinton told me I had a window of time, and that I should be strategic about how I used it. "You're hot right now, and you have a lot of opportunities. They won't be there forever."

He was right. I became a VP at a large company, the youngest VP in a company of thousands of people. Sure, I hated it and I quit after sixteen months, but by then I had leapfrogged several levels in my career, and was able to command good rates as a freelancer—plus, I could be more of a hermit.

Twelve years after that fateful lunch, I still use the leapfrogging strategy to grow my business without having to work too hard. How? I try to work on one or two "marquee" clients per year, no matter how low-paying. High-profile work boosts my business development, so I can get business through the door even in slow periods. When you say, "When I was working for so-and-so," the mic drops. If you're running your own business and want to find a way to enable a hermit lifestyle, get out there and land a big-kahuna client, or a viral campaign or a hot product. Then tell everyone you know.

Obviously, leapfrogging makes the most sense early in your career, when you have the least to lose. Kiva founder Jessica Jackley advises, "Try something big and bold and crazy right out of the gate. Give your life away for two years. If it works, it opens a lot of doors. Once you're older, it's a harder calculus to make." For Jessica, it was building a project she started in graduate school into a multinational organization. For others, it might be working at an investment bank for a few years, joining a start-up or political campaign, or any other high-risk, high-reward type venture.

There's tremendous joy, Jackley says, to being so deeply immersed in one's work, when it's for a limited period of time. Sometimes she misses the passion. "What if I don't get to be a part of something like that again?" she asks, almost wistfully. Now that she has three children, her priorities have changed. "I didn't think twice about throwing my life into something in that way. What if that's what's required to have such a big impact?"

I understand where Jessica is coming from. She feels limited and apprehensive. But look around: there are many stars of all ages in politics, tech, and innovation who take crazy moon shot jobs for short periods of time. When I worked in politics, our digital teams comprised young men in hoodies (which you'd expect) and older people who'd been through three or four careers already, all working insane hours. And not for the money!

Chunking Your Day

If you like your daily work schedule, you'll enjoy work more. Yes, a radical four-hour-workweek level of control is not realistic. But if your default is hiding in the bathroom, taking charge of your schedule to better fit your energy and moods can really help.

Lindy Huang Werges, whose financial services staffing firm grew 300 percent last year, has one of the most insightful takes on her workday I've ever seen.

Lindy schedules "clusters" each day. Her calendar is blocked out for production hours in two parts each day: 9–11 A.M. and 2–4:30 P.M. The production hours are her intense, revenue generating hours. Everything else is "non-production" time, the non-revenue generating work that is essential but allows her time to breathe a little bit. Lindy has a "blackout" on her calendar from four-thirty to eight. (But not necessarily because she's with her kids; because her brain is full by then.) Because Lindy is an incredibly vibrant, nonhermit person, seeing and hearing about the way she works felt like a sort of permission to schedule my day to suit my state of mind—so I thought about how I perform best.

What I found was, for my own schedule, I like to work in intense bursts, with two or three days of intense activity, and then days with a lot of alone time and quiet.

I have a job that demands a lot of engagement. It's embarrassing, but before I get on a call, I often have to give myself a pep talk, because picking up the phone can trigger social anxiety. On a bad day, even anticipating a phone call can make me feel like hiding. Although once I'm on the call and hooked into the other people or the work, I'm fine and happy, I schedule myself in a way that doesn't fill me with nerves when I review my schedule in the morning.

I have a similar strategy with my week. I've learned that to deal with my anxieties and reclusive tendencies, I have to dive in and keep going until I'm exhausted, and then schedule time to recharge by building in alone work time. My ideal week will have me tightly scheduled for two or three days with external-facing meetings, out-of-town travel, and lots of interaction and engagement with existing clients or potential clients, such as meetings or speaking engagements.

When I'm in the zone, dressed up, makeup on, I'm good. I forget I'm a hermit and get engaged in the work and people. The sheer act of looking like a grown-up reminds me I can do it. On the road, I'll do as many meetings as I can. On busy client days, I'll also try to schedule as many back-to-back phone calls as possible, so I don't have time to ruminate. And once I get on the plane or train, I turn off.

On quieter days, I'm a putterer. I try to schedule calls and meetings in the morning, when my energy level is higher. I work, then break, work, then break. I don't like to leave the house except for errands or kid stuff. Ideally, I will have at least a two-hour block with nothing scheduled so I can have some maker time to write proposals or memos and work on projects that don't demand interaction. And then I finish early, around 3 P.M. so that my brain and body can recharge. I'll usually log back on around 8 P.M. I love to write or really dig into projects at night, when it's quiet. I also use a service called Boomerang to schedule e-mails to be delivered during working hours so that a client won't expect me to work all the time, and my team won't feel obligated to respond.

My weekly podcast also demands a lot of personality, which means a lot of energy. When I recorded it from home, I was so reluctant to do it that the hours before we recorded would be ruined by anticipatory anxiety. But I realized that if I left the house to record and went to a real studio, I could get into the zone easily without losing my morning.

Christine Koh, my colleague at Women Online in addition to being an author, blogger, lifestyle influencer, podcast host, and Ph.D., is my hero and opposite, but she also knows her work style. She is focused and task driven and, unlike me, doesn't let a bad day send her back to bed. She puts in a solid nine-to-five, and then she's done. Her husband told her, with love, "You are like a robot. You go into your office and you just destroy, and then you come out and you look glazed, but you have conquered the day." Christine says her ability to switch quickly into parenting mode comes from feeling "the flock has been tended accordingly," just like mine comes from feeling I don't have to keep regular hours to do good work.

Get Your Ideal Workday

Only you can figure out the cadence of your ideal day, but to start, ask yourself some questions. Let your answers be as specific as possible; for example, "I'm most productive at five, when the people in my house are still asleep," or "I get my best work done on the train." Remember, your dream day may be very different from the actual workday that will make you happy, or the workday you get to do. But a specific list can help you develop ideas for maximizing your time.

1. When in the day do you feel most productive?

2. How long are you able to concentrate on any given project? Do you work best by doing one big one a day, or doing a little work on several?

3. Do you work on weekends? Do you feel resentful, or that you're finally getting a chance to catch up?

4. Do meetings inspire you, or feel like a waste of time?

5. On what tasks do you really shine? What work do you get praised for? Are they the same?

6. When you procrastinate, do you still manage to get your work in, or is procrastinating really having a detrimental effect on your productivity? How do you usually procrastinate, and when?

7. What distracts you? In what zone do you feel no distraction?

8. What are the tasks you dread?

9. What are the tasks you like?

10. At what time of day are you just done?

11. Do you get more work done around people? Alone? Do you waste time with colleagues, or do colleagues help you get motivated?

12. What tasks really bring in the bulk of your income? How are your earnings distributed?

Now, what are the limitations that affect your workday? For instance, you may have a boss who wants you on 24/7, or you may be a freelancer with monthly deadlines and little client support. A sample list might look like this.

1. I have to pick up my kids at five.

2. My job has project meetings every other day, and they go on forever.

3. My clients call me at all hours.

4. I need to set aside time for business development at least once a week in order to bring in enough work.

5. My boss wants me in at seven every day, and I can't leave until six.

6. I need to bring in [X] amount of clientele.

7. My job has a lot of paperwork that keeps me from my real work, but I have to do it.

Now make a wish list for the parts of your life that get affected by work. Go crazy!

1. I wish my house weren't such a disaster.

2. I wish I had time to go to my kid's soccer class.

3. I wish I made more money—I have no disposable income.

4. I wish I had more time. I have plenty of money, but nowhere to spend it.

5. I want to build up some savings for retirement, or to buy an [X].

6. I want to take one big vacation a year.

7. I wish I could go out on a Wednesday night once in a while.

Now give yourself some credit!

*1. At work, I really get praised for*_____.

*2. Strangers are impressed when they hear I do*_____.

*3. My secret hack for getting things done is*_____.

*4. In recommendations, people cite my*_____.

*5. I feel most proud of myself when I*_____.

Okay, you've got an enormous list now. Take some time with it. Use the information to think specifically about your hours, your goals, your productivity, and what's in the way. You may not be able to achieve the workday you want entirely right now, and you certainly won't always stick to it, but when you're stuck at work, go back to the list and use it for guidance.

Levels of Busy

Christine Koh notes the power of what she calls finding the "Goldilocks level of busy." (See later for my Goldilocks contract-size method. I guess Goldilocks was pretty smart: there is a perfect fit for most of us.)

Too big: You are overwhelmed—your inner hermit is in distress. You can't figure out how to structure your days. Review your calendar for the past couple of months. What weeks had too much? How many events were there? What pushed you over the edge?

Too few: What were too few events? When did you actually start to get antsy?

What was just right? Figuring out the happy number as a target and shooting for it is a good feeling. I can't take more than five meetings a week, with one evening event max. Christine notes, "There's always more work to do, so part of the challenge is giving yourself the permission to take the time you need. Try to build it into your routine." When you know what you want more of, you can craft it into your intentions.

THERE IS NO RULE BOOK

I've already shared my very strong opinions on establishing a vision, developing strong boundaries, and taking your time seriously. Lest you think I'm immune to doubt about all this, let me tell you a little about my friend Meighan Stone.

When I'm feeling frustrated with just how limited my boundaries can be, I think of her incredible work with some envy. When Meighan was president of the Malala Fund, she traveled the world with the Nobel Peace Prize winner to raise funds and implement programs that educate girls. A normal month for Meighan might find her opening a school in Nigeria, meeting with CENTCOM generals in Jordan, staffing Malala for an interview with Oprah, or fund-raising for the organization with the billionaire "unicorn" founders of Silicon Valley. She worked in different time zones, many hours a week.

The mother of a seven-year-old, Meighan does incredible work in global development, and her passion fuels everything she does. In her week off, she organized a faith community protest to support refugees at the National Prayer Breakfast in Washington, D.C., and helped an upstart candidate launch his gubernatorial campaign. But Meighan makes sacrifices to do her work, definitely with her time, and sometimes even with her health and her personal security. I admire her tremendously, and I would never have the fortitude or courage, or, frankly, the energy to do what she does. I just followed her updates with awe from the comfort of my couch.

She and I laugh about this. Sometimes I feel jealous of Meighan:

her impact, her role in such a powerful movement, her travels. I see what's she's accomplishing and I feel envy and admiration. She's building a school in a Syrian refugee camp; I feel hopelessly bourgeois and suburban. But even if I had her skills, I would not be happy doing what she does. It would tax me to the limit and defy all my boundaries about time and control. Knowing this feels good.

We're going to get really practical in the next chapter, and talk about how to find your niche at work. When you know exactly what you stand for and what you're here to do, you can channel your passion efficiently, then take a break. It's the opposite of always being on. If, like me, you find yourself feeling envious of someone like Meighan, but know that controlling your boundaries and time is essential to your well-being, you'll love developing a strong niche.

8

Go Niche

n January 2005, on top of a Mayan pyramid in Oaxaca, Mexico, I had a life-changing experience. I met Lisa Stone, the founder of BlogHer, the first community for women who blog.

At the time I was a political consultant in Washington, D.C. I had just finished three years in the trenches, working in Internet marketing for the Democratic National Committee and John Kerry's presidential campaign. I was beaten down by politics and its (mostly male) egos.

Every week I'd go to a gathering of young male "netizens": bloggers, activists, and pundits who were mostly under twenty-five. Now many have become famous. They shape Beltway opinions, and those gatherings are the stuff of political nerd legend. But back then, I'd sit at these meetings and boil at their myopia and ignorant swagger. ("I don't get why health care is a big deal to voters," is an actual quote. I wanted to scream! Only I was usually the single woman in the room . . .) I had no outlet, and I was frustrated and insecure.

But BlogHer changed all that. Writing about politics as BlogHer's first political director gave me a platform to share women's points of view—then and still now in short supply in Beltway culture, no matter how important women are as a voting bloc.

BlogHer came at a time when blogs were changing news and political coverage. In 2005, Facebook was a one-year-old platform for college students, and YouTube was brand-new. But suddenly blog-based activists and reporters were threatening the authority of major outlets and changing the media landscape. Which meant that all of a sudden a blogger like me and a reporter for the *Washington Post* were publishing major scoops.

I will never forget the moment when I got front-row seats at the YouTube presidential primary town hall in South Carolina next to Adam Nagourney. I sat there and I thought, *I'm a blogger, and I have the same access as the political reporter for the New York Times.*

I didn't know it then, but as one of the few female bloggers who covered politics, I had lucked into a powerful niche. As blogging gained popularity and authority, I often found myself fielding questions from curious political, marketing, and communications professionals: What was this blogging and citizen journalism thing all about, and could I explain it to them? Even better, I could blog from anywhere, and this allowed me more time to myself while still building professional influence. I knew I was onto something.

The Hermit on the Web

Contrary to what you might think, a strong online presence is a hermit's best friend. Indeed, if you're shy, a strong digital presence and online brand is especially critical, because it creates a powerful digital footprint that separates you from the competition and does your networking for you, even when you're away from your iPhone.

The best way for a hermit to build a strong online presence (besides saying smart things and creating great content, of course) is to focus on gaining expertise and awareness within a specific niche of your business or professional field. You spin fewer wheels when your offering is focused and your expertise is sharply defined. You also spend less time comparing yourself to others and trying to compete with bigger budgets and more business development resources. This is equally powerful whether you work for yourself or within an organization.

That doesn't mean tweeting every two minutes or constantly posting to Instagram. A meandering and banal Twitter account, for example, will not do you any favors. Nor will a company blog no one reads (I've been there). But a strategically crafted online presence is a potent business development tool.

That means the more niche, the better. Georgetown University's Cal Newport, a computer science professor who studies how to perform productive, valuable, and meaningful work in the digital age, argues that the market "rewards things that are rare and valuable. Social media use is decidedly not. Any 16-year-old with a smartphone can invent a hashtag or repost a viral article."[1] A hermit gains value from her unique online footprint and its smart content, not its popularity. Showcasing your niche allows you to stand out in a sea of blog posts and search engine optimization (SEO).

Go Hyperniche: Ana Flores's Story

Ana Florés, a former TV producer, created the "hyperniche" #WeAllGrow Latina Network, a powerful online community focusing on Latina social media influencers. By "owning that we are unapologetically about the Latina woman's experience," she's created a powerful business, unlike any in the marketplace. Laughing, she says, "With platforms and apps bombarding us all the time, the natural instinct is to compete with influencer marketplaces that are all about reaching everybody. But I think there is much more of a need for expert voices."

This extends to her specific brand: We All Grow Latina. The name derives from the company's mission, stated by Ana in a 2010 blog post: when one of us grows, we all grow. This reflects the open, almost sisterly vibe of the company's events both online and off. "Everything you see about us, from the pinkish colors, to the way that we speak to our audience, the way that we manage our community, what our events are about, the inspirational messages: They're not crafted through market research. They're crafted because that's who we are and that's how we want to be spoken to."

When she worked in TV, Ana created content for massive multinational companies like MTV and Univision, where, she says, "You are validated by their brand names." But even after the recession, she turned down job offers to stick with her blog, Spanglish Baby. "I just knew," Ana says, "that if I hung on to it for a little bit longer, it would bring me something. And my mom and everybody were like, 'Are you crazy? Take the job.'"

My beloved husband refers to my business, Women Online, as Vag.org. Every time I talk about my business, people remark condescendingly, "Oh, what a great niche." (Never mind the fact that women are 52 percent of the global population.) But I just smile and nod. If I decided to be a full-service marketing and PR firm, the pool of companies I'd be competing with would be much larger, and their resources far greater than mine. Not to mention I'd have to pay a lot more to market my services. The truth is, owning a niche is powerful.

Like Ana, I learned about the power of the niche by growing up professionally in online community culture, where people find others who share their very particular passions. I started my career at iVillage.com, the web's largest destination for women, where my job was to highlight stories of women's connections for the media and public-affairs campaigns. Our members were dealing with breast cancer, cranky toddlers, or divorce, and I could tell the connections were real, even though I was a twenty-two-year-old who knew very little about these topics.

Ten years later, BlogHer was the amazing natural evolution of iVillage.com, as well as the natural evolution of BlogHer cofounder Lisa Stone's work as editor of Women.com. Both early sites relied on message-board technology to connect women seeking advice and sharing stories. (For a taste of community culture's size and power, just check out Hermione Granger fanfiction communities.) And, like Ana, my niche business is driven by passion as well as intuition.

As a small-business owner who has built her credibility through her social media platform, I can say that the more authentic your online voice, the more response you will receive. You can take your life experience, distill the most meaningful pieces, and create a narrative that compels others. The key to building a strong online presence is ownership. You need to know what you want to say, who you want to say it to, and most important, *why* you are the right person to carry the message. You need conviction.

As Ana puts it, "It really has to be something that comes from you, that belongs to you, and that you are that topic—that *you* live it."

The thing that is so wonderful about creating your digital brand is that it truly is personal. I have interviewed many successful bloggers with millions of readers, and time and again they tell me that they view their blog or website as an extension of their living room, or perhaps as a small boutique or storefront. It's their personal space, a true piece of their life that is open for others to visit, as long as the visitors behave.

Why Women (Especially Women Introverts) Need a Strong Digital Brand

For women of any age, becoming social-network savvy isn't just about connecting with friends. It's about creating and maintaining the critical connections that establish your expertise and leadership, regardless of whether you're employed or own your own business. And even more than for men, it is critical for women to establish a strong online brand. While your career path may wax and wane as you start a family, care for relatives, and deal with any of the myriad of issues that can disrupt your climb up the career ladder, your digital brand stays with you. It is a crucial piece of your credibility as a professional and as a leader.

What do I mean by digital brand? I simply mean how someone finds you online, and what they find when they do.

The first step in a digital brand is a simple website or a blog that curates all of your professional accomplishments, interests, and opinions. You control the content, you control the message, and the site changes as your career grows. Think of it as your digital CV. It might include participating in marketing channels such as Twitter, LinkedIn, Facebook, or Pinterest, which are excellent places to find like-minded people. But ultimately, you cannot control the content of a site owned by someone else. And therefore, you need your own home on the web.

The Internet gives us the space to showcase the accomplishments of our less-than-linear lives, create new networks and professional opportunities that bolster our careers, and highlight our unique brands, all from the comfort of home. (I do always blog in bed.)

The web allows you to maintain relationships with colleagues and to forge new connections with thought leaders in your space—from *home*, at the time and place that's convenient for you. This is important for women who are on a break from a career path because of caretaking or childbearing, and for women who are introverts or hermits, who need to get out there without always getting out there.

It's important to establish a digital footprint to . . .

Access new networks. Research shows that women's social and professional networks are different from men's, and this can hurt us professionally. Women tend to have fewer weak ties, more all-female reference groups, more contacts who are peers, and fewer who are superiors. We're much more likely to form tight-knit groups of equals among ourselves. The way we form ties isn't necessarily wrong, but it can hinder our progress professionally. For the same reason finding male mentors at work is important, building a diverse online social network can really help boost your career. Having an online brand isn't just about creating Facebook, Twitter, and Pinterest pages; it's about forging relationships online that can propel your leadership potential.

Engage from anywhere. Women are still responsible for the majority of caretaking and domestic work in American homes, regardless of whether they hold a paying job. Our caretaking responsibilities can prevent us from being able to participate fully in the work culture outside of regular business hours. As the network scholar Howard Aldrich writes, after work, "Men head for cocktails, women head for the dry cleaner." But online media fundamentally changes this equation. Women can be at home and still engage in the virtual cocktail party happening across social networks.

Build a portable, permanent brand. Women can lose out professionally because most of us take some time out of the paid workforce to raise children. If you take time off to have a baby or opt out of a typical career-ladder progression, your online presence can still grow and burnish your professional reputation. Your online brand is layoff-proof and it can grow with you as your expertise and interests grow. In fact, according to the Families and Work Institute, jumping in and out of the traditional workforce is the new normal for all ages. Keeping up a strong professional profile online allows you to stay engaged even if you're not officially working.

Establish expertise and credentials. By creating a strong online brand through digital publishing, you establish expertise in your field while bypassing the traditional gatekeepers or barriers to success. A strong Google rank, along with links to your work, establishes credentials in the digital age. Research shows women feel the need to be more credentialed before assuming or asking for greater responsibilities or positions of power much more than men. Strong use of social media allows us to build credentials without having to break into traditional networks. (If we are part of those networks, even better—we can use our position to link out to more women.)

Create strong community ties. We get by with a little help from our online friends. These connections not only build social capital, they're also a wonderful addition to life. My entrepreneurial networks do everything from referring clients to helping me find resources like tax assistance and trademark advice, and I don't have to leave my house. Online communities can help busy people feel connected, listened to, and recharged. Online community ties help keep us from feeling isolated when our family and home responsibilities surround us. Perhaps more practically, staying connected to a professional community helps women stay on top of current trends in their professional space, helping us better prepare to reenter the workforce when the time comes.

GETTING STARTED

Twitter for Dummies (You're Not)

Twice a year I give a workshop at the Harvard Kennedy School to encourage students to think about using digital and social media to establish their professional brand online. I can't tell you how many really brilliant people have heard me speak about building an online brand, and responded sheepishly, "I'm not smart enough to do social media." Or "I'm too old." One was, I kid you not, an M.D./Ph.D. Another was a former member of Special Forces.

This mind-set is total crap. First of all, if you're a professional you are definitely smart enough to create content online. If a nine-year-old can make a YouTube video, so can you. Second, don't be ageist against yourself! The stereotype that only young people are good at social media and web stuff is damaging and untrue. Figure out which pieces you want to take on yourself, don't be afraid to hire help for the rest (freelance web design and social media help is copious), and get going. Here's my advice:

Morra's Guide to Owning Your Corner of the Internet

Identify your ecosystem. Your ecosystem is the unique set of players, circumstances, and organizations that create a professional field or topic area.

Define the work or mission of the marketplace. In this case, it helps to get as narrow as possible. You may think your ecosystem's work is accounting or public relations consulting, but it's a lot more effort to become a big fish in a giant pond, and tough on hermits. Get granular: perhaps the work of your ecosystem is accountants with a specialty in not-for-profit management, or public relations management for American cities trying to attract tourists from China.

Know the players. In any field, there are players. These could be individuals or firms. If you've worked long enough, you know them. You see them quoted and you see them receive awards and accolades. Get to know the players in your chosen field intimately. This is your competitive set. Review their websites, follow them on Twitter, understand their pricing and staffing, and suss out the secrets of their success as well as their vulnerabilities.

Think about how you or your firm would pitch against a player, and how you'd highlight your advantages over theirs. Once you find your target audience, and the specific tactics they are using to promote their brand, chew on what they are missing. There's your opportunity. Drill down as much as you can. If you're a company providing flexible jobs for moms, see who blogs about these issues both locally and nationwide. Check out the content, tweeting, and LinkedIn groups about your field. What aren't they covering that you could?

Establish your expertise and POV. Even though you're a hermit, you're still hard-core! Negotiation coach Tanya Tarr is a fan of using a portfolio as "hard evidence" of your accomplishments to establish credibility in the marketplace. When I started Women Online, I borrowed case studies from past client work, because Women Online itself didn't have any work to show yet. I was only partially bullshitting, because I'd actually done the work, and I knew my trade. The difference was now I could sell past results with a new edge.

Find some "boast bitches." But you don't need to brag yourself. In her book *Feminist Fight Club*, Jessica Bennett says to let these validators vouch for you. Your status also depends on praise from your peers, and with it, your status in the ecosystem will rise quickly. With peers you admire, you can return the favor.

What does your audience need more of, or what are they missing? Just as shoppers in search of homemade wedding favors are served by Etsy, your audience is served by the specific online ecosystem you're part of. Think about your brand in the narrowest sense, and identify your target audience. Even more important than understanding your marketplace and your competition is understanding your audience. What do they have plenty of and what do they need or wish they had more of? Where is the gap in the larger marketplace, and crucially, where is the gap in marketing and communicating the offering? This is where your online brand comes in. Do you know how much time I spent online searching for customized Easter basket liners for my kids? There are about three or four small online businesses who specialize in that offering. I bet they make a lot of money.

Where does your audience hang out? Define your audience's media choices. Understand where the audience hangs out online (even IRL), who influences their decisions, and what media you need to have a presence in. My clients are mission-driven organizations, but the consumer audience I need to work with every day is the vast and powerful community of women in social media who want to learn about and promote my clients. You might also have a consumer and a trade audience, or some other combination. Make sure you're considering everybody.

How can you reach them? So, for all potential audiences you need to reach, what conferences do you need to attend? What trade journals or B2B publications must you have a presence in? I literally draw a map and create circles for all the various points of contact I need to influence, from press to events to social media to professionals or thought leaders in my field. Use this research as a learning tool to enhance your strategies. The key to success here is to identify where your passions intersect with what's missing.

Finding the "Blue Ocean"

Normally I hate business school jargon, but this is a great one. Created by INSEAD professors W. Chan Kim and Renée Mauborgne, the Blue Ocean strategy is "the simultaneous pursuit of differentiation and low cost to open up a new market space and create new demand." In English: understand the marketplace and what the players aren't providing. Use your expertise to create a solution, and technology to price it well.

The theory goes that when you identify and create an offering in the Blue Ocean, competition doesn't matter, and your costs to entry are lower. You're not paying for as much advertising, and you've got far less competition. Widely available technology (such as Word-Press or an app builder) allows you to create a minimum viable product with little cash or expertise. In other words, it's a great approach for an entrepreneur who wants to do purposeful work and have a life. And it's especially helpful when you're in a large field, such as public relations, hair care, or apparel.

Swivel is an app that connects women of color with expert hair stylists, whether they wear their hair naturally or straighten it, and it seems to define Blue Ocean opportunity. "It's for when you put your hair in a bun after you get it done and say to yourself: 'Did she even use a flat iron? It's still so puffy,' says Jihan Thompson, a former magazine editor and founder of the app. "So many times I've left the salon feeling like I wasted my money."[2]

Now, that's a clear mission, a well-defined audience, and a big opportunity!

Create Your Offering

When I founded Women Online, I had a Blue Ocean: there are lots of marketing firms that specialize in reaching women, there are lots of digital firms that work with online communities, and there are lots of firms that specialize in mission-driven marketing campaigns, but to my knowledge, there still is no other digital marketing firm that helps mission-driven organizations and campaigns connect with influential communities of women online. I would be a service consulting firm but I also intended to build a product, a database of influential women online who care about social change. I could do that cheaply thanks to open-source software and blogs.

I made a little triangle diagram to define the intersection:

My research showed that, though our offering was specialized, the addressable market was huge. There are over four million mom blogs in the United States alone, at every income bracket, and the majority of Facebook's 1.6 billion daily users are women.[3] Women

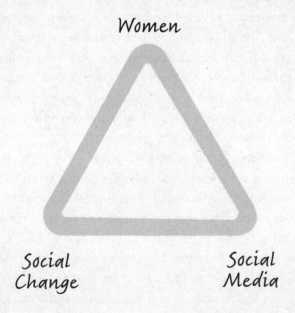

Women

Social Change

Social Media

are 1.5 times more likely than men to sign an online petition, and women make more frequent charitable donations.[4] My ideal clients were also an enormous field: political campaigns, not-for-profit organizations, foundations, and even companies whose issues and products women naturally cared about.

Still, I knew I would compete against three different kinds of firms: public relations firms that specialize in influencer marketing; digital agencies that also specialize in social media and content marketing; and social-impact firms that specialize in working for nonprofits, foundations, and political campaigns.

I defined a competitive set of about eight firms that I always seemed to be competing for business with, or that seemed to be winning clients I wanted. I set up a tracking system on Google Alerts, Mention, and Newsle to monitor the work of competitors, collaborators, and role models, and to know who was talking about us and what they were saying. This "oppo" research keeps us smart. Sometimes it causes a lot of FOMO. That is a very helpful reality check.

And in my weekly rounds with folks in my industry, I made sure to always be on the lookout for the scoop and gossip about my competitive set. What were they doing well? What were people saying about them that wasn't so great? And above all, how could we stand out? Defining the niche that only we owned against these bigger firms was most important of all.

Make Your Networking Niche

Even your networking can be niche—and hypereffective. This means small, specialized, curated groups for your field or niche might be a better use of time than a giant fancy conference with a famous keynoter—an especially great perk for introverts and hermits! Michelle Madhok, founder of SheFinds.com and MomFinds .com, notes, "I'm a member of a small, invite-only group for owners of websites in key content verticals. It's very specialized, and it's both networking and learning information from peers that isn't publicly out there."

Starting these private conversations can be as easy as retweeting an insightful tweet, commenting regularly on an active blog related to your work, or engaging others in an online group or forum. You can also invite friends in your field to write a guest post for your blog or invite a few colleagues to participate in a blog roundtable where they each share their perspective on a particular topic. If you're involved in an issue with public-policy or global implications, or cultural impact, you can organize a live tweet of an upcoming speech or event. Use a hashtag so others can participate, too.

Create Content That Supports Your Niche

Chances are, potential clients are going to Google you. Your search engine return page is frontline for your business or brand. Google juice and word of mouth are two of the most powerful allies you have as a hermit entrepreneur. And if you Google "Women Online"—guess who you see.

To ensure your search leads to accurate, useful, and professional results, you need strong content that supports searches for your name and related key words a potential customer might use to search for you.

Find your friends. Pick which platforms work best for what you do. For example, if you're a media commentator, Twitter will likely be much more useful for you than Pinterest. If you're a photographer, image-heavy sites like Tumblr and Pinterest will showcase your work brilliantly. Updating your social networks and blogging regularly will improve your SEO—search engine optimization—which is important for establishing your expertise and credentials. Remember, though, to be a good host at the party. Don't just promote yourself and your opinions. Acknowledge others, respond, and foster relationships. It makes for good karma and good business.

Start small. Maybe you don't want to commit to having your own blog or site just yet—and that's fine. Check out local online publications and volunteer to write a weekly or monthly column related to your work. You can also look for online publications related to your field and volunteer to write for them.

Stay current. Facebook and Twitter are the best places to post quick updates and interact on a personal level with your audience. Creating a fabulous e-mail newsletter, or using your Twitter feed or Facebook page or Instagram to "push" content to people, is important. Use your website or blog for posting the most important information you wish to expand upon. People don't often visit websites or blogs anymore without being prompted by a link in a social media field or an e-mail. However, quality is more important than quantity. Updating your content simply for the sake of updating could bury your best and most important updates, which you want to showcase.

Don't get stuck in traffic. Build influence by guiding audiences through the chaos of so much content. If your customers hang out in several places, target them where they are. Stacey Ferguson, founder of the social media community and conference Blogalicious, reminds us that now "everything is so divided up—you've got your blog, then Facebook, Instagram, Pinterest." By the same token, do your research! Creating profiles on every social network is not necessary, and trying to keep them all updated will drive you crazy.

Online PR. Even though you've rejected it personally, remember that you want to create a bit of FOMO in your potential customers, bosses, or investors. You can do this online without even having to speak in public or attend an event! The fact that I blog at prestigious outlets like the *Harvard Business Review* lends me an aura of credibility, and no one has to know I write my pieces in bed. Guest blogging, getting quoted as an expert, or freelance writing in a relevant business publication has a long digital footprint, and it's not just you talking about how great you are: it's a valid third party or a journalist. Resources like HARO (a free service that sends out multiple journalist queries every day) make it easier to get in front of media looking for experts.

Long form. Tweeting is great, Facebook is our home away from home, and we adore Pinterest, but the act of sitting down and giving voice to your opinions is crucial. Blogging is still a wonderful format to be smart and insightful. So is podcasting. Medium.com makes it possible for anyone to write on a forum shared by Melinda Gates and Bono. It's much harder on other platforms that contain your thoughts to a few characters. Telling the world what you think, but, more importantly, doing the work and asking the hard questions, is incredible for your professional credibility and your business development.

Think about a simple newsletter. Sending out a monthly or quarterly newsletter is a great way to update members of your audience who might not visit your website regularly but still want to be kept in the loop. And there's no better way to track influence than producing an e-mail people will actually open.

I'm a big fan of creating a delectable newsletter and building a CRM (customer-relationship-management database) to track customers. I have built up a "biz dev" list in my MailChimp with over nine hundred names of past clients, colleagues, and possible future clients. Everyone on that list has the potential to connect me to a new client for Women Online. And when I want to try to gin up some business quickly, I draft a witty newsletter.

There are several online services and templates you can use to create e-mail newsletters. My company loves MailChimp. Once you have a newsletter, know that your subscribers likely receive similar update e-mails from other organizations, so it's important that yours contains relevant content that is easy to read quickly. Make sure it has a fabulous voice.

Hermit freelancer, host of the popular podcast *Call Your Girl-*

friend, and feminist journalist Ann Friedman is the absolute gold standard. The popular and influential Ann Friedman Weekly is a must-read and gives her an instant way to connect with editors and TV bookers. Friedman's newsletters feel like sitting down to catch up and chat at the end of the week with your friend. She mixes links to her personal work with the best writing from around the web over the past week, plus funny pie charts, GIFs, and jokes. And she has used it to build a powerful business and platform as a feminist pundit, thinker, and writer.

She also has a great, no-stress method: she writes it partly for herself. "This is a nice way to give myself structure at end of week . . . what did I read? What did I produce? If you're not consuming interesting things, you won't produce interesting things."

If all this content participation is too much for your hermit nature, feel free to hire someone who loves it! That is okay. Many successful entrepreneurs with large digital presences outsource their social media communications and writing to someone who they trust, who can channel their voice.

WHAT'S YOUR FRANCHISE?

Many people I meet are simply scared to be as open and authentic as you need to be to be successful online. And it *is* scary! This is why the professional "franchise" approach can be helpful. Instead of simply tweeting, creating a franchise allows you to use a social platform to build something helpful for your entire field. Consider how to develop a digital franchise that shows off your unique smarts: something online that people love and rely on.

❑ Founded and hosted by Susan McPherson, head of McPherson Strategies, #CSRChat, a biweekly Twitter conversation, is a fantastic resource for anyone active in the world of corporate social responsibility, sustainability, and the place where social change meets the corporate world. As host of the franchise, Susan convenes the most important players in CSR to answer her questions. It's a PR win for participants, and for Susan, who "has proven to be the ultimate source of lead generation." It also began as a one-off, but after the first show, somebody e-mailed and said, "When's the next one?" Pay attention to what people respond to: you may have a possible franchise.

❑ Amy Webb is a prolific writer and creates more smart content than I can believe (her book *Data: A Love Story* was optioned by a Hollywood studio). Her company, Webb Media, helps clients determine the future, and how to cope with it. Each year, the firm produces a comprehensive "curated guide to digital media, design, and journalism conferences" that rates cost against the chance you'll actually learn something new. Webb Media also produces a great trend guide. These two franchises capture Webb Media's brand ("the future") and allow the company to reach new business leads without Amy having to get on a plane or train and hold a meeting. And— proof of the power of the franchise—you don't even have to provide an e-mail address to download them.

❑ Podcasting is the new blogging (and that is a huge compliment). I'm a huge fan, and I have one myself. If talking, not writing, is your thing, consider Carrie Kerpen's approach. In her podcast *All the Social Ladies,* Carrie interviews women in digital media about their careers, along with any advice they have for women trying to break into the field. Carrie says, "It was an easy way to overcome shyness about speaking to women in positions of power, and I also thought it would help with leading the next generation. I started getting business when guests and fans would refer me to clients. Now I have over 1,000,000 downloads of the podcast."

What's in the Name?

When I was twenty-three and working in London, a bunch of very cool ad guys taught me a saying I love: "Does what it says on the tin." Originally a slogan for wood sealant, the phrase means that the name on the packaging should never veer too far from the product's actual use. I always think of this when trying to name a project or help a client name a new brand. When clients are trying to be fancy, I stop and ask them, "Does the name do what it says on the tin?" In other words, does the name offer a clear promise of what you're offering?

Now, Women Online does what it says on the tin. The company is about connecting and mobilizing women online. However, my Google Analytics results frequently tell me that some of my most frequent visitors are those searching for mail-order brides and Eastern European women online. I bet they're disappointed to find my marketing agency! Oh, well. So much for the tin.

Still, another vote in favor of "does what it says on the tin" is the very prevalence of key words. In fact, when I was trying to develop the subtitle for this book, the very wise people at my publishing imprint, Dey Street, stressed the importance of using relevant and popular key words. How else, they pointed out, would the right audience find the book? That's why you see "introvert" in the subtitle: people often search for advice with that word.

So if you're struggling to create a name for your business or personal brand, use Google AdWords and trend data to find out what keywords your target audience actually uses when trying to find content like yours. If your company's brand name doesn't reflect such words, then ensure that supporting copy does. For example, leaders in the work-life field have fought for years to change public adoption of *work-life balance* as the term of art, because, as we've discussed, they think the idea of balance is a pointless exercise. Here's the problem: that's not what the public uses. It's not what the media uses. Everyone except leaders in the field uses *work-life balance*. For someone like Cali Yost, her leader branding might include her term *Work+Life Fit*, but you can bet supporting copy on her website references *work-life balance*, because that's how people will find her via Google.

You Must Also Buy Your Name

Owning your name online is a critical first step toward fully owning your online presence. Leave no stone unturned when it comes to establishing your name online across all possible social media platforms even if you don't use them now. Register a few domain names and all possible extensions. This can be done using sites like GoDaddy, BlueHost, or HostGator, or, if you have an existing site hosted on Squarespace (my personal favorite), WordPress, .me, or Blogger, you can register your domain name and host your blog there. Using Google's App Suite, you can give contractors or part-time workers an e-mail address at your firm in about two minutes, which is fantastic for branding and communicating with clients.

Also, be sure to use the same name across platforms. If possible, use the same name for your URL, Twitter handle, Facebook fan page, YouTube channel, etc. This will make it easy for clients to find you online and gives you a professional, streamlined image.

Your Look Must Also Be Consistent

For this one, you need to spend money to make money. If you're a hermit, your online look needs to do a lot of work for you. And so do photos of yourself on the web. Please invest in photography and a logo that are chic and professional. Graphics and image matter. Get a gorgeous head shot and use it for all your online properties. It is money well spent.

But People Online Are Mean!

In 2007 and 2008, I had a pretty good run as a pundit on CNN. But the worst part was the online comments after segments, because, when you appear on TV as a female political commentator, all commenters care about is how you look. I was informed on right-wing blogs that (a) I was completely unfuckable, and (b) I look like John Malkovich. (I suppose the two are related.) It didn't help that I was often paired against the Megababe of the Right Wing, Mary Katherine Brewer.

And that was nothing compared to one of my colleagues, who had to get an FBI detail because she and her kids kept getting death threats. She was an outspoken political blogger, and she was extremely in-your-face. She paid a heavy price, and I've seen a lot of friends braver than me go through scary, scary times.

The Internet isn't always a safe place, especially when you are a person with strong views. I realized that being a woman who wrote and spoke publicly about things like abortion rights and gun control meant strangers would say hateful things about me.

As of this moment I only have 6242 followers on Twitter. Certainly the owner of a social media firm should have more than six thousand followers on Twitter, no? But I am the least tough person out there. My skin is thin! Keeping my online presence narrow is deliberate. While I am turned off by trolls, the art of curating a gorgeous visual feed, say, on Instagram, almost scares me more. I just cannot be that fabulous.

But I know I have to accept some exposure, because every article I write that impresses potential clients means I can stay home extra days and not get on a plane.

Balancing my reluctance by consistently writing insightful (I hope) and professionally relevant blogs for elite online publications helps protect my professional credibility and keeps up my Google juice online. It also allows me the flexibility I crave, because I'm letting my online content work for me, even if I'm hiding at home or hanging out with my kids.

Writing professionally doesn't feel scary to me. It feels necessary. And when parties in power and policies change, it can feel *really* necessary. I had to find credibility in a way I can handle, which for many years meant staying out of personal or political discussions online, and keeping it strictly professional.

The challenge for you is to quit thinking of your online presence as a #FOMO-inducing Instagram feed of fabulousity, and shift your thinking into carving out your own unique space online. Your voice is valuable, professionally advantageous, and once you get into creating online content, it can be addictive. Best of all, you can do it anytime, anywhere, and especially from your couch.

9

The Hermit Entrepreneur

I n the next two chapters, we'll discuss how to maximize your flexibility and quiet time and minimize stressors at work. This chapter focuses on entrepreneurs, while Chapter 10 addresses the hermit who works within an organization.

If you feel like you aren't cut out to be an entrepreneur because you don't have a huge appetite for risk or you're not willing to sacrifice your personal life, I'm here to tell you that's crap. If you have a vision for your life, your work, and the impact you want to make, a small business just might be the right strategy.

Here's the truth: running a business is a skill, not an inherent gift. And it's not the exclusive province of extroverts or the carefree. With the right tools, you can grow your business, land new clients, and do the work you love, while keeping travel, networking, and extracurriculars to a minimum. In fact, being a small-business owner is actually a fantastic career for the hermit, once you know how to sustain it.

A hermit entrepreneur maximizes control over her pace, place, and space so she can do as much work from the quiet of home as possible. But a day in the life of a hermit entrepreneur might look different every day! One day you might be running around from business appointment to appointment, hustling as hard as you can, in full makeup and wardrobe, while the next might find you in sweats, working from your home office and venturing outside only to check the mail. That day might be full of back-to-back calls, or it might feature chunks of unclaimed time for writing on deeper-thinking work. For me, a good week sees me out and about two days and working from home for three. On top of that, at least one of the "home" days needs to feature almost no conference calls or web meetings.

Small Is Sexy

The media just loves an iconoclastic entrepreneur. That is, as long as their company is a "unicorn"—meaning, valued at a billion dollars.

But those million breathless articles and magazine covers are very far from the true story of successful entrepreneurs. These small-business owners actually create a thriving, innovative economy, and their companies reflect their values, not just their valuation.

Silicon Valley veteran Gina Bianchini, whose start-up Ning was once valued at over $800 million but never made that unicorn exit, has a different growth plan for her new company, Mighty Networks.

With Mighty Networks, Gina has kept her team at about 20 people and built a profitable business. The company creates social-networking software for professional communities. *Wired* notes, "As the current unicorns—from Dropbox to Snapchat—grapple with skyrocketing burn rates and build out expensive enterprise sales-forces to help them grow into their valuations, Bianchini is adding customers and banking revenues."[1]

The smaller the company, the more control you (the owner) have. This may mean you can keep better hours because you contain your workload, or it can mean you decide how to spend your company's resources or give back to the community. You can run a mission-driven business simply by directing dollars you would already spend in a good direction. Lindy Huang Werges started her executive recruiting firm, Integritas Resources, after years of working for both large corporations and start-ups. It's a revenue-driven firm that is focused on accounting and finance, and she controls how her firm's dollars get spent.

"Philanthropy is important to me," Huang Werges says. "I wasn't able to do it in larger companies. We are a woman- and minority-owned business, and we invest in minority- and women-owned companies." In 2015, her firm invested 33 percent of its earnings in giving back, and her revenues still grew by 500 percent. "We even try to take our clients out to lunch at local restaurants," Huang Werges says.

In a culture that idealizes the entrepreneur who's always hungry, it's hard to feel that small is, truly, sexy. Often I feel I'm letting people down by passing up opportunities to expand rapidly. I see colleagues and competitors staffing up, and can feel a twinge of envy and insecurity. But then I have to pinch myself and remember this is a choice. And it *is* a choice.

That's why the enterprising hermit must, above all, be realistic. Part of being realistic is having the systems and knowledge in place to control growth, whether to stimulate it or slow it down. Your career may not be a rocket ship. But it will keep rising steadily, and even if it's not a thrill ride, it will give you a great sense of satisfaction.

GETTING STARTED

To value your product, you have to figure out your finances, growth, and business type. Here's a step-by-step guide.

"The McKinsey of Mommybloggers"

Positioning your business means creating the desired perception of it, and when I was starting out, I hadn't positioned mine. I simply tried to price myself fairly enough to get hired. But after about a year of working and competing against other momblogger agencies or influencer marketing firms, I realized I wanted to be different. I jokingly said I was going to be "The McKinsey of Mommybloggers."

The phrase is tongue-in-cheek, but it means we hold ourselves to a high standard in a field that's completely unregulated and full of firms of varying quality. McKinsey is a legendary, elite, and high-priced strategy consulting firm. They hire the best, work with the best, and, in the market's view, do the best work.

That's how I wanted Women Online to be perceived—a challenge, since the company is about moms (undervalued in the marketplace), social media (a field with no barriers to entry), and digital marketing (again, not exactly Nobel Prize–level work).

Pricing is one of the most powerful tools to control your work life, and your choice is also a positioning statement. Like everything else in business, it's more art than science, and you need to be flexible. Here are the metrics we use to price our services:

Price: We are not the least expensive firm in our space, and that's on purpose. However, because we often work with nonprofit organizations, our fees are flexible and are managed on a sliding scale.

Clientele: We are extremely choosy about who we take on. If I wouldn't work for this client for free, I won't do it.

Quality vs. volume: Our sales approach, our pitch, and our very presentation is niche. Some pitches use low prices, some are about technology, some feature giant numbers of ad impressions, or sheer volume of business. Ours emphasizes our quality, our excellent strategy and field knowledge, and the fact that we work with world-renowned clients. It's social proofing. This approach says: if we're good enough for them, surely we're good enough for you.

Staying low-tech: My firm will never earn awards for its infrastructure or tracking. Our website is, frankly, meh. I'd like a better website, but the investment required for such infrastructure would strain me as much as bringing on extra staff, and it's not part of my plan.

I know other small firms run by hermits who have done the opposite: invested up front in incredible technology, high-tech websites, databases, and tracking for pitches that use metrics and results to get business. It works beautifully. I think the key is knowing what kind of business you're going to run.

Six years in, my business has stayed small while competitors have grown exponentially, sold to big firms, or taken on outside capital. We are not for everyone, and we lose as much business as we win. That's okay, though, because our clients tend to stay with us, and they refer other new clients to us.

That's where the aspirational piece of pricing comes in, and why it's important for hermits. When you price your goods or services slightly higher than market average, you can shoot for clients you want instead of shooting for volume, which helps stave off work-life conflicts right out of the gate.

Pricing 101

First, you need to learn the landscape. Having some basic guidelines on how to price your work is very helpful, especially if you bill by the hour or on a project basis. If you are starting a business in a field you currently work in, this won't be too hard. If you're doing something new, creating a competitive set is really helpful, much as you did when developing your brand niche.

You can make this set both aspirational (building in some profit, or competing with the players) and realistic (making sure it covers your monthly nut—and we'll define that and learn how to figure that out in this chapter).

What kind of firms do you want to be considered alongside?

What kind of firms are you actually competing against?

This is really important because clients or hiring managers will group you in a cohort, consciously or unconsciously. And if you are responding to RFPs or government contracts, you'll need a solid sense of pricing.

Women and the Underpricing Trap

I have a tough time being taken seriously as an expensive strategist because I work in a space that's entirely about reaching women. I still have to fight all the time to get paid the rates I want. (You know that pay gap between men and women? There's also a pricing gap for women entrepreneurs.) Obviously, if you're undercharging for your work, you have to work more! That makes it difficult to be a successful hermit.

One counterintuitive way to get a sense of what to charge? Ask some men.

Data show men set higher reference points on income: they always aim higher, and they often get it. Traditionally, when pricing, women tend to consult more female reference groups. Our fellow entrepreneurs, clients, or experts in your field—that is, our professional networks—look more like us. This can be a real disadvantage when it comes to evaluating your worth in the marketplace. (Later, in Chapter 12, on negotiation, we'll learn the basic tool kit to ensure you're paid your worth.)

Do the Hustle

Yes, you have to value your work, but sometimes you'll have to compromise. That's where hustling comes in.

Real estate mogul Clelia Peters explains it well: "I define hustling as what happens when you realistically survey the marketplace and strategically choose to offer your services at a discount or with more favorable terms than competitors 'purely to gain a foothold among new clients.'"

Hustling can also mean doing whatever it takes to win new business or establish your foothold, but should not be about selling yourself short. There's the kind of hustling that verges on being taken advantage of, like doing work on spec, and there's hustling with a contingency plan. If a potential client asks you to do some free work, you can say yes if you like. But sometimes what you think might be hustling is someone taking advantage just because they can. I think our record for putting together and then tweaking new proposals for a potential client lies at four iterations. That's about twenty hours of work, all unbillable. When it all comes to naught, you can feel angry.

This effort is key, so either build time that you may never win back into your budgeting, or build in a hustle with contingencies, for example by writing free articles or planning an event from which you can draw lasting credibility and accolades, whether or not the client comes through.

Going all out is also a way to develop a portfolio. A blogger I know began by simply doing that: blogging about her passion for free. But, because she entered the fray just as blogging was started, she was able to establish a foothold in the field, which led to several high-profile paid gigs writing, teaching, and speaking, as well as a full-time job to support her and provide health care as she built her business. In time, that exposure led to a book deal—one entirely unrelated to her blog—and she was able to go freelance full-time.

Hustling is part of the life of an entrepreneur, hermit or not, and it's essential when you're starting out (and probably when you're well established, too). You'll have to take less than you're worth at some point, but make sure it's only a short-term strategy. Be careful not to price yourself too low, though: in my experience being too "cheap" often suggests to clients that you are not good enough at what you do.

Remember, too, that you can hustle from home. It's great to get out there and meet potential clients or customers face-to-face, but follow-ups and relationship development via phone or e-mail works well. Most important, hustling is a state of mind. Even the most introverted entrepreneur needs to hustle. If you love your work and you feel in control, you won't mind it, and you'll probably even enjoy it.

Feathering Your Nest

A wonderful lifestyle is a curse if you wake up ten years later with no financial security.

Financial planners will tell you that you must have a cash cushion of six months while also saving for retirement, a house, or college, and paying yourself. This might not be realistic for small-business owners; I have never done it. Feathering your nest is being intentional and smart about where all your money is going, and making sure your business venture is really taking care of you.

Too many people have escaped the reality of their daily work lives to create an entrepreneurial dream that not only fails, but strips them of whatever financial security they have built up. Remember, you are becoming a hermit entrepreneur to try to reduce stress and anxiety in your life. If you don't have the money saved to float yourself for six months while your business ramps up, reconsider why you're doing it. If you're launching a product or opening a store and you're planning on cashing out your kids' college funds or refinancing the house, reconsider.

Start-up veteran Lane Wood puts it like this: "Entrepreneurship is something we sell motivated individuals in the same way the beauty industry sells women makeup or shoes." Like *Sex and the City*'s Carrie Bradshaw, who realizes she's spent over $40,000 on shoes with nothing to show for it, people may be buying a dream with damaging effects. Smart people quite literally mortgage their futures.

This is because sustainability works both ways. Your lifestyle must be sustainable emotionally, physically, and financially! I might be an anxious wreck full of migraines if I'm on the road selling every day of the week, but if I stay home and hide for too long, I can't pay the bills. That's pretty stressful, too.

So how to take care of your finances and your emotional health? Feathering your own nest could look as simple as pulling out pretax dollars every month to fund a SEP-IRA. It could mean keeping up a highly paid consulting gig while you're launching your business so you can keep earning cash and maintaining your health insurance. It could mean keeping a job while you work every night on growing your business, with your living room filled with boxes of your product. You'll know what's right; just don't ignore your finances.

Having a Knippel

My most powerful early experiences around money were shaped by my father's moving out when I was eleven and sometimes refusing to pay the bills (simply because he felt like it).

Like many women of her generation, my mother is an educator. She earned a good living as a learning-disabilities consultant. And, like many middle- and upper-middle-class women of her generation, she stopped working when my sister and I were born.

As privileged as my childhood was, it was peppered by constant stress about money: Would we ever have enough? When I was accepted early into Brown University, an Ivy League school, I called my father excitedly to let him know. "That's great, honey, but you have to go to Rutgers [the state university of New Jersey]," he said. That's a good problem to have, but it also highlighted the truth that my sister, mother, and I were completely dependent on men. I hated that feeling, and I was determined never to depend on a man for my own income. Thankfully, the Brown volleyball coach magically made some funding appear, and indeed I packed up and left for Rhode Island.

When I was about twenty-eight and getting serious about a man, my mom told me about her *knippel*. It's a concept that is crucial for women entrepreneurs . . . and in fact, for everyone.

In Yiddish, a *knippel* is a knot, like the kind you might make in a handkerchief. The phrase comes from the old country, where women would hide jewels or a few coins in those knots or in the seams of their dress. That way, in case their husband died, left, or they had to flee during a pogrom, there would be a little cash. Now a *knippel* just means a little money on the side that your partner doesn't know about.

In my mom's case, her *knippel* was a secret stock account. Her friend Barbara's *knippel,* Mom proudly reported, had recently done very well in an AT&T stock split. But when she advised me to have one, I recoiled, because my marriage would never be toxic like my parents'.

I'm happy to report my marriage is not toxic. It's great. But I still have a *knippel* and so does my husband (I think).

You don't need to be married to have a *knippel*—you don't even need to be in a relationship. Think of it as your own knot for your future self. It's another way to feather a nest, because life brings us surprises, and sometimes, as hard as it can be, we have to handle them alone.

GIVE YOUR MONEY A GOAL

There's a common saying: the only difference between an entrepreneur and someone with a dream is money. But all money isn't equal, and to figure that out, first, you need to accept that money is an emotional topic. Think of money as the principal element in how you make choices, and how you establish what your financial values and priorities are.

I've learned the hard way that, for an entrepreneur, emotions and money don't mix. In my case, my emotions revolved around credit use. I had a serious shopping problem in my twenties. (I was interviewed on TV about my staggering $12,000 debt!) That's why the first time my bank gave me a line of credit, I felt ashamed to use it. It felt like running up debt on Daddy's credit card.

Then my stepfather, an accomplished businessman, told me this wasn't debt: it was growth. Was I ready for it?

Well, at the time, I wasn't, and that's why I was anxious about using the credit line. My money didn't have a goal.

The advice of financial therapist Amanda Clayman is something to take to heart. She stresses that a goal, when budgeting your business, can be transformative. She recommends choosing one even before you launch that business.

Paying attention to how money comes in and out is key to stress. For instance, in my case, when I was younger, failing to set appropriate boundaries in my work made me spend impulsively on expensive self-care. In effect, I was reinforcing the system, because the more money you spend, the more chained you are to your job.

By the same token, not budgeting can lead to overwork, another violation of boundaries. "We put such a high value on being a hard worker," Amanda says, but people also need to give themselves permission to say, "I only need this much money."

Any money that doesn't have a direction is vulnerable to being misspent. That's why, Amanda says, it's so important to set an intention. Money set aside will still actually change our behavior in the moment, if it doesn't have a goal.

That doesn't mean you'll find the solution or answer immediately. Realizing what goal to give your money takes time and experience. But allowing yourself to reflect how your emotions affect your spending or saving is the first step to letting your finances make you happy, which is the goal of an entrepreneur.

Figure out Your Monthly Nut

My husband's great-uncle John had a funny story about how we spend money. When his father-in-law remarked that John must be doing well if he could afford a new Cadillac, John replied, "Of course I can't afford it," then added, "If I could afford a Cadillac, I'd be driving a Rolls-Royce."

We might chuckle, but how true is this for you? I know it is for me. (See my aforementioned TV interview about my shopping-inspired debt.) The American Dream is built on overextending ourselves. Symbols of success like cars, watches, and handbags are expensive, and, unfortunately, there's a very eager consumer credit industry to enable us. Endless exposure to American Express commercials in my youth—"Membership has its privileges"—had me whipping out my Amex with way too much gusto. I thought the color of the card signified something about what I'd achieved in life. I'm much better now, though I would be lying if I said I was left with a huge amount of money at the end of every month.

I can't tell you how many people have told me the biggest barrier they feel to launching a business is dealing with cash flow. They're right to take it seriously, because control over your cash flow is what buys you freedom and flexibility. If you're going to be a hermit, you need to figure out how to pay for it!

So, before striking out on your own, figuring that out is certainly important. That's where a "monthly nut" comes in. Here is how it works if you own a small business. Your monthly nut is all of your business expenses, and the cash you need to generate in order to cover the nut.

Your accountant might use a financial statement for this, but I find accounting-speak, even after all these years, confusing, so I put the terms in my own basic language.

Set up a spreadsheet (I use Google Docs) and add a line for all your fixed expenses.

ITEM	COST (ESTIMATES ARE OK)
SALARIES	
RENT + CAPITAL EXPENSES	
ADMINISTRATIVE (AN AVERAGE OF YEARLY LEGAL, ACCOUNTING, INSURANCE PAYMENTS, DUES, ETC.)	
TAXES (ESTIMATE QUARTERLY PAYMENTS)	
CREDIT CARD/TRAVEL & ENTERTAINING (PUT IN A HEALTHY AMOUNT BASED ON YEARLY AVERAGE)	

The total is your nut. If your business's nut is $34,000, you know that every month, to break even, you need to earn at least $34,000 in revenue.

Other expenses will come and go, of course. For example, I usually have several contractors working on projects; I pay them out of the specific contract fee they are assigned to. I might have a trip that comes up that I need to pay for. You can handle these kinds of things as they arise. The nut is simply those bills you need to pay every month. Once you know this number, you know how much you need to earn.

The comfortable monthly nut keeps you motivated, but not stretched too thin. If you are consistently going into debt to cover your monthly basic expenses, you have four options:

1. Get a new job and earn more money, or keep on your current path if you're due for a big promotion.

2. Cut down your expenses.

3. If you have one, ask your partner to float more of the expenses while you figure things out.

4. Win the lottery.

If you want to be a successful hermit, I suggest number two: try to pare down your expenses. This is good discipline while you figure things out. Then, once you know how much you need, you can put systems in place to earn it.

Here's a way to calculate your personal monthly nut that is especially helpful if you are a freelancer, or your business income and personal income are one and the same. I realized I was never going to download receipts or actualize my spending into Quicken or another budgeting platform. But every six months or so, I adjust our monthly personal budget and make sure it's as accurate as possible.

(Feel free to swap out for relevant categories.)

ITEM	COST (ESTIMATES ARE OK)
MORTGAGE OR RENT	
UTILITIES (HEAT, CABLE, PHONE, WATER/SEWER, LAWN)	
GROCERIES	
TAXES (ESTIMATE QUARTERLY PAYMENTS)	
CAR + GAS + AUTO INSURANCE	
DINING OUT/ENTERTAINMENT	
STUDENT LOANS	
529/401(K) OR SEP (IF NOT TAKEN FROM PAYCHECK)	
LIFE INSURANCE	
DRY CLEANING	
GYM	
PERSONAL (CLOTHES, FUN)	
CHILDCARE OR SCHOOL	
HOUSEKEEPER	

Scoping Your Work

Scoping is the key to maintaining your boundaries as a hermit entrepreneur. According to the business dictionary, the "scope of work," whether you are in a service business or producing product, means, "The division of work to be performed under a contract or subcontract in the completion of a project, typically broken out into specific tasks with deadlines." Usually contracts will have a Scope of Work attached, which holds one accountable.

But I also like to think of scoping as an everyday discipline that allows me to protect my time and sanity. Scoping is basically boundary setting. You could even scope out the work involved in throwing a dinner party, a kid's birthday, or in planning a vacation.

One of the keys to scoping effectively as a homebody entrepreneur is right-sizing your contracts. (Goldilocks again.) The first step is a more global decision than creating a scope for a particular project. Every project has a specific impact on your time management and your boundaries, and you have to be honest with yourself about what pace you thrive on. At some level, only experience in your business will truly teach you how to create the work product that's right for you.

Over the years, my team has learned how to sniff out the right-sized project for us. Our contracts tend to be smaller than those of other digital marketing firms, but we can do a lot of our work independently, and we don't usually do work that is super-deadline-driven. At kickoff, we set up milestones. When we meet those milestones, it means no frantic calls from our clients, no working weekends, but also no huge rush when we finish a giant, stressful project. My colleagues running huge social media projects or planning major events or building amazing websites get the glory and a bigger seat at the table, but they often have to go 24/7, and and the work is stressful the whole time. It's an emotional trade-off I willingly make.

Scoping can also be seasonal. In your business, when to grow and when to stay status quo probably has a rhythm all its own. I know that the period from Christmas to Valentine's Day is always quiet.

Work wraps up at the end of the year, and new business doesn't really get going until mid-February. Summer and fall are usually very busy and profitable. I never get to take a summer vacation! So I try to save cash for winter, and also know I need to pump up business development in early February. Then, instead of panicking, I work less in January and try to enjoy it.

The scoping process, in which you determine how you're going to get a task completed, is crucial for hermits. Whether creating a product or offering a service, I'm shocked to hear how many business owners continually overpromise, erase all their boundaries, and fail because they're not being honest about the kind of work they need to do and the scope of their work. Now, we all fail; it's a natural part of work. But incorrectly scoping is a correctable failure. You miss deadlines, can't deliver what's promised, and feel miserable. Your boundaries are erased because you think about stressful work all the time. Even worse, your valuable word-of-mouth referral pipeline can get damaged, which means you need to start the hunt for more work from scratch. This makes you feel you have to overcompensate in business development. It is no fun.

Here are four steps to consider:

❑ The meta-question: What kind of work product do you want to deliver? Learn to specify the kind of project your business does, and the impact it will have on your schedule and boundaries.
❑ Determine what you are good at and what you can safely say good-bye to.
❑ Find the right tools to plan, and learn to be realistic about scope.
❑ Determine what you have the capacity to deliver—and again, be realistic.

There are lots of web-based or SAAS tools out there to help you scope a project. Most are designed for creative agency or service-based teams. Software company 10000ft offers several versions of an easy-to-use and comprehensive online tool for scoping and project management.

A simple spreadsheet will do. You want to list every aspect of the job, line by line, and estimate how many hours you think each element will take.

Every element of the project should be accounted for in terms of hours and cost estimates, low to high. That allows the development firm to budget the project and allocate staff resources. As the proj-

EXAMPLE: SCOPE CHART
FOR A DIGITAL MARKETING AGENCY

EXPENSE	HOURS	COST ESTIMATE	SPENT TO DATE	EST. TO COMPLETE	NOTES
PROJECT MANAGEMENT					
CLIENT MEETINGS					
STRATEGIC PLAN DEVELOPMENT					
EDITORIAL CALENDAR					
DESIGN					
SHARE GRAPHICS FOR SOCIAL MEDIA					
CONTENT CREATION					
COPYWRITING FOR FACEBOOK					
TOTAL					

ect evolves, keep accounting for hours and costs up-to-date so you
know how you're pacing.

While it's essential to scope out a project so you know how much
to charge, it's also essential to scope a project so you know how the
work will affect your life for the next six months or so.

It's also helpful to think about how you can scale production or
a client engagement without adding too much extra labor or time to
the scope of work. Ask yourself as you're preparing a contract, *How
big should the project be, and how can I scale without including too much
extra labor?*

I can scale a project in my field (social media–content creation)
without adding too many extra woman-hours. The fee for a campaign that produces forty pieces of content isn't four times higher
than one that produces ten pieces, but the volume of social media
impressions the client gets will be much higher. On the other hand,
there are project tasks a client could double or triple, and it would
impact the budget and time spent by a corresponding amount.

For example, if you develop software for one customer and new
customers want the same exact software, you can probably scale up
without too much impact on time management or the bottom line.
That's why companies that scale and can produce lots of work product without adding much extra labor make a lot of money! Unfortunately, that is not my business and I am not rich. But I have learned
how to realize my own little economies of scale.

THE WORLD'S MOST BASIC SCOPING TOOL

Total project budget: $25,200
Length of project: four weeks

TEAM MEMBER	TASK	HOURS/ WEEK	COST/ WEEK	TOTAL COST	% OF BUDGET
JEN	METRICS AND TRACKING	3	450	1800	6%
AMANDA	SOCIAL MEDIA– CONTENT CREATION AND COPYWRITING	20	3,000	12,000	48%
JAMES	LANDING PAGE DEVELOPMENT AND GRAPHICS	15	2,250	9,000	36%
ANA	PROJECT MANAGEMENT AND MEETING FACILITATION	5	600	2,400	10%

Capacity Plan

Your capacity plan is the total sum of all your scopes of work. It details your current workload, and when individual tasks begin and end, to determine what you actually have the capacity to do. For instance, if you have ten clients and ten people, the capacity plan should, at a glance, reflect how those people are using their time. It's key to maximizing your profits, because you can actually lose profit when you overpromise and underplan. For instance, the artisan sellers on Etsy.com are full of cautionary tales of business owners who scaled quickly, experienced great demand for their products, and simply didn't have the staff time or resources (such as a hard-to-source ingredient) to meet the demand. There's even a term for it: "handmade business burnout."[2]

For simplicity's sake, say you have four employees, and four projects at your company.

(HOURS PER MONTH)	EMPLOYEE 1	EMPLOYEE 2	EMPLOYEE 3	EMPLOYEE 4
CLIENT 1	10	40	20	
CLIENT 2		40		80
CLIENT 3	70	20		65
CLIENT 4		40	60	
BIZ DEV	60			10
ADMIN	20	20	20	5

If everyone works 160 hours a month, then who has capacity for a new project? Answer: it's Employee 3—she still has forty hours free per month. The next question is whether I can staff Employee 3 on this new project. If the scope of the project is more than she can take on and the other staff can accommodate, then I need to bring in new staff to service the client. Now, this question is a personal and financial one. Is bringing on someone new worth potential added stress? Or is the upside of winning this new client going to pay dividends in future business development—say, if it's a vanity client or high margin?

Jen Vento, the managing director of Women Online, also warns about "scope creep"—when you wind up providing much more on a project than originally specified. "Be very prescriptive," she advises. "If we're going to post five original pieces of content per week on a project, and then we're going to curate another ten or fifteen, I'm going to plan that out to the individual piece."

After every engagement, we also like to look at the hours we actually spent on a project and divide it by the budget so we can figure out our effective hourly rate. Meeting what we set is our goal. It doesn't mean you have to meet the budget exactly for every project, as long as your overall time sheet balances out.

Jen and I both tend to offer too much for free, so we have built in traps to catch ourselves. One of these is sussing out our future clients before we even sign the contract. "The personal dynamics between a customer and your firm can hugely impact scoping," she says. Take note of the process leading up to the signing: Do you have to micromanage already? How many people are you working with on a regular basis? How many group meetings will there be a week? On some level, Jen says, you just have to trust your gut. "Is this a person I want to be with?" she asks. "There are some clients we have a relationship with. And some I never want to talk to again."

Choosing Your Clients

Not all clients are equal. Part of growth is choosing clients that will allow you to maintain boundaries but also earn money. This is not about "reaching scale." It's about sustainability and profitability. Your client mix can also help the introvert with business development, because your clients speak for you.

Here's how I think about my client mix in terms of public perception and business development:

❑ **Vanity clients.** These are the big names I can brag about. They instantly give me credibility in the marketplace and increase my firm's value. They are less about income maximizing and more about doing a fantastic job. Nothing is better biz dev than a happy, big-name client.

❑ **LTRs.** Long-term relationships. Just like in marriage, sometimes things can get a little stale and eyes might wander. But you're always there for each other, and you have deep ties and institutional memory. These are usually multiyear, retainer contracts.

❑ **High margin.** I'm not going to brag about these clients. However, they pay really well, are low churn (meaning they don't turn over often), and are wonderful for a cash infusion in uncertain times. Last year I had a large corporate client who paid us $50,000 for about thirty hours of work. All the work we proposed got stuck in legal and bureaucracy and no one seemed to mind. And of course, good work is always great for word of mouth, so make sure to do your best for these clients. You never know who knows whom.

❑ **Just for the love.** You would do this for free, because you love the cause or client, or you want the experience. Price it low, or do it pro bono, and dive in. Because Women Online works with many not-for-profits of varying size, I have learned how to "mix" clients so I can make a profit while working for both small nonprofits, who offer a lower hourly rate, and large companies with bigger budgets.

❑ **Short term.** These are a lot of work to set up and are high churn, but they can lead to long-term work.

For me, the ideal mix is 50 percent long-term retainer clients, with a contract of six months or twelve months. Another 40 percent of the client work will be short-term engagements—six-week or three-month projects. Then I always save 10 percent for pro bono work, just for the love (and the brand boost it can give to my firm). For you, this might be totally different: you might want to do 30 percent pro bono work and 70 percent short-term projects, with a complete stoppage in the summer so you can take time off. (Ken, a highly skilled database developer in Seattle and a friend of my husband's, works ten months a year because he likes to save the summers for camping.) Acknowledge your hermit self, and decide what percentage of work you can devote to what.

Realization and Utilization

Even short-term clients or work products are not all created equal. I may have a short-term client that is very profitable, and one that is a money loser. The difference comes in how long it takes to win the business, from first meeting to contract signing (sales cycle), and how many hours I spend on work winning the project. It's very simple math. Figure out the hourly rate for the project, then multiply that by the hours you spent wooing them. That's deducted from your total profit.

See below. Not only is Client A less profitable because I'm spending valuable hermit time wooing them, I have to wait six agonizing months to know if they even sign the contract or not! Also, don't forget

	CONTRACT VALUE	SALES CYCLE	BIZ DEV HOURS	EXECUTION HOURS	IMPACT ON PROFIT
CLIENT A	$30,000	6 MONTHS	15	150	($3,000)
CLIENT B	$30,000	3 WEEKS	3	150	($600)

the paperwork time it takes to get a customer signed up in your system. Factor that in. For instance, six hours of contract negotiation is a lot less painful on a six-month client than a one-month engagement.

And because the time you spend to develop a client or customer relationship is unpaid, you need to guard that time carefully. Every hour spent courting a client in person, on the phone, or by writing a proposal is an hour lost to earning revenue or spending time at home.

I refer to this as utilization rate; it's also sometimes called billability or profitability. This is how much of you and your staff's time is being billed to clients vs. being spent on business development, overhead costs, or administrative time (time that comes out of your pocket, not from client projects). If I work two thousand hours during the year, for instance, and one thousand of that is billable to the client, my utilization is 50 percent. My accountant, Alicia, says that for a midlevel worker, you should shoot for 65 percent utilization (meaning 65 percent of their time is directly billable back to clients) and about 50 percent once they're senior, while brand-new staff should be at least 75 percent, because they're not doing development and sales.

So how do you plan for utilization? Alicia says it's complicated, and depends on how many clients you have for the year, and what your goals are. "Say that it's my first year and I only have two clients signed up," Alicia says. "I know that my utilization is going to be very low. My goal is to have ten clients by the end of the year. So I should only be spending 20 percent on utilization, while 80 percent should be working on closing those new deals. That means I've got to have enough cash in the bank to cover for the fact that I'm only billable 20 percent of the time."

My biggest lesson on the big picture of sales came when I started a new department at a large communications firm. My boss told me I'd have to bring in a certain figure of revenue in order to be able to hire more people for my fledgling department. I expected the revenue number to simply cover the salaries of my new hires, but that wasn't the case. My boss told me that for every new hire I brought in, I would need to earn 2.5 times that person's salary! This was to cover business development time, overhead expenses, and administrative costs. Never forget the hidden costs.

Putting Systems in Place

I have four different financial reports that I consult at all times. These reports are applicable if you run a business, work freelance or are self-employed, or work on any sort of commission structure. Here they are:

❏ **Cash in the bank.** Know your cash position at all times. This can be as simple as logging into your online account frequently to check, or setting up a daily alert to send you your balance in the morning. You can even set an alert for every transaction. If you want to take it one step further and have decent projections and a good system for cash-flow management, you can use a simple document called a FINMO, which stands for something like "financial info monthly."

❏ **Accounts receivable, or AR.** Use a simple online software program such as QuickBooks or FreshBooks. Especially if you're a service business, it's essential to know your booked revenue.

❏ **Accounts payable, or AP.** These are the invoices you owe. Obviously, these are important to keep current.

❏ **Pipeline or biz dev planning doc.** My wonderful accountant, Alicia, taught me this one. I use a spreadsheet and I also keep a pipeline at the bottom of my FINMO, with a cell estimating the likelihood that business will close. For every proposal or strong indication of interest I get in a new project, I log the client, contact, last meeting date, scope of work and contract size, and potential to close (WARM, COLD, DEAD, CLOSED). I can quickly scan it and see, for example, that I might have $250,000 in biz dev prospects but only $25,000 in my bank account. Time to get moving and close some of those prospects! If I have $250,000 in my bank account but only $25,000 in prospects, I need to turn up some business development levers, although I might take a few days off to enjoy in the short term. The pipeline document extends years back, and so it not only shows me what potential new clients are in play, but also allows me to review my "win" rate over time.

Michael Ansara, founder of the Share Group and Upsource Inc, who actually lives my fantasy of owning a horse farm and making jam, notes that business people who only look at their numbers backward are missing something. Once you're halfway into the next month, he says, "It's kind of hard to do much about the previous one." Instead you should be projecting a few months forward, then asking, "Whoops, we've got a hole. How are we going to fill that?"

"We're not doing this as an exercise in accounting," Michael says. "We're doing this to see where the opportunities are, and where [there] are problems we need to correct. There's hundreds of numbers, but what are the really critical ratios? And which ones drive profitability and success? And now, how do we move them the way we want to move them?"

The thing I like about Michael's approach is its humanness and practicality. I don't have an MBA, and I've always been intimidated by those who have them. But it's in talking to experienced entrepreneurs like Michael that you realize, running a business is mostly common sense.

Speaking of common sense, I want to talk now about a topic that seems to defy it: growth. It's easy to all assume that the purpose of starting a business is to grow. But for the hermit entrepreneur, this may not make sense. Ask yourself, whether you're about to start or you already have a business, how much bigger do you want to get? How much risk can you handle? If the answer is "not a lot!," read on.

Are You Building to Delegate or Staying Small?

There are two basic models for a hermit entrepreneur who's starting small.

1. Use your own labor and time to earn the bulk of your income.

2. Manage others' time, delegating tasks to them and earning a percentage of others' revenue.

Successful solo players I know have two strategies to keep boundaries and coffers well balanced. They almost always have a strong administrative assistant or junior person to take on tasks that suck time and don't earn money. This is a powerful opportunity for you to secure your future by investing a little bit of money into something that will pay dividends.

They also have a network of colleagues whom they can team up with, and to whom they can refer extra business with confidence or subcontract overflow. If you're a solopreneur or a small-business owner, your Rolodex of fellow travelers is key. If a client suddenly demands time you do not have, or needs a skill set you do not possess, you can phone a friend, and maintain your limits.

You can base your monthly earning on available time. And about this, too, you must be realistic. My friend Margie Cader runs a successful PR consultancy and is rigorous about turning down new work if she is booked. "What works for me is to charge by the hour, or to really base a retainer on hours—but not go over," she says. "There have been times that I have overserviced clients, of course. And sometimes you do this at the start of a relationship. But I've gotten better at it over the years and I never lose my shirt. So, I'm less concerned with a big retainer or a big contract than I am with making sure I am being properly compensated for my hours."

It may seem counterintuitive that someone who wants to avoid interaction as much as possible would want to choose a life in which they constantly manage others, but there's a wonderful magic to it. The less time you personally need to bill and the more time you can delegate to your staff, the more free time you have to pursue the work you want to do and maintain the boundaries you need. Become your own delegator in chief. This is not an income-maximizing approach, but it is a flexibility-maximizing approach.

You could build a business with a small number of employees whom you really trust and still maintain most of your boundaries. However, you cannot micromanage, and you cannot expect perfection. If you set up a system where you bring in the majority of the new business (say that's ten hours a week) and work on clients with a light touch (say that's twenty hours a week), with another ten hours for admin, you're working forty hours a week on what should be a pretty profitable and well-run business, as long as your staff is billing enough to support their time as well as most of yours. That means you must ask, if, say, your firm's blended hourly rates equal $150 per hour, how many hours a month does everyone need to bill to pay for the whole company? Your staff should be billing more time than you are, and the numbers need to account for that.

Here's a very simple way of looking at it:

Your business has a $45,000 monthly nut (this includes all salaries, taxes, expenses, and administrative and capital costs).

After doing your research and determining your pricing strategy, you have arrived at a rate of $150 per hour for your company's services, based on the marketplace. This is a "blended" rate: a junior person might only be worth $50 per hour and you as the owner are worth $300, but it works out to a good average rate of $150 per hour.

At $150 per hour, a team of five needs to bill three hundred hours to meet the $45,000 threshold.

Say you earn $8,000 per month, but your time is only 50 percent billable (you work twenty hours a week on billable client work, or $12,000 per month in revenue).

The other four people need to reliably bill fifty-five hours a month (or $33,000) each to make up your monthly nut.

That's pretty manageable, and actually, they should bill more. But this model shows how you can build a pretty successful business while controlling your hours.

Now, using this model, you can size up or size down. Probably you wouldn't have five full-time staff at this level of income, but you might have consultants who work on specific projects for you.

If you manage other people, the key is to understand how much revenue each person is responsible for, including yourself, and to be laser-focused on and realistic about how everyone is using their time.

Once your business reaches about fifteen employees or more (and mine never has), it is hard to take time away. I have interviewed several small-business owners about this shift, and the truth is, once a critical mass of income, staff, and clients is reached, the business becomes more consuming.

Assuming they don't have start-up capital, most businesses follow a pattern of growth that looks like a staircase: one or two employees at first, working for a while, and then growing to more. But I have known many service consulting firms, for example, that staff up quickly because they start off with a large client, and then actually shrink over time because that may prove easier to sustain. There is no single right answer. Be realistic about your revenue, monthly nut, and your boundaries, and you'll find the right number for you.

BRINGING IT ALL TOGETHER

Don't ever let anyone tell you that you can't be an entrepreneur because you're risk-averse, like to be at home, or because you are allergic to working twenty-four hours a day. (I have heard it all a hundred times. Still do.) You may not be able to be *their* definition of an entrepreneur, but you can be your own.

I hope that the chapters of this book feel like building blocks. Your vision to live out the success that's right for you requires strong boundaries, control over your time, a strong niche, and the basic skills to make a business run. Add hustle, craftsmanship, and subject-matter knowledge to the mix, and you can absolutely build a wonderful and strong small business while protecting your time and emotional needs.

And now let's talk about the hermit at work in a larger organization.

10

The Corporate Hermit

Many years ago I interviewed at a large corporation where all employees literally had to clock in and out via a swipe card, all day long. Everyone I asked about the company raved about the incredible cafeteria. But all the free food in the world couldn't get me to focus in my interview because I was stuck on the swipe cards. Every instinct in me said, *Forget this,* while the good girl in me kept saying, *This is a very prestigious place to work.*

I've always been frustrated by glowing press for companies like Google that offer employees lots of time to think, and encourage introverts and quiet-seekers to use nap pods and to play pool while creating brilliant products. But that organic sushi at the cafeteria comes at a cost. What Google and its perk-ridden Silicon Valley compatriots don't offer is freedom.

A lot of us are work-life rebels. It pains us to show up every day somewhere at the expected hour. Unfortunately, in overachieving circles, it's socially unacceptable to say that. You seem lazy. And admitting you try to work as few hours in the office as possible can be corporate suicide.

So what's a hermit at work to do?

I admit, I had to work really hard to find stories of successful corporate hermits. I'm not sure if it's because people didn't want to admit they are hermits, or because it's very hard to achieve. After all, if I had been able to build one alone day into my ambitious schedule without feeling like a loser, perhaps I wouldn't have left corporate work at twenty-nine.

So those who advance in their career while replenishing their resources have incredible skills to teach the rest of us—whether we're hermits, or introverts, or both. These are work-life leaders who have learned how to feel they have space and alone time, even within a large organization, and they keep a low profile while also rising in the ranks.

The successful corporate hermit knows that to do her best work, she needs more control over her schedule and space than the average person. This could be as simple as having a day a week to work from home, coming in a bit later or leaving early, or chucking a meeting-heavy culture in favor of creating more "maker time." It's control over place, space, and pace.

Being a hermit at work isn't about being mediocre, and being an introvert doesn't condemn you to making a less-than-stellar impression. It's not about working less hard than your colleagues, but about working differently. It's about being awesome when you need to be so you can earn the autonomy, alone time, and freedom you need in order to thrive.

Making the Change

We learned many years ago that in the workplace, autonomy and control help engage people. It doesn't matter whether or not you're a parent. It doesn't matter whether you're married or single. Doesn't matter whether you're Gen Y or a Boomer. For example, accounting giant EY has measured retention from a flexibility perspective for a decade, and they know that the top 25 percent of teams in terms of levels of flexibility—meaning team members can determine where, when, and how the work gets done—have five points better retention than the bottom 25 percent.[1]

Work culture is changing, and breaking the hermit's way. Technology, of course, has ushered it along. Since many office workers don't literally need to be together to get work done, it's now much more acceptable to work away from the office. Things that would have been considered shocking just twenty years ago (replying to your boss at eleven thirty at night in a nonemergency situation, for example) are now quite normal. And here's what's really interesting: Americans don't seem to mind feeling tethered to office work by their devices as long as they don't have to physically be at the office. Gallup polling finds that among U.S. workers who report they frequently check e-mail away from work, 86 percent say it is a somewhat or strongly positive development to be able to do so. The same poll finds that when "asked how much time in a typical seven-day week they spend working remotely using a computer or other electronic device, such as a smartphone or tablet, employees who report checking their e-mail frequently say they spend nearly 10 hours working remotely."[2]

Many freelancers can also live with it. Talia Borodin, who recently opened her own consultancy, has a policy that directly addresses her life as a freelancer: "I frequently respond to e-mails after hours," she says, "but since I work one tenth the hours I did when I was full-time, it seems like a fair trade."

Perhaps the biggest change is the sheer variety of working styles we have now, from people who happily work at coworking spaces like WeWork or Workbar, to full-time office workers, to people like me who are 100 percent work from home. Indeed, all three work styles may even be collaborating on the same project or working for the same company! Maryella Gockel, who has pioneered flexible work at accounting giant Ernst & Young for years, likens the evolution of work styles to the famous "quiet car" on commuter trains and Amtrak. Some love it, some hate it, but it's a great option to have. In innovative environments, she says, work is moving away from "all day, every day." Instead there are all-hands-on-deck times, and time-off times.

In newer companies where digital natives increasingly prevail, "flexibility" can be baked in. Kathryn Schotthoefer, President of Heavenspot, a part of advertising giant M&C Saatchi, notes that in her fast-moving digital entertainment company, "As long as everyone gets their job done and can work collaboratively with other people, it doesn't really matter to me when they're in the office."

When you're just starting out in an office environment, of course, you most likely will need to put in the face time, especially when you're in an environment where being present means being committed. But as you advance in your career, you can negotiate from a position of power. And if you're an executive with hermit tendencies, you do have the power of changing culture at your company.

Mighty Networks' Gina Bianchini laughed when I asked her if she knew any powerful hermits in Silicon Valley. "Everyone I know is a hermit," she said. At Mighty, employees weekly work from home, coming into the office for scheduled meetings and check-ins.

SLUDGE

We've all heard it:
  "Nice of you to finally join us!"
  "Leaving early?"
  "Is he ever at his desk?"
  "Must be great to work from home every Friday."
  "Another sick day?"
There's a very specific kind of workplace passive aggression: sludge. The term was coined by workplace innovators and consultants Cali Ressler and Jody Thompson, who write, "Sludge is the workplace chatter that reinforces the idea that people can't be trusted with complete autonomy."[4]
If you are an office hermit, you're probably familiar with it. In work

systems where rules and rewards are based on traditional values, someone who tries to make her own schedule and rules of engagement is going to get some flak. (There's even social sludging: if you don't want to go out to the office lunch, or you skip happy hour, you get a reputation as a pill.)

Maryella Gockel smiles at how her firm's quest to create a flexible environment sometimes backfired. "We put in these great, comfy chairs where you could put your feet up with your laptop," she says. "But the minute folks said to people, 'Gee, you look comfortable,' people stopped using those comfy chairs. It was code for 'Are you really working?'"

You can try to ignore the criticism, knowing your results are great, or engage your colleagues to change their view of commitment. But let's face it: people can be petty assholes, and there's only so much you can do to change others' perspectives. It's probably easiest to try to understand that sludging is often unconscious, and their comments have less to do with you than with their own insecurities or their own business practices.

Or, you can always sludge back. One great suggestion from Thompson and Ressler: if a coworker says, "Leaving early?" say, "Oh, I'm sorry, did you need my help?"

In such a short amount of time, the concept of working from home has changed so dramatically and allowed for a hermit lifestyle in the corporate world. From 1998 to 2010, tech giant Sun Microsystems' philosophy of "open work" meant around twenty thousand Sun employees spent an average of three to four days out of the office, wherever they wanted to work. When they wanted to get out of the house, remote employees could check in at Sun "drop-in" stations, plug a data card into the system, and pick back up on their work. This innovation helped pioneer cloud computing! And the company saved over hundreds of millions in energy and real estate costs.[5]

Now, mega-corporations like Deloitte, IBM, Dell, and United Health Group not only have strong percentages of employees who work remotely, they have assigned aggressive targets to make half their workforce remote in coming years.[6] My friend Casey Carlson, for example, manages a thirty-person Deloitte team in India from her home office in suburban Boston.

Work+life fit is becoming less gendered, and that's essential. Take for example Nirad Jain, a New York City–based partner at Bain, an elite consulting firm where the average partner earns $1 million per year. He is proudly quoted bragging about his work+life fit: When his two-year-old daughter, Isha, woke up with a temperature of 104, he stayed home from an important client meeting while another partner "insisted on flying to the meeting, both to help keep the project on track and to support Nirad's parenting needs."[7]

If a high-status executive dad can brag in a national magazine about taking time for his children, a person in middle management should be able to point out that the world won't end if she misses a meeting, too. We can only hope that what's happening at Bain bodes well for the rest of us looking for flexibility when we need it most.

Finding the Right Role, in the Right Environment

My mom, an only child who grew up feeling lonely, loved working in a hospital because, as she said, "It's like working in a family." She thrived in that committed group in an intensely human setting, and loved teaching for the same reason. My father, at the other extreme, always said to me, "The best boss in the world is an asshole." He was a labor arbitrator and an art dealer on the weekends, and was proud to be self-employed. I can still hear the tap-tap-tap of his typewriter and smell the cigarette smoke as he wrote briefs from his home office in the attic.

Both my parents liked their work well enough, but they especially liked the environment in which they worked—even though, in my dad's case, his freedom came with enormous financial instability. For the workplace hermit, environment is key, and some workplaces are far more hermit-friendly than others.

Leah Ginsberg, now Deputy Editor of *Forbes* Women's Digital

Network, started out in a very "old-school" media company. "It was ten to six on the dot," she says, "and if you were two seconds late, it was, 'Where were you?'"

Leah loves her work as an editor, because "You're in your own head a lot," she says. "I love to just fall down a research rabbit hole." She also understands that her best ideas don't come in meetings. "I don't work exactly the way other people do in terms of brainstorming," she says. "I prefer to be able to think about things on my own beforehand."

A great deal of Leah's satisfaction is because she knows herself well. She's an introvert, not a morning person, and she doesn't like her every movement tracked by a boss. She has a lot in common with many of us hermits, and she's made her corporate job work for her; she found the right kind of role, and she knows exactly what kind of office culture she thrives in.

GETTING STARTED

The Questions to Ask

Like Leah, I've talked myself into many jobs that weren't a fit because I was a fan of the company or attracted by the prestige or the money. But when, like Leah, you know your own boundaries, you can avoid a bad fit right from the start by tuning into signals even before the interview.

Mercedes De Luca, COO of Basecamp, says e-mail can be the first sign. "If the HR rep is e-mailing you at midnight and scheduling interviews for Saturday afternoons, those are red flags," she says. Another warning sign is the immediate e-mail response. "You know they have an always-on-e-mail culture," she says. "It can be hard to work in that environment, and people often wind up catching up weekends and nights." Social media chatter is also revealing. "If your candidate company skews negative on platforms like Twitter, LinkedIn, or Glassdoor, reach out to your networks and raise questions in your interview to fact-check your findings."[8]

It's also important to simply observe the office on your first visit, Leah says. In one job she took, "When I went in to interview, you could hear a pin drop. It could've been a clue for me." A sneaky trip is to schedule a meeting very early or very late to see how full the office is. Best of all is to have a friend or the friend of a colleague give you the inside scoop.

Then, once you're in the interview, it may be beneficial to ask what a day in the office is like, or how many meetings you would typically have in a week. Most of us can't just say, "I want to be able to come in when I want and I want to do this," but you can listen for code words. *Entrepreneurial*, Leah says, can mean managers encourage innovation—or that you're expected to have no life outside of work. Having to interview with an HR gatekeeper first may be another sign of corporate inflexibility.

One of the biggest bullets I ever dodged was being turned down for a CMO role because I asked to temporarily work from home a few days a week while nursing my four-month-old baby. Even though I lived ten minutes from the office, even though half the company was located in another state, and even though they were ready to make me an offer!

THE JOB SHARE

It's not always about switching careers. If you're in the right role for you, it's picking the rhythm and pace you need. And finding a creative way to shift your pace when you know you're in the right job can be the key to a happy work life.

Take Maisie Pollard. She's a C-level executive at a major hospital, a powerful role. She defies the stereotype that an atypical work schedule automatically means less prestige or salary.

Maisie was one of the youngest-ever chief administrative officers at Beth Israel Deaconess Medical Center in Boston, working a typical sixty to seventy hours a week, when she had her first child. She wanted to cut her hours, so her boss suggested she dial down to four days a week in the office.

The problem was, she says, "It was sixty or seventy hours in four days instead of five days. So I thought I needed to switch careers. I went to a career counselor, and we circled my ideal jobs from the newspaper. Lo and behold, it kept coming back to, I'm in the right job and I'm in the right career, but it wasn't right for my work-life balance."

The woman who had held Maisie's job before was still on as an internal consultant. Slowly, this position started to evolve into a job share. "She knew everything, and it allowed me to work less," Maisie says. "She did a lot of clinical work. I did more of the management and business side." Maisie saved budget on additional roles that weren't needed because she and her partner could do so much more.

"The other wonderful thing," Maisie says, "was that our kids were at different points in their lives. Hers were older, mine were little. We evolved into [working less] when the kids needed us in different ways."

Maisie's story highlights an important thing to consider: You might be in the right job, but you simply have to alter the structure of that job to keep going. Or, you might be in the right field, but in the wrong position. To me, this is the true definition of flexibility: crafting the day-to-day realities of your work so you can thrive and be amazing at what you do.

Finding Your Team and Communicating Well

The hermit executive can do a lot to create a culture that empowers people to work in the way that makes them thrive. Good teams understand their members' work styles, and, like good teachers, create an environment that encourages tolerance and collaboration. And the corporate hermit must seek that kind of environment.

We all know the difference a bad boss and a bad team can make. (Think of Gary Cole in *Office Space*, surveilling the floor and taunting staff if they aren't there when he's looking.) Flexible work environments have less tolerance for bad managers and poor communication because tyranny doesn't work well. Maryella Gockel explains how work at innovative companies is changing from merely creating policies for flexible work to helping managers create teams that can thrive as a flexible unit. "You've got a raging extrovert who gets energy from office conversations, and someone who needs more space and quiet," she says. "How do you create that inclusive team where people understand how people do their best work?"

You may be lucky and work in an environment with flexibility and autonomy baked in. Workplace expert Cali Yost calls them high-performance flexible environments. In this kind of flexible work culture, employees don't ask for permission, but they are proactive in planning and communicating. "Everyone has a responsibility for their plan," she says. "You've got to make sure you're updating them on where you are and what's going on. Expectations have to be clear with your manager and your team."

STAYING ALERT

"I'll be online later."

We all say it, and we all feel we have to. These four little words that make us feel better for taking time out during the day or finishing early. They're like an insurance policy against being sludged.

But, if you're a work+life rebel, you do mind the expectation that even though you're leaving at a reasonable time, or on a flexible schedule, you have to be available whenever, wherever.

Because smartphone technology is fairly new, we're still creating norms and ways to cope with the always-on expectation. There is no single answer. But if those four words are ruining your happiness at work, here are some enlightened approaches to curbing your accessibility.

Core hours/norms. Blocking off availability is the first step to freedom. Web-development business owner Lauren Bacon sets the norm for client expectations up front: her firm doesn't return calls after business hours. (She and her cofounder make sure to model respect for the rule: if they do work late, they take the equivalent amount of time off.) At the business accelerator Bionic, founders have established a company norm that staff are only available via e-mail/phone/text between 7 A.M. and 7 P.M., Monday through Friday. Other firms set core meetings hours from 10 A.M. to 4 P.M. One friend has an easy-to-follow "go dark" rule: if it's dark out, she is not expected to be on call.

Schedule your e-mail traffic. My life changed when I discovered Boomerang, a software tool that allows me to schedule my e-mails. (Basecamp has a similar feature.) This means I can work late at night or Saturday morning (my favorite), but recipients won't see my e-mails until Monday morning. Scheduling your e-mails is a wonderful gift, because, as we know, one sent e-mail can start a hamster wheel of activity. Professional services firm JDI's CEO Josh Jones-Dilworth uses the Slack program to indicate team availability: he knows that if he e-mails a client late at night, what started as a simple message can escalate into a late-night full-on work session.[3]

Institute a "Sabbath." Nowadays, renowned business leaders are all about the "digital Sabbath," when you unplug from Friday night to Saturday night. If you're in a position to do so, pilot a Sabbath with your team. If not, take one yourself, and talk about how wonderful and healing it was. People might get the message.

Find a job where extra time costs extra money. Most salaried positions don't pay overtime, so your management doesn't care how many hours a week you work or how many e-mails they send you at midnight. But for jobs with overtime, any work above a certain number of hours must be approved. When your boss has to pay more to e-mail you, suddenly your time off becomes sacred to her. You can institute "overtime" into your work as well. Lauren Bacon considers contact outside of office hours to be overtime, so her core hours save her clients money.

Own your time. Until every country adopts a version of the French "right to disconnect" law in which employees have a legal right to take a break from e-mail and accessibility (and I'm not holding my breath), office hermits may have to cobble together solutions. But remember expert Cali Yost's advice: your boss doesn't want you to be so unhappy that you're at risk of leaving. So here's an idea: take control, and just stop responding after hours unless it's really urgent. Don't send texts after appointed off time, don't promise you'll be available. Be the work+life rebel. My team at

Women Online has done this for years. I must admit it annoyed me until I just accepted it and gave up. If I really need them, I call.

Skip "shallow work." As Dr. Cal Newport says, "No one ever got promoted because they were great at answering e-mail." Newport argues that maintaining your in-box, or posting basic social media content, is low-value, or "shallow," work. Shallow work might help pay the bills and manage your logistics, but deleting e-mails is not adding your unique skill or voice to the world. To maintain a true competitive advantage, you should be engaging in "deep work," which Cal defines as a skilled activity applied at a high level—in other words, your expertise. I don't know about you, but I don't get many e-mails at 10 P.M. that require me to dive right into deep work.

Try a Hermit Pilot

As you know, I'm a big believer in the value of pacing and cycles. If you're a hermit executive, you probably don't want to be White House press secretary or an ER physician. Talk about extreme working environments. If you're an ambitious corporate hermit, it's crucial to find not only the right culture but the right pace at work.

The successful hermit works in a flexible team that doesn't sludge, and also takes advantage of the cycles of a typical office job. For example, if you are in professional services, different clients will have different expectations, and it's hard for most managers to defy those expectations. If you have a very demanding client, flexibility may be limited for the duration of that engagement. On another assignment, a client might be okay with letting you set the pace. Of course there are intense times, but honestly, if there's a crisis every single day at your white-collar office job, something is seriously wrong with the company.

Even if you have a rigid manager—one who doesn't understand why anyone might want to work from home, you can set up a pilot. It can begin with one person saying, "You know, I need four hours of unbroken time this week, and here's how I'm going to do it." Don't be afraid to ask for a "hermit pilot," where you try the job for three months or some other specified period of time. It may be that with some tweaks, you're able to find a rhythm you all agree with—and you may even get some company. (And probably some sludging.)

"You don't say, 'I want to be a hermit,'" Cali says, "because many people can't fathom why you would want that. So you want to say, 'Hey, I'm more productive if I get these chunks of time where I can just focus. Here's how it's going to help me, here's how I'm going to do it, and here's how people can reach me if you need me.'" In her experience, being responsive and accountable is the main thing managers want. If you are able to be 100 percent committed when you're required to be on, you can earn a lot of slack to control your time and place.

Cali says there's a common problem among workplace hermits: they quit before even asking. She says, "I have had managers tear up and say to me, 'I absolutely would have listened. I didn't know!'"

Failing to negotiate a better schedule with a boss before leaving is like getting divorced without telling your partner you're unhappy. But Cali notes that our work culture makes people afraid to ask for what they specifically need. Instead they go global. "They'll come into the office and say, 'I can't travel anymore,'" Cali says.

Cali has interviewed hundreds of managers, and she knows what they want from their employees: a plan. "What are you going to do on your out-of-office day? Who is covering for you? If people do need you, how do they communicate to you?" You must advocate for yourself, she says, because another thing managers want from their employees is to not have to micromanage. Cali says, "You've got to think first, 'What do I need? What does it look like this week? How, when, and where can flexibility help me do that?'"

There also needs to be a check-in in place. "Across the team, there needs to be a mechanism to make sure everyone's tasks are coordinated, and that expectations are clear," Cali says. In other words, making sure stakeholders don't feel like you're a pain in the ass.

Remember, other people on your team may have work+life fit goals, too! Your team can change as you do. Your best team doesn't care that the next day after you're wiped out from a huge pitch you're working from home. They think, 'Wow. She did a great job on that pitch.'

Obviously, it also helps to do your job really well. Think of it like this: the most successful salesmen might spend a hell of a lot of time on the golf course (or in strip clubs). No one judges them for it because they bring in a lot of revenue.

Sales: A Hermit's Paradise

Being on the road and pressing the flesh may not seem like the obvious choice for a hermit, but for making your own hours and being free of supervision, it can't be beat.

Anne Greenwood, who managed hundreds of people in the brokerage industry on Wall Street notes that her sales staff "had total freedom." What she focused on was results. "As long as you're building your business and keeping your clients happy, it's up to you. I literally had people who I didn't see for two weeks."

She adds, "If you're in sales, you will never have to miss a kid's soccer game, a school play, or the tea party with the teacher in first grade on Fridays. And no one is going to ask you where you are."

Another great job is pharmaceutical sales rep. (I'm sure you've seen them while at a doctor's office, with a little rolling suitcase and a nice car.) In fact, pharmaceutical sales gets top marks as the best overall job for working mothers, according to *Forbes*.[9] In a survey of 250 pharmaceutical sales reps this quote stood out to me: "Feeling like I'm self-employed, because I have flexibility in my job."[10] They get the perks of being self-employed, but they have the back-office support and compensation that small-business owners rarely achieve.

If sales scares you, change how you think about selling (we'll tackle this in Chapter 11). Being judged on the revenue you bring into a firm is a lot of responsibility, but the flip side is control and freedom.

Surviving the Open Plan

I can't tell you how many times I've been at a client's office space and needed to pump breast milk, and I've found the reserved and private "wellness" rooms occupied by workers seeking refuge from their open-plan offices. Indeed, "how to survive an open office" is a very popular search on Google.

So here are some strategies.

Open-plan offices became en vogue in the postwar era as architects and management theorists tried to break down social and human barriers by removing doors and walls.[11] The first iterations of open plan featured rows and rows of desks in a line. In the 1960s, cubicles came into fashion, sort of a compromise effort to offer junior workers some privacy, while employees of a certain status had private offices that ringed the cubicles. Now trends are leading back to desks and tables without any barriers, often referred to as "pods," that are even for senior leaders. After all, open plan saves money and space and increases transparency (it's tough to check Facebook or shop for shoes when everyone can see your monitor). A recent meta-analysis of open-plan workers found that open office spaces cause conflict, high blood pressure, and increased staff turnover.[12]

Office design changes with time, and it has an enormous effect on how an office culture functions. Alan Dandron, a design principal at the Architecture and Interior Design firm Mancini Duffy, says that the hierarchical and transactional layout of many offices is gone—and Alan says he's seeing more offices without desks entirely. Now, he says, spaces reflect how work is more collaborative, "but the design industry has been slow to take introverts into account."

A few tips from the experts:

"Face outward," says Geoffrey James, contributing editor at *Inc.* magazine. This gives you a sense of privacy, and you can't be taken by surprise by a coworker sneaking up on you or reading over your shoulder, which can trigger a cortisol-upping startle. I'll never forget the day I was instant messaging a colleague about what a "dumb fuck" the new CEO of my start-up was when, of course, he instantly appeared over my shoulder. It was a move worthy of Ilana in *Broad City,* and needless to say, I left the job soon after the incident.

The stress of an open-plan office led Elan Morgan, who was working in development at a local university, to crack her molars from anxiety-driven jaw clenching. But she loved her work, so she tried to adopt a new philosophy to manage her cubicle. She bought a coat stand to create the illusion of a wall (some people buy plants or another curtain-like object). She built in time for walks and lunches outside or at places she enjoyed, and she created signals (such as wearing headphones) to make sure colleagues knew she couldn't be bothered. A colleague in her office taught her a true pro tip: observe the pattern of the week. There are quiet times you can count on. "It turned out that Wednesday afternoons were when everyone in her office was out at meetings," she says. Elan's colleague took that time to lie down in her cubicle and meditate.

"One day it occurred to me that no rule said that meeting rooms could only be booked for groups, so I booked myself a room for two hours and worked alone without interruptions. They were the two most blissful hours of my open-plan office life." Booking a small conference room on a regular basis, just for yourself, could provide the decompressing time you need in the workplace.

Office design trends are shifting in response to a zest for "collaboration" and also to the way technology is changing work styles, but office designer Alan Dandron says there's a bit of a backlash against all that open, collaborative space. His clients want more small rooms and hideaways. His challenge is to balance corporations' desire for efficiency with humans' desire for some privacy.

Spaces are specifically designed to support a behavior, which means there's less waste, Dandron says, "but also we know you need support spaces that make the open spaces work." In private offices, his clients frequently "request a little living room set up—sofa and all. They want offices to feel more homey, and they know they need to create private spaces for phone calls and conversations within the open plan. At the same time meditation rooms, gyms, and lactation rooms are becoming more and more common."

One day, I hope, all companies will design work to suit many different temperaments, including neurodiversity and those of us who react strongly to sensory stimulation. Imagine if you got to choose what kind of physical space you worked in every day, just like you might choose your health-plan option or order office supplies. Someone who needs quiet could be in a quiet space, and the extroverts could all sit around a big table. Then everyone could come together for meetings or very focused sessions. As demand for highly skilled high-tech talent and high connectivity further impacts how we work, those days can't be too far off!

Until then, if you must work open plan, there are ways to hack it. The good news for hermits: what's really shifting is that offices are becoming about places to meet, and much work can be done anywhere.

When Corporate Life Just Doesn't Fit

Sometimes, even the most flexible environment isn't right for you. But, when even a schedule can't change, there are still ways to keep the relationship. Think about becoming a consultant to your current organization—this can be a great strategy when you need to dial down but aren't ready to completely change things up. You'd be surprised at how many organizations are open to employees going 1099 (e.g. becoming a consultant) or part time. Think about particular tasks you could continue to do as a freelancer, from home. Perhaps there's one part of job you are spectacular at, and everyone would be fine with you continuing solely on that.

I counsel many people who leave steady and prestigious jobs for the unknown of freelancing or small business. I try to help them be realists and not fantasists, because even the happiest hermits can have a bittersweet relationship with their new, leaner life. Just like any job, working for yourself provides good and bad days. Just remember, if you're ready to make the leap, you don't have to storm out the door and never return. You can ease your way out of the nine to five and learn if self-employment is for you.

EARN IT. THEN OWN IT.

I believe that if you do a great job and work hard, you've earned the right to control your own time and location at work. You're a grown-up, you'll do what you need to do and show up when you need to. Autonomy shouldn't be a perk. And yet: I can't tell you how many very senior and acclaimed professionals I've interviewed who show up, day after day, at the office, simply because that's the norm.

Here's the thing: taking control of your time might actually earn you more power at work. Next time you feel cowed in the face of a culture of face time, channel the privileged white male.

In my career, I've always known successful men who come in early to prove their eagerness, then disappear for much of the afternoon. It's assumed they're off doing something important. Patriarchy wins again. Watch the senior executives in an organization (who, let's face it, are probably privileged white men). They work hard, but at any given time, do you know where they are? No! They could be out on a sales call, on the golf course, or at home napping, for all you know. And they like it that way.

High-status men understand how to use the system to have their cake and eat it, too. Recently, a study of 726 MBA men and women showed that though both sexes preferred flexible hours, the men did not take advantage of formal telecommuting programs as frequently as the women.[13] Instead, when they wanted to work from home or remotely, they simply did. They didn't feel the need to ask permission. Perhaps they understood that simply being flexible without asking for it maintains their power.

Most professional women only begin to take advantage of official workplace flexibility policies when they have a caregiving crisis, whether for a baby, partner, or elderly relative. This automatically positions their flexibility as a perk.[14] It strips power from the worker who uses it. It mommy-tracks us, when instead, our autonomy should be valued and rewarded.

I'm going to say it again: control over pace, place, and space is NOT a mommy issue! Everyone has their own work+life fit, and if you're an introvert, yours may not include sitting in an open-plan office fifty hours a week. If you love your career and you want to stay in it, don't let lack of flexibility or a poor work+life fit chase you out! Remember what workplace expert Cali Yost says: most managers feel shocked when employees quit over a work+life fit conflict. They don't want you to leave. So next time you're chafing against silly face-time rules, think like a boss and take what you need. Try a stealth pilot and start working from home more. Do an even better job while you're taking what you need, and I promise you, no one will complain. Build in what you need, communicate wisely, kick some butt, and bring your manager along.

Finally, if you're just starting out, this all may seem unrealistic—and it might be. You might have a few more years of proving yourself. I started out as an executive assistant, and for the first few years of my career it was my job to be chained to a desk (so my bosses could come and go as they wanted!). That doesn't mean you can't prepare for more flexibility a few years on. For now, spy on the more senior people you respect. Monitor their comings and goings. Are there any who seem to have worked out a really great gig? Ask them how they did it.

When you know what you want, and you see role models who've figured it out, you'll be on a much quicker path to autonomy and your happier hermit work life.

11

Sell Like Yourself!

G et out there!"

"Dominate."

"Always be closing."

When we think of sales, we think of the iconic image of Alec Baldwin in the film *Glengarry Glen Ross*. "Put that coffee down!" he yells at a terrified Jack Lemmon, Baldwin's alpha lumbering over Lemmon's beta male with Donald Trump–like predation. "You can't close shit, you are shit," he sums up, wearing a watch that costs more than Lemmon's car.

I call this the "fuck you" stance of sales.

Like the patriarchy, the image of the salesman as an alpha male asshole is internalized into our work culture. Worse, the obnoxious, dominant salesperson can be extremely effective in communicating power. As Courtney Nichols Gould, CEO of SmartyPants Vitamins, an eight-figure company she started in her house, puts it, "What makes you a great entrepreneur can make you a crappy person."

Because we think success is about being a shark, we forget that kindness, caring, and pride in your work is one of the most powerful tools. We worry we'll be stereotyped and our work devalued. But the gifted introvert salesperson is a secret weapon for any organization or small business.

My heroes don't use fancy watches to win business. They own their worth and their expertise, and get paid. Pride in your craft is one of the most successful selling points anyone can have. It beats a hundred hours of schmoozing. It inspires clients, drives word of mouth, and it keeps your shop humming, because the easiest new business to win comes from someone who is already your customer.

Bathroom-hiders face many common hurdles when it comes to selling a product or negotiating a deal. But know that your wonderful empathy plus a commitment to doing great work make you a strong salesperson and negotiator. You just need to stop trying to be someone else.

Suiting Up

When Courtney Nichols Gould was a new media executive, she modeled her sales technique after the top performers in her field, which meant taking her clients to strip clubs. She was competitive about it, too; she even knew the names of all the strippers. "I was going to out-dude every dude there," she says.

But, once she was flying high as the top salesperson at her company, Courtney says, "It felt wrong. Wrong like, 'This isn't me.'" She didn't feel dominant. She felt sorry for the women working in the strip clubs.

"So much of what we are taught in sales comes from a place of scarcity," Courtney says. But as CEO of SmartyPants, her perspective has changed. "I believe when you're pursuing your passion, you're not selling as much as you're inviting customers to join you."

Like Courtney, I learned how to sell by watching people around me; when I ran marketing departments I was constantly being sold to, and I tried to pay attention. As a client of ad agencies and digital publishers, I, too, was invited along to strip clubs (I said good-bye at the door and let the guys go on without me) and enjoyed some great steak-house dinners.

Many gifted salespeople come up through the ranks selling like everyone else, until they reach a point where they're confident enough to sell like themselves. And that doesn't have to mean always playing hardball, like the real estate agents we watch on *Million Dollar Listing* or the cast of any number of films and TV shows about Wall Street or Washington, D.C. When I started my own business and had to start selling rather than being sold to, I tried to mimic everything I'd learned. I tried to act like an alpha dog.

The problem was, I always felt like I was playing dress-up in someone else's clothes. As a green entrepreneur, I was definitely selling out of someone else's playbook, and I'm pretty sure people could tell I was new to the game. It finally hit me that I needed to own my sales style at a meeting with a potential client at Henrietta's Table, the power breakfast spot for much of Boston and all of Harvard.

The client I was courting was a wealthy man pushing sixty. He ran a cool new "one for one" start-up (think TOMS shoes: buy one, and the company will donate one to a person in need). I had been working for some time to get his digital marketing business. In fact, by the time of the breakfast we were on proposal version four—i.e., four executions of my free ideas—for him to consider. (Talk about taking advantage of hustle.)

In my mind, this breakfast meant we were finally sealing the deal. When the check came, I reached for it. "I always pick up the check for my clients," I said. "And you're my client now, right?"

He looked at me as if his teenage daughter had offered to pay.

After years of watching my husband and past vendors always treat at client dinners, I thought it was how it was done. But this client didn't respond to me when I mimicked being an alpha male. We had both internalized the patriarchy, me by mimicking "male" negotiating, and he by seeing me as a thirteen-year-old.

Needless to say, I didn't get the business. And that was the moment that convinced me I had to sell like myself.

As I grew as a salesperson, I kept pieces I really respected from past mentors (always be responsive; turn around proposals quickly; play the long game; and don't be afraid to act against your best interests if you think it's right for your client). Slowly, I stopped trying to change personalities in a sales meeting, and I began to I use my tune-in skills to read situations. Closing the deals became much easier.

Passion as a Sales Tool

You've got to be hungry to close a sale, but we're trained to play it cool. (There's always another customer waiting in the wings, right?) Selling, we're taught, is like dating: play a little hard to get (i.e., create FOMO) and they'll want to be on board.

Well, I don't roll that way. In fact, the thing I hear most when I'm pitching is, "You are so passionate!" And I'm not afraid to show I'm hungry: I've even been known to say, "I want to work with you so badly," or "You are my dream client."

I used to take the comments about my passionate pitching as a compliment. After all, I love what I do and I am proud of what I know, and it makes me excited to talk about it. But displaying passion runs counter to our cultural norm of playing it cool, never wanting something too badly.

When I started talking to other entrepreneurs and leaders, I started to see that noting someone's passion can be dismissive, whether it's a man saying it to a woman, or even a woman to a woman. Tereza Nemessanyi, one of Microsoft's entrepreneurs-in-residence, points out when someone invokes your passion, it can be condescending, and, ultimately, dismissive. "There's a fine line between passion and 'crazy.' And passion and collaboration imply emotion—which isn't seen as bankable." (Why are we so scared of emotions in business?)

After all, Tereza says, you never see a male thought-leader or market-mover lauded for his "passion." (Think of calling the president or Bill Gates "passionate.") Men are celebrated for their courage, strength, and acumen. As Tereza points out, they don't have "passion," they have "focus." They're not "collaborative," they pull together an A-team.

I think this is less about gender, than about the dominant alpha-dog "fuck you" sales stance we all inherit. I know many authentically passionate men who absolutely love what they sell. And I know many men and women who are absolutely talented—and terrifying—at playing hardball during a sales process. What matters is selling like yourself, and not assuming a posture. And, after all, if you're an introvert or a hermit, owning your passion is essential. You don't need to schmooze clients over dinner if your product is going to rock their worlds when you talk about it on the phone.

I've also found that if you own your passion in the moment because you truly take pride in your work, you cultivate an infectious quality that drives incredible referrals from your current customers. You can also have personal passion for the relationships you develop along the way. If you care for your clients as you do your colleagues and friends, you will find your clients actually do become friends.

I have been with my clients through cancer, deaths in the family, babies, miscarriages, frustrations with bosses, desires to quit, and everything else in between. I try to convey to them that it is a privilege to work with them and share the journey. And I believe, in most cases, people buy the products and work with the proprietors they feel good about.

Susan McPherson, owner of McPherson Strategies, is one of the most generous and caring people I know. She owns a leading corporate social responsibility consultancy, and she's an angel investor and board member of the UNHCR's nonprofit arm. She's *also* a powerful superconnector and an incredible networker. When I asked her how she got most of her business, she told me it was almost all inbound: people came to her. When I asked her what her secret was, she told me it was being good to people (and I can personally vouch for the fact that she is!).

And the connections she built weren't all necessarily face-to-face. "Years ago, before the Internet," she says, "I used to go through my Rolodex once a month, call my clients, and say, 'Just want to thank you for your business.' It was a human touch point. And because I was on the phone, it wasn't as scary as going to an event."

And way before Twitter, she was clipping articles and stuffing them in an envelope. Now social media lets her find a new platform to showcase the wins of others. "I know it's commonplace now to tweet something somebody says, but I've been doing that since the dawn of time."

So now, when people call me "passionate" and "collaborative," I say thank you. I own my niche, and I take pride in the clients that sign me up.

The Ask . . . Without Asking

When I meet someone, even a client, and I can tell they aren't happy where they are, my brain starts creating new career opportunities for them. Ironically, this has turned out to be a great skill for biz dev. Sometimes I have even placed clients in a new role—and then I get to work with them again.

Stew Friedman, a renowned leadership professor at the Wharton School, notes that the connections we make through the sales process, networking, or negotiating are actually foundations of the social capital that drive our world. "When you approach a social encounter as an opportunity for you to discover something about other people that you can help them with, as opposed to take something from them, then you are inducing long-term reciprocity," he says.

The most successful business owners I know always go the extra mile and build toward that longer-term relationship. But it's not always directly related to their business. Some are excellent sources of recipes, travel ideas, child-rearing techniques . . . even tarot-card readings.

Even if it's unconscious, working toward that long-term relationship and discovering the interconnection between client work and life can foster both professional and personal success. Christine Koh has brought her love of blogging to several clients of ours, and helped them find their online voices. But, more importantly, her instinct for helping stressed-out parents pare down (beautifully expressed in her book *Minimalist Parenting*) has helped so many people in our professional network manage the overload. She's so passionate about her work and about helping other people that the interconnection between "client work" and life projects feels seamless.

Like Christine, Michael Ansara, a successful entrepreneur who's built and sold two companies in call-center and customer-service technology, believes in getting to know the real person behind the client, and sparking a relationship that leads into a sale. And this is the key for introverts in order to sell with authenticity—that passion we spoke about earlier. Michael is also a feminist hero. When his daughter Meg was battleground states director for Hillary Clinton's 2016 presidential campaign, she delivered her third baby six weeks before Election Day. Michael stayed with Meg those six weeks in her tiny Brooklyn rental, taking care of the newborn and bringing it to campaign HQ for Meg to nurse, seventeen hours a day, seven days a week.

As Michael explains, he builds loyalty by being interested in the actual client and what's going on in their world. "I'm a great believer in sending articles, books, magazines—anything that you think will be of interest to either a past client, current client, or prospective client—with no ask attached to it." Paradoxically, that leads to more sales than a hard ask ever would. "I always found that when you could become pretty much an indispensable source of ideas, many of which had nothing directly to do with your specific service that you were selling, then it becomes very easy to sell it," Michael says.

Mixing your business goals with your real passions means you'll enjoy the sales process more and remove any remaining ick factor. SmartyPants's Courtney Nichols Gould puts it perfectly: "I went from doing sales as selling something into doing something I believe in and inviting people to join me in what I love."

Craftspersonship

Imagine your passion was building houses. If you knew a wonderful family planned to live in one, to raise their children there, you wouldn't treat the building as just a job. You would pour your heart and soul into the work, and after it was built, you'd check on it.

That's being a craftsperson. Craftspeople care about their work long after the contract is signed, while salespeople just cash the check and move on.

There is a firm that I consider a competitor, although they barely know who I am. Still, we share some clients and we have competed against each other for work. This firm wins big contracts and I often feel very envious of them. But over and over, I hear that they don't fulfill the promises they make. They're all razzle-dazzle. The firm focuses on selling, but not on their craft. And their clients don't leave happy.

Hillary Moglen, principal at the issue advocacy firm Rally, which helped win marriage equality, has won a reputation as a must-hire in a very niche but key field. She hates networking and "selling," and actually left a firm that wanted her to be more "market-y, shmooze-y, and network-y." They parted because she had proved herself in work, but not in bringing in business.

"Since then," she says, "I've had to find my own way of bringing in business. My philosophy is to find opportunities to talk specifically about the work we've done, and work that I've been particularly involved in. When I'm having to talk about our company and what we do broadly, that's less comfortable."

Hillary has cultivated craftsmanship, not salesmanship. She's no schmoozer. But get her in a room of public policy nerds (who are exactly the people who will hire her) and she is like a movie star. And almost 100 percent of her new business comes from referrals from past or current clients who love her work.

GETTING STARTED

Cultivate the Craftsperson in Yourself

Hands down, the easiest way for a hermit to keep business going is to do great work and then figure out some painless ways to drive word of mouth among happy customers or clients. Here are four steps toward building a craft-based business.

Check your sales. Obviously, you shouldn't lie to a client (although a little embellishment is expected), but it's just as important not to lie to yourself. You need to look at how you feel while you're actually *pitching*. Do you feel like you're saying what you think the client wants to hear, or faking what you think you should be saying? Does getting the project give you a sinking feeling? Sales are about more than a healthy spreadsheet (though that's great!).

Check in. Not only should you check in with clients as a good business practice, you should want to check in—to see how they're doing, to let them know what you're doing, and, most important, to see if they're happy. If not, you should offer to fix what they're unhappy about. A good craftsperson wants what they build to be working for the client, not only to lock down the sale.

Deliver. It's better to set clear boundaries about resources and time right from the beginning, because, in the long term, a client respects a contractor who can deliver the work, not only a promise.

Examine your clientele. Are you proud of those you work with? If you're not, chances are you're not proud of the work either. This doesn't mean everything you do needs to be glamorous and high profile, or the work you've always dreamed of. (You can even take on a stinker for the pay from time to time.) But you should take as much pride in a teeny, low-paying, low-profile project as you do a major one—and treat the client the same.

Pitching for Introverts

As BlogHer cofounder Elisa Camahort Page puts it, the first part of a great pitch is owning your expertise. When you own your expertise, you are very clear in why you are an expert in what you do, you express it clearly, people feel it, and the benefits of working with you become clear. Being a master craftsperson means you know exactly why and how you own your expertise.

Selling like yourself requires a lot of practice. It must feel authentic, but it must also be effective. However you feel it, you have to be able to put it into words, and these words should be flexible. And you must be able to pitch for your company, a specific product you sell, or your professional services—for instance, as an expert speaker, writer, or teacher.

How? One of the most effective tools an early boss taught me was to develop a "boilerplate" pitch. This is about two hundred words of focused bio sentences mixed with a lot of specifics. It's your "who I am and what I will do for you." If you have the basic language, you'll be amazed how it will carry you through many growth experiences in your career.

And, if you're worried it makes you a braggart to sell yourself, don't. Experts offer good counsel and get things done.

OWN YOUR EXPERTISE IN TWO MINUTES

by Katie Orenstein, Founder of the Op-Ed Project[2]

Begin by filling these in. Don't overthink!

Hello, my name is_____

I am an expert in_____

Because_____

I admit, when I first did this exercise in a workshop, I said I was an expert in . . . "cats." It was funny, but it was also a cop-out. That answer was a way to defuse any bragging or hubris I might feel. But owning your expertise isn't hubris. It's what your client hires you for. When someone pays me tens of thousands of dollars or more in professional fees for my expertise in marketing and mobilizing women, they're not interested in how modest and self-effacing I am.

When you first do the exercise, you might find yourself adding qualifiers, like "I think I'm an expert because . . ." or "I suppose it's because . . ." Take those out. It's hard to be declarative and it feels weird, but it's the first step, and it's good practice for your pitching. Even your language in this exercise should own your expertise.

Once you have your basic pitch of who you are and why you're awesome, you'll need to develop some talking points that work effectively in a sales situation. Talking points support your expertise and give clients concrete evidence about why you're worth it. One example might be, "Our approach will save you X percent, because we are so much more efficient that other firms. In fact, when we worked for [insert impressive client example X] we saved them X percent over six months and increased their customer satisfaction." Talking points are some sales numbers, some razzle-dazzle names to drop, and some major successes. Focus. Quality beats quantity.

Think of your boilerplate as your outfit, and talking points as accessories.

My basic pitch is below. Talking points I might throw in vary. All are time-tested, and while they speak to different strengths, they reassure potential customers.

BOILERPLATE:

I'm the founder of the award-winning social-impact agencies Women Online and the Mission List. I can help your organization create an effective and efficient digital campaign that will mobilize your women consumers and turn them into advocates. I've been working with women online since 1999 and (fun fact) I helped Hillary Clinton log on for her first Internet chat. I've worked on over 175 online action campaigns, including four presidential campaigns, and raised over $100 million in online donations in my time. I've helped President Obama, Malala Yousafzai, the United Nations, the Bill and Melinda Gates Foundation, and many other leading figures and organizations create effective campaigns that mobilize women. I'm also a blogger, author, and podcast host. Online community changed my life, and I'm extremely loyal to it. I was founding political director for BlogHer.com, and have written for the Harvard Business Review, *the* Huffington Post, MomsRising, *the* Wall Street Journal, *the* New York Times, *and the* Guardian.

Here's a guide to how I've developed the talking points for Women Online. You can apply them to your own:

Numbers and efficacy: Our work offers serious return on investment (ROI), and it's often more effective than traditional advertising. I like to have some impressive numbers to throw in here.

Authenticity and deep community expertise: I've been blogging since I got my start at iVillage, the original online community for women. All of my staff are content creators and influential bloggers, so we not only understand what moves women online, we work in a community we are part of and value deeply. Our work is built on relationships, not pitches.

We're grown-ups: When you hire us, you work with the senior-level talent, including me. You're not passed off to a junior account executive.

We're experienced, and that experience translates: We helped X organization build their entire online strategy, because our experience raising money for nonprofits and political campaigns meant we had a unique understanding of how to build a communications campaign that supports the growth of your donor base.

Here's how we help clients solve problems: Harvard Law School called us when they needed to get more women in their executive ed program, so we devised a strategy that reached women decision makers through the business media they consume. (This is a great one. Remember Michael Ansara's tactic? Throw in some relevant examples of how you helped past clients solve thorny issues.)

Now that I've been pitching for almost twenty years, I'm here to tell you, I could do it in my sleep. I still get nervous with in-between strategy talk and negotiating, and cocktail-hour banter makes me hide in the bathroom . . . but I can get up in front of any-size room and talk about my work.

That means it takes practice. Sketch a draft of your pitch. Show it to friends and trusted colleagues to make sure you're showcasing all your accomplishments. (You'd be surprised at how many you can forget!) Practice your pitch in front of a few friends, and get their feedback. Pitching them is more nerve-rattling than any future client will ever be.

The Ask . . . for Money

If, like Alec Baldwin in *Glengarry Glen Ross,* you drive around in an $80,000 BMW and wear a watch that costs more than most cars, folks will assume you're worth whatever you ask. The "fuck you" method works here, too: when you assume that stance, your clients immediately assume you're worth every penny, whether you're in a hoodie or Céline. I always marvel at competitors who successfully charge triple what I do, simply because they assume the "fuck you" stance.

When you're passionate and nice, people can forget you actually need to earn a living. Doing incredible work for clients who love you doesn't ensure you're paid top dollar, or even what you're worth in the marketplace.

As the kinder, gentler seller, you need different strategies to ensure you're paid what you're worth. Here are three of my favorites:

Invoke the cause. Women experience 15 percent more success in a negotiation if they negotiate on behalf of someone else.[1] (I know, I know, it's ridiculous!) After maternity leave, women who state clearly to their bosses, "I need to work to support my family," get better opportunities and are paid more. (Don't get me started.) I find it helpful to remind people that my business is not for vanity and that my household depends on me, and I talk about the larger impact of supporting women's businesses. Women on average get paid seventy-seven cents on the dollar, and you don't want to be one of them.

You can even invoke the cause to yourself: if I'm feeling insecure or even greedy about quoting a high rate, I remember the people who are relying on me getting paid.

Name-drop. You may have noticed that in my pitch, I drop some pretty heavy names. Don't think of it as obnoxious, like it might be in a regular conversation. Putting forward strong credentials or clients is a great way to communicate how much you're worth. People want to be in good company. And it reassures them to know that other large outfits have trusted you. A brand name will do more for your market price and business development than a year of networking, and it prevents you from being devalued. If I'm sensing a potential client isn't taking me seriously, or we're negotiating on fee and they don't want to pay my rate, I'll make sure to weave in, "Well, when I worked for President Obama," or "When we won the award for promoting Malala's film."

Be matter-of-fact. Hillary Moglen, principal at the issue advocacy firm Rally, is not cheap. She knows exactly how much work goes into the end product, she knows how to make it successful, and she knows how much it costs. You get what you pay for in her shop, and it's not an emotional decision.

To get your facts in place, know your market and how much competitors charge. Scope carefully so you feel confident in your price. If you need to cut off 5 or 10 percent to get the job, fine. Then *be* confident. Sometimes you will try to achieve a certain sales price and you will fail. And sometimes you'll be pleasantly surprised.

I like to think that I'm evolving after years of invoking causes and dropping names. The older I get, the more I just want to say, *This is what I cost: take it or leave it.*

But as an anxious introvert, my ruminative nature can be difficult when I'm trying to sell, because I always second-guess everything and am convinced my client thinks I'm not worth the price I'm asking. Even worse, my general anxiety about money and bag-lady fears can make me feel desperate while I'm trying to sell, which is never good for the outcome. In my head I'm saying to myself, *If I don't get this contract I'm going to have to shut down the business,* while on the outside I'm trying to smile and close the deal. It's never a good combo.

If you get anxious when asking for money, channel the facts. You've done your homework, you know what you or your product is worth. If you get anxious, say in your head, *This is a fair price.*

Most important, be yourself. If you're a generous person, be generous in business. If you have a tendency to be Mama Bear, be Mama Bear with customers. If you're anxious, don't hide behind a fake set of armor. Your authentic self can drive your success. Listening to your authentic self is probably why you run a P&L in the first place. Some inner drive and sharp instinct brought you to this place. Now learn to define that instinct and make it work for your business and your life.

Whether you're selling a product, a service, or your company, use these strategies to see yourself past salesmanship and into craftsmanship and selling like yourself.

Accepting "No" When You Feel Things in Technicolor

When I was working in corporate jobs, whenever a boss would give me negative feedback, I'd cry. They'd get upset or uncomfortable (of course). But whether the criticism was slight or major, I cared about the work, and hearing I was less than perfect literally made me feel like they were ripping my heart out.

Entrepreneur Christina Wallace calls this "feeling in Technicolor," and it's something we sensitive Hermits need to accept—and plan for.

Because here's the deal: if you're selling something, you will be turned down. It's a fact of life. If you're an anxious, introverted overachiever, though, you need to prepare yourself. A no can be made for any multitude of reasons, but chances are, you will hear no as "you're not good enough." Everyone hates rejection, but if you're already prone to rumination and overanalysis, the effect can feel like personal failure. You may catastrophize and blow things way out of proportion. (If I get negative feedback from a client, get passed over for a big new contract, or a client doesn't renew, I immediately assume I'm going broke.) Add your passion and craftsmanship to the mix, and you're likely to feel like they're turning down *you*.

But this is a moment that you can't let being über-sensitive win.

You can't grow in your career until you get rejected. Frankly, rejection is actually a sign your business is healthy—because it means you're casting a wide enough net both to get clients and to get important feedback.

If you're a Technicolor feeler, you've got to practice getting rejection and negative feedback. The best way is to find a trusted counselor who feels in black and white—ideally, a successful extrovert. (Mine is my husband.) They respond to rejection in a way we hermits can learn from. I have watched my Nicco and his alpha-dog colleagues shake off noes and think it's the other party's loss (even their fault!) because they don't let the no disturb the solid inner core of who they are.

When I'm castigating myself over a rejection, I try to remember all the guys who run our country. (Privileged white men, or PWM, as we call them in my house.) These men come from a world of abundance, so if they encounter a no, they assume it's just a temporary roadblock, and a yes is just around the corner.

And you know what? Even though they screw up right and left, say ridiculous things, and even commit crimes, they just keep going, rising to higher and higher levels of power.

So the next time a no sends you questioning the viability of your entire financial future or existence, brush it off. Instead of imagining you're going to get fired, lose everything, and become a bag lady, force yourself to be generous and expansive. Channel your inner PWM. Give yourself a break. Tell yourself, *That's okay. There's plenty more.*

12

Claim Your Negotiation Style

The stereotype about a negotiation is that it's a game of chicken: someone has to leave the table or die. This approach is called combative, or positional, negotiation, and it's the alpha-dog territory we see in my personal favorite reality-TV genre: real estate shows. Think of the real estate agents saying "Do we have a deal? on *Million Dollar Listing* or any real estate reality show; think (gulp) of President Trump's bloviating tweets and what he calls "the art of the deal." It sounds like macho bullshit to me, but, apparently, many of our countrymen think that's what strong negotiation skills sound like. (I blame the patriarchy!)

Guess what: bathroom-hiders, counterintuitively, actually have a great advantage in negotiations, since we're strongly attuned to both others and ourselves, and we can sniff out bullshit. This lets us adjust to diverse situations and other people's expectations, which is crucial to successful negotiating. We know we need to prepare for several different outcomes because that lessens our anxiety. We want everyone to leave happy, and so we are great at making that happen.

Now I know to trust my gut and handle negotiations in my own introvert style: by doing my homework, asking lots of questions, and finding a common thread between me and my client.

I used to think negotiating was just for alpha dogs, and so when I did it, I quickly became a puddle. Meaning, I was so nervous that I said yes too quickly, and didn't fight for my terms. Instead of understanding that a negotiation isn't personal, and that a counteroffer doesn't mean the other party doubts your worth, I'd take everything personally. And give in. I left a lot of opportunity and financial benefit at the table simply because I was too scared to ask.

When I own my own style, I still don't always get exactly what I want. But at least I'm not a puddle.

What's the Deal?

Nothing brings out my impostor syndrome more than asking for money to do work. When people balk at my figure, I'm usually pretty sure they're right: I don't deserve it. Even worse, it's hard to find a model negotiator, since most examples show you can only get what you want by being a shark.

Before I found my own style, the stress of negotiating made me so eager to get it over with (or avoid it altogether) that I usually left with less than I needed. This wasn't only about lining my own pockets; it also meant less for my employees and our consumer audience: the bloggers and content creators we hire. My insecurities were hurting my business.

Negotiation coach (and my personal guru) Tanya Tarr notes that the way we think about negotiating is as a "sledgehammer form of power." But there's a more flexible form of power, she says, one in which you are not married to options, but "inventive and imaginative, which makes it easier for another party to make a decision." This is called collaborative, or value-based, negotiation.

In value-based negotiation, unlike a shark, writes expert Natalie Reynolds, you want the other party to feel like they've won. "Otherwise," she explains, you'll have a client who leads with dissatisfaction. "They'll start asking for more, making late payments, not prioritizing your requests, or just being generally uncooperative."[1]

GETTING STARTED

Get Emotional

You may think that emotions and negotiations go together like chalk and cheese, but when it comes to emotions in negotiation, says Harvard Medical School associate professor Dr. Kimberlyn Leary, we don't have a choice. "You're always engaged emotionally if you're relating to other human beings," she says. The key is to use your emotions as a tool.

Dr. Leary says, "Emotions are really like a set of sensors that give you all kinds of valuable information about the other person, about yourself, about the interaction. If you can learn to use those as sources of data, you will get better outcomes."

If you're not a psychologist with years of training, how do you get in touch with your emotions and then determine how to handle them? Here's Leary's advice:

Locate the trigger. First you need to understand what emotions a negotiation is triggering (mad, sad, nervous, ashamed). If you can identify and regulate your emotions, you'll be more in control of how to handle the person or scenario. As the "getting to yes" guru Roger Fisher says, "Just because you're mad with your negotiating partner doesn't mean that the only thing you can do is raise your voice."

Write about it. Psychologist James Pennebaker has shown that as little as fifteen minutes of writing a night can help people significantly to understand their emotions, make connections between this event and that event, and actually contribute to their overall mental health.

Picture it. Harvard Business School's Mike Wheeler suggests using question prompts such as, what emotions do you typically feel before a negotiation? What would you like to feel? What are the ways that you can typically cultivate that feeling in your life? How could you adapt that behavior into the scenario?

Tune in to your body. Because often a negotiation happens fast, you can't analyze in real time, and your physical feelings are an actual clue.

Check in, even at the table. "As you're calculating the figures, calculate the emotional equation. Then you can catch up to yourself with the next thing that you say or offer, or don't say or don't offer."

Talk back. Negotiations and challenging conversations bring up all kinds of memories and baggage: of past bosses, stressful situations, and even your parents yelling at you. When you know what sets you off, you can set it aside. "So, this reminds me of my father, ex-boss, professor," Leary says. "Tell yourself strongly: they are not my father, grandfather, and professor!"

GENDER'S ROLE

The weight of thousands of years of patriarchy manifests in every deal we try to make, and the system is rigged against us. Ask for too much, and it can backfire. (Even while negotiating with women.) And if you are anxious *and* asking for more, you are even more likely to be penalized.

I fondly call this the Bitch Tax.

Unfortunately, I'm not alone in doing this. According to Linda Babcock and Sara Laschever, authors of *Women Don't Ask:*

❑ Men initiate negotiations about four times as often as women.
❑ Women are more pessimistic about the how much is available when they do negotiate and so they typically ask for and get less when they do negotiate—on average, 30 percent less than men.
❑ 20 percent of adult women (twenty-two million people) say they never negotiate at all, even though they often recognize negotiation as appropriate and even necessary.[3]

Blech.

It's hard not to feel like a feminist traitor when you negotiate "like a woman"— i.e., think about communal benefits and shared values, and hold back from asking for the moon and stars. (Yes, it shouldn't be this way! Screw the patriarchy.) But negotiating "like a man" or judging yourself when you negotiate "like a woman" can be a mistake.

More and more, data show that acting like a man disadvantages you because either you don't seem authentic, or another party might punish you for assuming a traditionally male stance (the Bitch Tax). However, avoiding negotiation is very damaging for women. The key to staying at the negotiating table and achieving your desired outcome is to negotiate like your true self, accepting the role of gender norms and making them work for you.

Hannah Riley Bowles, one of the world's leading scholars on women and negotiation, has immensely helpful words of wisdom to make you feel okay about the tendency to be nice instead of a shark.

First, deliberately trying *not* to act like what Bowles calls the feminine ideal can backfire: "If acting forceful is your personality, great," she says, "but many times women change who they are in negotiations because they believe it's the only way to be successful. But if you start to say things that sound different than who you are, that's a red flag to the other party."

And avoiding certain negotiations may be an act of wisdom, not fear. A 2014 Harvard Business School study shows that though women avoid negotiations more often than men, it may be because they instinctively know when to negotiate and when to hold back.[4] They avoid strategically—either because the situations are not favorable to their negotiating style or because they're not experienced enough to negotiate that deal successfully. Whatever the reason, being attuned—not blindly ambitious—kept them from wasting time.

What matters is you getting what you need and deserve. I try to bring in a larger sense of purpose and use my natural self-deprecation as a tool. Few of my negotiations are about me becoming richer, much to the chagrin of those who depend on me for income. (Oh, well.) But that style translates as authentic to the client, who is more likely to respond positively—and actually make the negotiation successful—and I have become confident about rejecting negotiations that may not be fruitful before they begin.

Collaborative Negotiation 101

What if you thought about a negotiation not as a win but as a success—one that makes both the client and you happy?

The first step toward a successful collaboration is attuning yourself—both to the situation, to your needs, and to the needs of your client. This work sheet by Tanya Tarr is an excellent way to lay out the basics of any negotiation.[2]

Collaborative Negotiation Prep Worksheet
Courtesy of Tanya Tarr

Goal:

Objective: What's being negotiated:

PEOPLE

PARTY 1	PARTY 2

Interests: What are my motivations, needs, concerns and fears?

Motivation:	Motivation:
Needs:	Needs:
Concerns:	Concerns:
Fears:	Fears:

What standards or values will guide making a decision?
(Ex. Fairness, accessibility, utility, tradition, market value, etc.)

What happens if no agreement is reached?

What is the minimum set of options that MUST be included for an agreement to occur?	

What are the maximum resources available for an agreement to occur?	

Do we have a NOPE situation? (No Options for Possible Engagement)	

What are the potential options that could be a part of the final agreement?	

Final Outcome?

Shooting the Moon

Once you realize negotiating isn't just for Mark Cuban wannabes and you can use your fantastic negotiation skills to align with organizations that share your values, not just maximize your money haul . . . you'll probably get what you always wanted. Because the bro-tastic (as Tanya Tarr calls it) version of negotiating is asking for the moon and stars, the rest of us may feel like we need to raise our price just to keep up. But actually, doing your research and being realistic is more likely to place you in an organization that shares those values—and where you can advance.

Tanya Tarr relates a story in which she and a "tall, good-looking white male" were candidates for the same, very competitive job. "We had roughly the same qualifications," she says. After doing her research, Tanya asked for $75,000, smack in the middle of the pay range for the job, but a healthy bump up from what she was already making.

The other candidate asked for $95,000 a year. Tanya found out later that that's why she had gotten the job, since when the other candidate overshot the range by $15,000, it made the company feel like he didn't know the sector and lacked expertise.

"P.S., in two years," Tanya adds, "I was making $95,000."

If the organization does reward the candidate with blind ambition with the job, Tanya suggests, "Think of that as a clarifying event that helps you understand that you probably don't have the same values the organization does. Is that really somewhere you want to work?"

Your Negotiation Tool Kit

If you negotiate without a plan or a firm grasp on your emotional investment, you're much more likely to turn into a puddle, or try to act tough and be caught out. These steps can make sure everyone emerges happy.

What motivates you? First, you must know what's motivating you to get to the table. Tanya Tarr says, "If you don't know what truly motivates you, you really don't know what will satisfy you." The first question is tactical. Are you gunning for a new job for the salary? The new title? The opportunity to work with a new boss, or escape an old one? The second is what fundamentally motivates you as a person. For example, in working with Tanya, I learned I was less motivated by money or status than by the need to protect the ones I loved and those I care about.

Know your BATNA. BATNA, or best alternative to a negotiated agreement, is especially important when you're very attached to the outcome, and gives you a sense of power even in the most risky negotiation. For example, if you're negotiating for salary in a prospective new job, your BATNA could be that you'll remain in your current job quite happily.

Know the zone of possible agreement. Tanya Tarr interviewed ten CEOs about their approach in naming the first figure in a negotiation, termed *anchoring* in negotiation-speak. Half said never name the first number, and half said always do. Advice from your elders can help. Keeping it realistic is a strength, not a weakness. The zone of possible agreement gives you a basis from which to operate, however you negotiate; so you can feel comfortable being flexible.

Remind yourself of your mission. As you sit at the table, ground yourself by remembering your values and the larger purpose of your work. You should feel confident in what you're asking for, not just because you deserve it, but because it's right. Then, before you're tempted to say to yourself, *I'm asking for too much,* you can remind yourself that getting a raise sets a great precedent for others in the firm, or you can help pay off student loans, or provide a better life for your kids.

Give evidence. You may not feel empowered or deserving in the moment, and so it's important to have your reasons nailed down. Evidence might be that employees who work part-time in your field have focused contributions, or that your fee for a certain service is the lowest on the market. And it's not only valuable for the other side of the table: Tanya notes that the best way to squelch impostor syndrome is to have evidence ready of why you're asking what you're asking. Remember the idea of a "portfolio" of great facts about your work and awesomeness, or Jessica Bennett's concept of a Boast Bitch—an outside validator who can vouch for your worth.

Practice. Like most things in life, negotiating gets easier the more you do it. That said, no two negotiations are alike, and your stance might change given different scenarios. So role-play your terms with someone you trust, and in real life, experiment with different situations and personas. Negotiate everywhere! You might see what works best when seeking a lower price at the consignment store, for instance, or a better seat on the plane. When flying, I've learned that I can get an upgrade when I'm sweet and kind at the counter, not tough and threatening. I've been an upgrade queen ever since.

Find your lucky socks. Tanya Tarr wears Wonder Woman socks to situations that make her anxious. I have my go-to outfits, and believe me, the woman wearing them looks much richer and put-together than I actually am. Find the outfit that gives your confidence—even if it's superhero socks.

Understand your counterpart's motivations. Here's where being an anxious, hypersensitive soul really works for you. Put your attunement to work. When does the other person sound fearful? Angry? Relieved? Bored? What aspects of the situation seem to motivate them in conversation? Your observations can steer your responses and your strategy.

Research, research, research. Buying a car is one of the most dreaded negotiations out there, but I'm awesome at it. Why? USAA, to which I have a family membership, tells members the wholesale price of any car, features and all. I walk into the dealership armed with objective, bulletproof data, and I automatically win.

YOUR EMOTIONAL BATNA

When I was younger, I went through a months-long, multiple-interview process at a hot start-up. I had to sneak out of my day job to meet them, and every time I got on the subway, I felt nauseated. When an e-mail from the hiring manager came into my in-box, my first instinct was to hit delete. I was so caught up in the notion of winning, I was ignoring its effect on me.

There's an emotional BATNA to every negotiation, too, and listening to it will keep you from wasting their time and yours. For example, if your asking price is keeping you up at night, consider lowering it. If negotiating a huge fee out of a contract is going to give you crippling performance anxiety, take less. Advice from Wall Street and Sheryl Sandberg notwithstanding, your emotional well-being is part of the cost-benefit ratio.

I'm going to contradict myself right now. Sometimes you need to toughen up and let go of fears that hold you back while still acknowledging and accommodating for the very real triggers that create unnecessary anxiety. My mentor Lisa Stone, cofounder of BlogHer and self-confessed "shy girl," reminded me that introverts especially have to get tough when it really matters.

Before she started BlogHer, Lisa was a journalist and reporter. When her divorce made her a single mother and her fear of the spotlight kept her from the managerial roles she needed to support herself and her son, her little brother gave her a talking-to, armed with his own facts. "Get over your desire not to lead teams. It's the only way you'll be able to support your son in Silicon Valley," he said.

Lisa realized her comfort zone behind the reporter's notebook would only get her so far. When she stopped being a solo contributor and became Executive Producer, she was supervising thirty-five people within the year. In the next decade, she would cofound BlogHer.com, the largest community for women in social media. In addition to the financial pressure, realizing her ultimate purpose, to break into the males-only zone of digital media, was key: "My discomfort was overcome by the need to actually change things."

Always Consult Before Deciding (ACBD)

The bestseller *Beyond Reason,* by Roger Fisher and Dan Shapiro, discusses how we shouldn't pretend negotiating can or should be separated from emotions and interpersonal relationships. Consulting with others—whether they are involved in the negotiation or not—has three crucial benefits.

1. Other parties feel included in the decision making.

2. You might learn something through a consultation.

3. You still maintain veto power in a negotiation, but consulting another person allows them to give input, which can be valuable.

But more than even these points, ACBD provides checks and balances and a clear strategy for those of us who don't trust our instincts.

When I was in graduate school at Harvard, I cofounded a skills-building series for women graduate students called Effective Strategies for Powerful Women. A core team of women students convened six sessions led by big-name Harvard professors on everything from negotiating to strengthening communications skills. I loved working on it so much. I was a very gung ho member of the group, and at times I went too far on my own without consulting my other team members. As a result, the de facto leader of the team, who originally conceived the idea, froze me out, and I got none of the credit for organizing the sessions. By going too far on my own steam, I accidentally ensured I'd reap none of the rewards of my great work.

Like much of business, ACBD isn't rocket science, and it strengthens the notion that having a strong kitchen cabinet is one of your best strategies for success. If you're an introvert or a hermit, it may be hard for you to reach out, and in the middle of a tough time, you may be feeling low or depressed, making asking for advice even harder. One of the key signs of depression is a sense that you're not worth considering, so my telling you to consult someone for advice on a tough question at a tough time may feel rich indeed. But trust me, try to force yourself. Write out a script if you have to; ask for solid advice and engage another party in a big decision.

We're in this together. Columbia University scholar Beth Fisher-Yoshida lays out this intuitive approach, which I love to try to apply to negotiations and sales. It's simple: seek to establish an interdependence of goals. Meaning: if I succeed, you succeed, and if I fail, so do you. It's the opposite of a zero-sum shark negotiation, in which one person succeeds at the other person's loss. Fisher-Yoshida writes, "When we have familiar interests and attitudes, it is easier to believe we share common goals. This alignment is more likely to induce cooperative behaviors."[5]

Use appreciative inquiry. The practice of appreciative inquiry seeks to search for and activate the best in people. Tanya Tarr frames it this way: "Imagine how much fun a negotiation with a potential customer could be if you could activate your counterpart's sense of pride and wonder, because you feel it, too? Imagine if you put your natural sense of curiosity and interpersonal radar to use in a negotiation?"

Wharton's Stew Friedman reminds us that in any transaction, you can find a way to change it from taking to giving—to help the other party, either directly by serving them, or indirectly by connecting them to other people that you may know. This induces reciprocity, the engine of any good relationship. You can apply the relationship building to negotiations, because it's so important to engage the other party and learn about what makes them tick.

"One of the basic tenets of all modern negotiation theorists," Friedman says, "is 'the more you know about your partner's interests, the more likely you're going to get a better outcome for yourself.' What do you care about? What are you interested in? What matters to you? The more I know about that, the easier it is for me to fashion ideas for resolution that work for both of us."

NEGOTIATING ISN'T EVERYTHING

I want to stress that yes, you can negotiate a great deal by employing your intuitive introvert skills. Your anxiety might drive you to prepare so well that you achieve an absolutely phenomenal outcome.

You might also decide to negotiate for just enough, and be happy anyway. Like so many things, the concept of negotiation is deeply affected by achievement porn. Real life isn't *Million Dollar Listing* or *Shark Tank,* and negotiating the most killer deal doesn't have to be a badge of honor. Think of Tanya's story; she didn't push for the absolute maximum salary in her initial salary negotiation, but she soon ended up making it anyway. She wanted to make sure she aligned with the organization, where, after all, she'd be spending at least nine hours a day.

The idea of settling for less in favor of achieving an outcome that would make you content feels foreign, I know. But if you decide that, as an anxious introvert, you want to minimize unnecessary stressors, or in a move to commit to a hermit lifestyle you also want to reduce maximizing your output, getting to just enough might be great. I often think of negotiating the way I think about setting the scope of work in a contract: I want enough work to feel committed and well compensated, but not too much to lose sleep or control over my time. All that matters in the negotiation is that you and your counterpart walk away feeling good. If you're trying to create a life for yourself that doesn't have you running for the bathroom, or suffering anxiety every day, just enough is perfect.

13

Be a Player from Your Home Office

One of my superconnectors (you know, the person who always introduces you to the people who power your career forward), a former client, now a friend, invited me to the White House Correspondents' Dinner, aka "nerd prom." I was ten weeks pregnant and so sick I could barely focus. The thought of swanning around with five hundred people more important than me filled me with existential dread.

But I did it. I squeezed into a fancy dress, ate some saltines, and had a good time. I really did. And, when I went to hide in the bathroom, which I did quite often during the terrifying predinner cocktail period, legendary journalist Andrea Mitchell and I bonded over our mutual dislike of high heels. And I peed next to Sofia Vergara.

In the months to come, as I headed into pregnancy's familiar weight gain, lethargy, and anxiety about my business future, the image of me at that event, literally rubbing shoulders with my heroes, gave me faith in my ability to succeed. A ticket to that event is hard to come by, and I felt honored that my former client thought of me as someone worthy to introduce to his professional network.

Your superconnectors are probably not your best friends or closest colleagues, because they share a similar network with you. Your best superconnectors may simply be acquaintances—in social-networking theory, "weak ties." And in a network, they're much more important than your closest ones.

How to Create a Great Social Network Even If You're Not That Social

Networking for hermits can be summed up in one sentence uttered by a fellow small business owner, who observed, "I don't know why I bother to go anywhere. The same ten people always refer me all my business."

We all have superconnectors: folks with large and diverse social networks who are key to our success, though we might not have noticed it. There are three events a year that I will always attend, because year after year they are intellectually stimulating and they enhance my professional network. I meet people who drive my business forward in a superconcentrated time frame. Not surprisingly, two of these events are hosted by my superconnectors.

Superconnectors are generous and helpful because that's who they are. And, if you cultivate powerful superconnectors and nurture a strong online social network, you can keep actual in-person networking to a minimum while still advancing in your career (ideally from bed).

Any social network is made up of nodes. These are the individual actors or people in the network. Some of the nodes in your network are more powerful than others in introducing new relationships. My superconnector from the White House Correspondents' Dinner was a node with a lot of access to other nodes.

Networks aren't only for our personal lives. They build our civic society because they form social capital and interpersonal ties. As defined by Wayne Baker, professor at the Ross School of Business at University of Michigan, *social capital* refers to the resources available in and through personal and business networks. When it comes to work, social capital is pretty much everything that propels careers forward: relationships, financial resources, leads or new job opportunities, mentorship, and Baker notes, intangibles like trust, goodwill, and cooperation.[1]

Can I Have Strong Social Capital When I'm Not That Social?

Absolutely! Even the biggest hermit needs strong social networks.

Building networks is a skill I had to learn. When I left college, I felt so sad that no professor had ever taken an interest in me, and that I had no relationships with anyone besides my small group of friends. I looked in wonder at friends who got recommended for scholarships or great opportunities, who had dinner at professors' houses. How did they do it? I knew I was smart, but I had no idea how to nurture professional relationships (I wasn't so great with personal ones either).

Why hadn't I formed those social networks? Well, I was convinced that no one older or important would ever want to spend time with me. I never wanted to ask for their time or attention. I was socially anxious, and when I did reach out, my tactics were artless. In my early career, I was mentored by some incredible people, but I never kept in touch. I didn't reach out or offer to help others naturally. It wasn't because I was a mean person, it was because I was scared. I felt worthless and very alone professionally, outside family and friends.

Even if you were born into privileged circles, networking can be very very stressful if you're shy. The secret is that, for hermits, front-loading the hard work of building strong relationships actually means you have to travel and work less when it comes to business development for your job or company. And for introverts, knowing your superconnectors and having them in your corner can save you a lot of networking angst. If you can develop close relationships with a few superconnectors with access to diverse networks, they'll do the connecting for you.

Sometimes a superconnection doesn't even need to be a person. It can be a passion project.

For my beloved editor, Lizzie Skurnick, it turned out that the biggest superconnector in her career was her blog. (I totally relate to this, because blogging changed my life forever, too.) Her inspiration to launch one of the first literary blogs, Old Hag, led to her career as an author, publisher, *New York Times* columnist, and much more—and, most important, let her make her living in the book world. Lizzie says, "My entire professional life and my dearest closest friends spring from a blog. If I hadn't started it, and connected with the three people who also shared my passion, I wouldn't have the life I have now."

In 2003, Lizzie was sitting in her apartment, forty pounds overweight, recently fired from her job, her only income coming from a still-new relationship writing about books for a local indie paper. But from a major writer she profiled, she learned about blogs, and joined the fledgling world of literary bloggers. At the time, she says, "You could get fired for blogging, and we all either hated our jobs, or were about to get fired." None of them had any idea the media was about to become obsessed with blogging, and she and her friends were swept up in it, some founding new Gawker blogs, some going to *The Daily Show,* some making a splash in print media.

For Lizzie, it led to writing reviews for the *New York Times Book Review.* It also, through a friend who read her blog, put her on the radar of a local teen-girls magazine that let her work part-time but still gave her health care. Another blogging friend introduced her to the new editor in chief of Jezebel, and she launched a column on YA books that the major author (remember her?) recommended to her editor. That became a book, as did her *New York Times Magazine* column, which another blogger friend had recommended her for.

That in turn led to her YA imprint, Lizzie Skurnick Books, which put her in the *Times* again, but now as a subject.

"Everything, everything I have came from the blog," she says, "but I was just noodling around. At the time, using a blog to be ambitious would have been crazy. So never underestimate the value of just fooling around with what you love."

When Hiding Changes Your Life: Cheryl Contee's Story

Cheryl Contee isn't a hermit, but for years circumstances forced her to hide her real identity behind a pseudonym—"Jill Tubman"—on the influential blog Jack and Jill Politics, which she cocreated. "Outspoken black people have a pretty long history in America of getting shot at, or hung," Cheryl says. "Blogging was very new then. Certainly being an outspoken black person taking on the Congressional Black Caucus or the Bush administration had not been done before."

Working eighteen-hour days, Cheryl was passed over for a promotion and finally decided it was worth it to take in a fraction of her former salary to work for herself. One tweet announcing her free-agent status led to her future tech-founder and business partner, and to a shift: she started managing her identity as Jill, shifting that identity into her real self.

"I think there were a lot of people who were surprised," she adds, "including one friendship that I almost lost because he felt that he had a relationship with Jill Tubman, and didn't realize it was me."

Jill, who, Cheryl says, is "probably funnier than me," was more confrontational, angrier, and blunter, as well. But the blog and the business allowed her to put the two together: "I felt the need to move forward in one direction rather than having a semicompartmentalized life."

Bringing them together was more rewarding than the corporate job had ever been. "I never dreamed that by launching the blog I would one day shake the president's hand and that he would know who I was and thank me."

Having to hide was, Cheryl says, very similar to the process of becoming an entrepreneur. "When we were starting, and my family was concerned for my safety, I decided that it was worth the cost, and I think, as an entrepreneur, it's a similar process. You're going to pay a heavy price in some ways. You have to be willing to go to the mat. Am I willing to put it all on the table in order to achieve my dream and the dreams of the people who joined me in this venture?"

Cheryl is truly a brave and original thinker. But her adoption of an alter ego who was just a little more out there than her true self at the time helped her grow into her current life as a leader and tech entrepreneur. Being anonymous gave her the courage that she couldn't give her true self.

Although it wasn't her goal, Cheryl's brave dive into the world of politics and cultural commentary opened up entirely new networks for her. By the time she was "outed" in the press, she was ready to leave her corporate job and start a company, and her bold voice and online leadership had paved the way, even though, ironically, it had been constructed under a fictitious identity.

GETTING STARTED

Find Your Superconnectors

Ask people how they got to where they are and you'll hear, over and over again, that they built on their relationships.

Connecting dots is what superconnectors do all the time, and you can learn a lot from them. One of the quickest ways to do it yourself is to start identifying the superconnectors already in your network. (If you seem a bit light on them, don't worry—we'll talk about building your superconnector stable in a minute.)

❑ Think about the last five years of work, or school, or the last ten projects you've worked on. Write down everyone who introduced you to a new boss, job opportunity, or client; recommended you for a speaking gig, professional organization, board, or blogging opportunity; or introduced you to a new community or social network that has added value.

❑ Go through the past few years of customer engagements, or look at your biggest contracts. Think about who introduced you to new employers, recruiters, or strong connections for advancement. In the cases where someone referred you to a customer, who was it? Is there a pattern?

❑ Take a large piece of paper or a whiteboard and draw circles; these are your nodes. Write down all the nodes that refer you business—don't be strict with the definition. Here a node can be a person, but it can also be an event, a professional organization, someone's website you're listed on, or a partner firm. Is there one client who always sends you new prospects? An event that results in new clients?

❑ Look back over the signature moments in your professional life: Which people helped facilitate them? Whose faces pop into your mind?

Eye what you've written critically. Is there one particular "superconnector" in your life that has widened your world? This could be a person, a yearly event, an organization. You will see common threads; I guarantee it. Challenge yourself to look critically at who is in your network, and if the list is not diverse enough or full of enough weak ties, you'll need to work harder to expand it.

What If I Don't Have Any Superconnectors?

Don't worry if you're reading this and feel like you don't have any superconnectors. It sounds so trite, but if you do things you like to do and seek out places (online and offline) where people with shared values tend to be, pay close attention to possible kindred spirits, and take a small risk now and then; you'll build the network that's right for you.

When I researched articles and books on building strong networks and making superconnections, everything seemed to be written by white men, which disappointed but didn't surprise me. The very spirit and language of networking and leadership culture in this country is what I like to call "enlightened bro." (Tim Ferriss, I'm talking about you.)

But in truth, the art of making wonderful connections through acquaintances or strangers is introvert-friendly, because it's about being attuned to another person and reading subtle signals. It's the risk part where you may need to practice.

In his book *Achieving Success Through Social Capital*, eminent social-network scholar Wayne Baker tells a great story about how his wife, Cheryl, forged a superconnection (I will use quite a bit of Baker's theory in this chapter, because I think it's great and enlightened). New to a city and unsure of her next career move, she bonded with her superconnector when she admired the flyer the woman was printing at Kinko's.[2] "The page that faced up was the woman's picture, along with her bio," Baker recounts. "Here was someone who had her own unique path. Here is someone who had done it." She asked for a copy of the brochure, and called the lady out of the blue. It turned out she and Cheryl shared many professional and spiritual interests—ones that created further relationships and connections.

To forge a connection with a stranger or someone you don't know well, you have to take a risk. You have to strike up a conversation, as Baker's wife did in Kinko's, or as KJ Dell'Antonia did when she chatted up Nicholas Kristof in the hallways of the *New York Times*. And for every great connection, you'll face a rejection, or simply a nod, and you'll have to move on. The good news is that superconnectors tend to adopt people, so you may only have to make the first move, and you'll be in good hands thereafter.

My favorite failed-connection story is very typical of D.C., which is why I don't live there anymore. I was invited to an exclusive Georgetown party at the home of Nancy Jacobson, a legendary political fund-raiser, and her husband, Mark Penn, famous pollster, CEO of PR giant Burson Marsteller, and, at the time, top adviser to Hillary Clinton.

As host, Mark was making the rounds, and he came upon me. I was very eager to meet him because I really wanted a job with Hillary Clinton's 2008 presidential campaign. I wasn't wearing a name tag, not that it would have mattered. He asked me, "Who are you?" but then got quickly distracted. When he asked again, clearly not interested, I simply replied, "I'm no one you need to know." He seemed relieved, and quickly moved on.

The point is, your superconnectors may not be who you think they will be, or even who you hope they will be. No matter. I still worked for Hillary in the end, because another one of my connections brought me in.

Calendaring Your Superconnections

Once you've found your superconnectors, whether personal or professional, you must tend your network like a garden. Relationships from past jobs, past schooling, industry events, and even kindred spirits are the soil from which your business will grow.

When I met Nicco, I was amazed. Here was someone who kept in touch with everyone from his first job onward, and beyond that, who had the richest network of experiences, friends, and supporters

I'd ever seen. It spanned generations, and included a diverse set of people, some very important. Many in his professional community were real, dear friends.

I also saw how Nicco puts a tremendous amount of work into keeping up his relationships, and is never scared to pick up the phone. He values everyone in his life and he works hard for them.

Nicco is an avid reader and poetry aficionado, and he loves to send people books. When I first met him, it seemed sort of crazy, to meet someone and then after just spending a few hours with them to send them a book. But I realized over time that that's how he loves to connect with people (they always end up talking books) and it's a passion he loves to share.

In our digital era, you can even tag someone with love and consideration. Susan McPherson is wonderful at surfacing a useful or compelling article on Facebook and tagging someone with a "thought of you." This tiny gesture feels generous and helps people stay in the know. Likewise, you could go through LinkedIn once a week, check in on what your contacts are doing, and comment on a few of their updates, endorse a few more. A digital acknowledgment of someone's worth is meaningful and builds social capital.

Camille Preston, who coaches people on finding their flow, sends past clients, friends, and colleagues articles or little snippets of information that she believes will help them work toward their personal goals, or conquer their personal demons. For her, it's a daily practice, and she sends a few people a "nugget" each day, just via e-mail.

If I have twenty free minutes, the last thing I'm inclined to do is pick up the phone and call someone. But what I have learned from Nicco, and practiced hard, is to honor my professional colleagues and work hard for them. I often have to go outside my comfort zone to do it, but I always end up having a good time. And I've adapted ways that I can stay in touch and tend my relationships in a manner that doesn't give me too much angst. Technology and online tools really help. I'll never be like Nicco, but no longer do I feel alone professionally. Instead I feel deeply blessed and supported.

I think the key is that your effort must be authentic to who you are and what you care about. It can't feel phony. Review those contacts, consolidate them, and develop a CRM. Message them with love, respect, and great stuff.

The "Ten Touches" Rule

Nicco owned a small business for years. As the company grew, the team considered how much to invest in sales and marketing: maybe hire a PR firm, or develop sales collateral, or host events. Before they made a decision, he tried to figure out what made the business come in and go out.

"It became pretty clear that my relationships with people and the amount of contact I had in a week had a direct impact on how much business came in," he says.

So he made a new rule: check in with ten people from his Rolodex—i.e., Facebook, LinkedIn, and e-mail—a week. "Maybe the exchange is an e-mail, maybe it's a phone call, maybe it's lunch or dinner or coffee—maybe it's sending them a book or an interesting article," he told me. "It very rarely leads directly to business. But imagine you reach out to someone in your network and have a good conversation. Then, the next day that person is having lunch with a colleague looking for help. You are the top-of-mind recommendation."

This method doesn't just work for small-business owners. Silicon Valley entrepreneur and power saleswoman Joanna Bloor noted a senior vice president at a tech company in San Francisco whose sales team had a target of over $200 million per year. This leader worked four days a week. She had figured out that if she made the requisite number of contacts and dates between Monday and Thursday, she'd meet her sales goals and be able to take Fridays off.

Is Managing My Social Network Slimy?

In *Achieving Success Through Social Capital*, Wayne Baker asks this question flat out: "Is it unethical to consciously 'manage' a social network?"[3] In essence, what kind of mercenary would treat relationships and human beings as useful tools for bettering her own life?

It is not unethical.

Thinking that managing our network is slimy assumes we are only using people for our own ends. But in true networking, that's a happy side effect, not the point.

Wharton's Stew Friedman says, "When you approach a social encounter as an opportunity for you to discover something about other people that you can help them with, as opposed to taking something from them, then you don't feel slimy. And if I find whatever resource I can provide, then you're going to want to help me in the future."

Your network doesn't have to be a scary thing; play to your strengths. As Stew Friedman tells us, "Think about networking as a contribution to your capacity to make the world better some way, to use your particular talents, skills, passion, interests to create value, to be of use, to have a life of significance."

And think about it: you are managing relationships throughout the day. You take your partners' clothes to the dry cleaners to do something nice for them; you flex a little to make room for a colleague's scheduling needs. You drop an endorsement on LinkedIn for someone you don't know well, just because. If you needed the favor returned, you hope they'll do the same for you. But this expectation of "ongoing reciprocity" isn't greedy. It's a positive view of how we operate in the world. As Friedman simply puts it, "We try to help each other."

Managing a relationship is as simple as learning about another person, being attuned to their goals and needs, and staying open to chances to help. It's bringing people, ideas, and resources together in a way that helps everyone involved. Consider Wayne Baker's take:

"It's not the management of relationships that is unethical. It's what we do with our knowledge that makes the practices ethical or not."

There's another positive side effect to managing networks. Generosity, as we've discussed throughout the book, is not only an underappreciated value in business, it's an incredibly effective tactic for reducing anxiety. If you flip the script in your life from trying to prove how interesting, intelligent, or effective you are into an inquiry into another person's needs, you forget yourself. You get out of your head and into relating to another person. You use your skills as an empath and a sensitive soul to attune to another, not to beat yourself up or force yourself to be something you're not. It's the social-capital equivalent of bringing homemade cookies into the office.

My favorite hermit social-capital discipline is to connect people to jobs or opportunities. When I see a posting on one of my networks, I'll think of five people to whom I could send it. It feels great, is great, and it's bringing good energy into the world.

The Power of Online Professional Social Networks

No doubt, the digital age is a blessing and a curse. For hermits, it's mostly a blessing, because it means we can build an empire from bed (which is where I wrote this sentence from). The digitally connected member of society can meaningfully participate in the world in yoga pants.

But for that, you need an online social network.

This is much more serious than your Facebook page. An online professional social network is your entry point to the world, to news, to opportunities and connections far beyond your home office. To be effective, it must have many of the characteristics we just talked about in relation to superconnectors: diversity, weak ties, access to new opportunities, and social networks beyond our own.

Now we'll focus on the key digital skills and tools to build and foster powerful online networks from the comfort of your laptop.

An online network can be just powerful as one in real life—and the people you find in it may surprise you.

Why Women Need Great Online Social Networks

I had a bitter laugh recently with my husband as he told me about the great new after-work cocktail spots in Harvard Square. "I wouldn't know about that," I said dryly. "I'm usually at home with the kids, drinking alone."

Work-related networks have traditionally been less effective for women because women tend to move in and out of the workforce due to childcare and family responsibilities. Instead of a wide-ranging group of weak ties, we have strong support networks. That means we have wonderful friends to call for advice on diaper rash, but fewer contacts who can put us in touch with a potential investor or patent lawyer.

Conversely, men benefit from an organized social life that promotes entrepreneurship. This network of weak ties contains valuable advisers who are their lawyers, accountants, business partners, or other power brokers.

But now online social networks, accessible from anywhere, prevent women's work networks from being interrupted by childcare. They can even create entrepreneurs: mom-blogging culture was built from online friends from Facebook or Twitter who only caught up in person once or twice a year at BlogHer or other community conferences.

Here's more good news. All-female reference groups have garnered power because of the vast marketing and political organizing opportunities they represent, and because online networking allows women to ignore barriers of place and life stage and connect with people from many walks of life. In the old days, power and access to capital was traded at the Yale Club, or on the golf course, among small groups of white men. Now women can form their own clubs, online. Some easy ways to start:

- **Find your online colleagues.** Tapping into professional networks in your field requires sleuthing and research more than anything. You don't need to start from scratch. Once you find one hub of activity, others will follow. It could be a blog, a Twitter feed, a message board. If you attend a professional conference you really like, research the conference organizers and speakers online, and see where they hang out. As in any social situation, you want to be with people you like and respect, so be choosy and take your time to find the right community.

Follow your bliss. Often, professional communities evolve from other passion projects you take part in. I think of Pantsuit Nation and a myriad of other pro–Hillary Clinton online communities that developed during Election 2016 and grew from there. The power of Facebook showed us all the professional colleagues who were part of our political networks, and gave us a great deal in common with new weak ties.

You may find the same if you get involved in a more local or regional issue, such as a municipal funding push, volunteering effort, or civic campaign. A few in-person meetings can pave the way for a strong online network, even if it's just conducted via e-mails. I find that I tend to bond with other working mothers who fly a lot, and I love the community we created. I've even met some by commenting on blogs or following women on Twitter who cover travel and working motherhood.

Contribute content. Andrea Sparrey, now the immediate past president of AIGAC, the Association of International Graduate Admissions Consultants, began her career by editing the trade association's blog when she was just starting out as an MBA admissions consultant. In so doing, she met everyone influential and powerful in the field of business school admissions—her chosen field, because she interviewed and edited them.

At the time Andrea didn't have much choice: she needed to conduct most of her networking online. Because of her husband's job, she'd uprooted her life and moved from New York City to San Diego, far from the locus of elite business schools and the consultants, bankers, and entrepreneurs who applied to them. "I was willing to write articles—and it gave me a platform to call up the most important people! I then helped organize the conferences, and then I had the chance to go out and meet people at all levels of the field," Andrea says.

Find, or create, communities of practice. I would not be where I am today were it not for several specific, professionally driven online communities. These are simple listservs or Facebook groups, invite-only, and they not only keep me up-to-date on professional development and trends, they continuously supply weak ties to my social network. And, because we're bound together by "The List," we all go the extra mile to help each other.

Scholar Wayne Baker calls these "networks of practice": a formal or informal network of people who work in the same function or process but are geographically distributed.[4] Until I had my lists, my social networks were limited. I had a personal CRM and I went to the same events each year; everyone knew each other and everyone ran in the same professional circles, so at some point, getting new business and new clients tapped out. When I joined my "lists," all of a sudden my network broadened.

Use the algorithms. We're all used to finding the "People You May Know" feature on Facebook creepy (and when it pops up an old boyfriend from high school, it kind of is), but when you're a businessperson, it's free research. Ditto for Twitter's "Who to Follow," LinkedIn's similar feature, and any other social-network algorithm. That doesn't mean you should follow people blindly—it means you have an opportunity to find some people you really would like to know.

Mighty Networks founder and Silicon Valley executive Gina Bianchini calls these identity networks, and believes they are the future. "No matter where you are in the world, you should be able to instantly connect with people with a shared identity, a shared interest, a shared condition. And software is now smart enough to play the role of the fabulous host." No more endless searching through the web forms on alumni or professional directories. My wrists hurt just thinking about that.

Use social proofing. Earlier I mentioned the concept of social proofing, which means that people tend to "assume the actions of others in an attempt to reflect the correct behavior for a situation." This concept has been co-opted by marketers and social-change agents alike. Think about it the next time everyone in your social network turns their Facebook avatar a certain color for a cause. If I post "Je Suis Paris," or if I "Stand with Planned Parenthood" and change my Facebook profile to reflect my stance, chances are other people in my social network will see the change, assume it's what's expected, and turn their profiles, too. This adds power and currency to online social movements, but you can use it in business development and in online networking. (And I will say that sharing your social activism on your online profile can enhance your appeal to like-minded clients or employers, and scare off those who might be a bad fit.)

You can use social proofing to align your work with the people, organizations, and places that command the most respect in your given field. If you are part of a community with inherent value, others will assume you have professional value, too. It's the equivalent of why people carry status tote bags: they want others to know where they've been and who they've been with without having to actually say it.

You can even use social proofing "aspirationally," optimizing your LinkedIn and Facebook profile to sound as prestigious as possible by aligning with groups, institutions, and people who are desirable in your field. And you can be in the know on new trends, actions, or other acts of meaning that will advance your currency among your online networks. All this sends subtle signals to online connections that you're *someone*. Even if you're in your sweats.

Peak event and the power of the online keynote. If you are at a point in your career where you're asked to speak publicly, write, and offer expertise, you might feel compelled to give lots of talks and fly all over the country to enhance your market value. But Gina Bianchini believes we're at "peak event," and she's done her own analysis of why an important keynote isn't nearly as fruitful for her business development as a well-crafted blog or Q&A session on Quora.com.

Unless it's on video a live talk doesn't have as much staying power as an article, which is easily re-shared. And preparation is a multi-day process. Gina says, "I need to think of the presentation, write out all the slides, write out the script, memorize the script. Not to mention I have to sit in traffic, get my hair and makeup done, arrive early so I can sit there for an hour because they want me to be there early and mic'd up, practice my speech."

Gina can get a million views for a Q&A on Quora, her online keynote equivalent of sending out a fundraising email to raise $4 million instead of a political candidate going to a four-hour-long rubber chicken dinner. That's why political campaigns love online fund-raising—entrepreneurs should love online visibility.

Social capital online. There are about six professional friends in my life who I will do anything for, no matter what. Two are on-again, off-again clients, two are colleagues I frequently collaborate with, one is a longtime friend who helped launch me way back when, and one I have never met IRL! (We e-mail and have chatted a few times by phone.)

When I took his class in 2008, legendary social theorist Robert Putnam was unconvinced that computer-mediated communication could make our investments in social capital more productive. More recent scholarship suggests information technology enhances place-based community and the generation of bridging social capital.[5] Increased participation in social-network sites such as Facebook or blogs seems both to predict and contribute to increased interaction in offline social networks.

In short: online communities are not for losers.

Social scientists such as Harold Rheingold argue that not only can one truly care about online "friends" and neighbors as passionately as the real thing, the anonymity and invisibility of Internet communications prevent some of the biases and discriminations of face-to-face contact. Online communities grow and deepen through years. Strong online communities have the power to replace many lost community elements. They also have the power to invent new ideas and allow ordinary citizens to drive social change.

ONLINE SELF-CARE

I could not be a hermit entrepreneur if it weren't for my strong online networks and incredible superconnectors (made easier to maintain because of my clear, strong niche and online brand). They have been the lifeblood of my business, allowing me to build my little fiefdom while in my pj's.

But as an introvert and someone who gets nervous when I engage too deeply, there are pros and cons to connecting online. As more and more of our social lives gets conducted online or via mobile, digital connections begin to feel just like IRL ones. You need to respond right away; the sheer volume of communication can be overwhelming. And then there's our old friend FOMO. The more you engage in high-quality online social networks, the more you will be daily faced with the incredible accomplishments of colleagues and friends.

I've talked about The List, the incredible online community of businesswomen I belong to. I truly love this community, which is technically just a Google group. Still, I have a secret way of coping with all the wonderfulness, which is sometimes too much for me to take in. If I'm having a melancholy day or need some quiet, I turn my e-mail settings to digest and only get the updates in my in-box once a day. It's the digital version of shutting out the world.

So as much as I advocate cultivating your online network, I also advocate turning it off or tuning it out every once in a while. In the same way as going out to a function every single night, engaging online professional communities each day can wear you thin. After the contentious 2016 presidential election, many people quit Facebook and Twitter for a period of time, simply because they were overstimulating at a time when they needed to be quiet, to grieve, and to take stock. I encourage you to use the same intention with your online professional engagement, monitoring your own reactions for burnout, and recognizing when you're overstimulated by all the energy of online conversations these days. Turn your feeds to digest, guilt-free.

And hey, you might even call a friend and take a walk, IRL.

14

Getting Out There (When You Have To)

I have a secret: sometimes, if there is a professional event I should be at but can't attend, I just use the hashtag and tweet as if I'm there.

This is because I'm torn about these events. I never want to go. When I'm there, I have to force myself to go into rooms, and my anxiety has made me get straight into a cab and head to the airport, days early. But if there is an important gathering and I'm not invited, I have insane FOMO.

Sometimes even the most committed hermit has to get out there. Meeting clients, attending conferences, giving speeches; face time matters. But if you have a plan and you know how to take care of yourself, you can make the most of your time in the wild. Whether it's choosing the conferences that pay off, knowing how to make your speeches count, and—yes—figuring out when to say no, identifying the characteristics of going public gives you space to psych yourself up.

Choose wisely and prepare well, and you might even enjoy yourself.

The Temporary Extrovert

The star speaker you heard during the plenary session? Hiding in the bathroom during cocktail hour. Those superstars holding drinks, laughing and charming everyone? Also angling for the exit. The only difference between them and you is that these leaders can tune in to a room and direct their energy outward in short bursts. They pitch, charm, and emote with the best of them. They just know to book in some quiet time afterward.

Life is not high school or a popularity contest. You don't need to be BFFs with your colleagues, or make sure there's a party to hit each Saturday night. (Isn't being a grown-up great?)

However, good social skills really, really help in business. And ironically, the more out there you are when you're out there, the more downtime you can pack into your schedule when you're "off." So I don't want you to feel you need to transform into a schmoozer. You just need to practice being a great extrovert for short amounts of time, and learn some powerful coping skills for when you simply must get out there.

GETTING STARTED

Morra's Fourteen-Point Plan for Surviving Events

By this point, you've learned to think about selling and negotiating in a way that's true to yourself and doesn't spike your cortisol. Now, what if you could do the same at cocktail hour? There's a way to work a room and leave a calling card that's authentic to you—and lets you banish stay-at-home FOMO.

Channel your inner Oprah. BlogHer cofounder and CEO Lisa Stone's former career as a journalist was key to helping her learn to work a room in Silicon Valley. "I've always been that person behind the reporter's notebook, asking other people their opinions," she told me. "What I don't like is the spotlight." If you feel alien, unworthy, shy, or nervous in a room full of powerful players, pretend you're there to report a story. Ask people lots of questions—this is your strength as an introvert! Listen actively. Draw them out. Even the most powerful person enjoys telling their own story. You can even use it to produce content. And the truth is, when you ask people lots of questions about themselves, you're remembered as a great conversationalist!

Wear your battle gear. My therapist once said to me, "The world doesn't have to know you feel like shit." Before I head to a business trip or a long day of meetings in the city, I wear one of my three fabulous outfits, get my hair blown out, and put on tons of makeup. This armor helps me transform from my homebody self into someone confident and open enough to make friends and charm people. I look like the best version of myself, and, often, I can actually be her.

Be prepared. On the few occasions I have been asked to give a keynote speech, I've channeled Hillary Clinton, who once said, "If you're not comfortable with public speaking—and nobody starts out comfortable; you have to learn how to be comfortable—practice." When I have to go out in public and be awesome, I'm training for the Olympics. I rehearse every word. I rehearse the room. I find my inner Gary, Julia Louis-Dreyfus's body man in HBO's *Veep*, and create a briefing book of attendee details for small talk. I even practice names before I walk in.

Only connect. Professional superconnector Susan McPherson says introducing others (known as the "cocktail bump") is the kindest and fastest means of escape for a hermit. "One of the reasons I love to host parties is I can introduce everybody else, and then I can run away. The conversation can go on without me, and people feel good being brought together."

Chunk your time. When you are at a conference, set a minimum target, pace yourself, and then give yourself a time-out treat. "One hour on earns one hour off," says Kate Gardiner. If you schmooze for an hour and meet three new people, you can allow yourself to go hide in your hotel room. The same goes for attending sessions, which can be a great way to learn new skills and meet people in a less pressured environment. One big chunk works, too. If I have to fly to New York or Washington for a client meeting or conference, I force myself to schedule five meetings that day. I'd rather be exhausted than fly back again.

Remember, you are there to work, not make people like you. For all of sixth grade, none of the girls in my class would eat lunch with me. Twenty-nine years later, the memories of sitting by myself for a year come flooding back when I enter a professional networking event. But here's the great thing: you're a grown-up, it's not middle school, and you don't need everyone to sit with you anymore. "I make it a point to ask questions and chat with the speakers during sessions specifically so that I can duck the networking," says financial therapist Amanda Clayman. "Then I don't have to feel like the unpopular high school dork."

Find a conference "spouse." When you're alone, establish a power duo with someone else for cocktail chatter, attending events, and standing in lines. Conference BFFs also work, as do actual partners, whom you can call for a quick pep talk when you're alone at the bar. (They'll be glad you're not off with your conference spouse.)

Never, ever be afraid to hide in the bathroom. Whether your kindred spirits are also hiding or they're just in there to pee, something about being in that shared space lets people's guard down. Either way, you can strike up the most informal and interesting conversations while putting on your lipstick. Even a short, friendly conversation by the sink will get your social juices flowing and make entering that large room easier. All you need to do is smile at someone in the mirror.

Once, I was feeling particularly bad about myself. I had been eclipsed on a client team by someone new, younger, and cooler, and I felt left out. Suddenly I recognized the woman at the sink next to me from her Twitter photo. We began chatting. She knew who I was. I remembered that indeed, I had a good professional reputation, relationships that had lasted years, and I would survive. Even better, I had someone to walk out of that room with into the fray.

Make someone else comfortable. BlogHer's Lisa Stone recalled something her mother told her as a girl, as Lisa was working on her own shyness. "You can take the responsibility to help other people feel like they belong, and make them feel good just by smiling at them." She adds, "Asking a stranger 'how are you?' is the gateway drug to feeling comfortable." Research backs Lisa up: the mere act of smiling at a stranger makes you feel more socially connected to others immediately after.[1] So even if the person you're smiling at doesn't notice, you'll feel more confident and connected when you emerge from the bathroom.

Have a job to do. Silicon Valley veteran Arvind Rajan, former executive at LinkedIn, the mother ship of networking, has social anxiety. "I can speak in front of two thousand people with no problem, but if there's a chitchat session after, I get anxious and drained." Arvind has learned that for him, structure is key to his comfort level. For the cocktail party, build in structure in an unstructured situation. It can be as easy as finding a person you've been meaning to meet. Talk, exchange e-mails, and then you're free to leave.

Share your expertise. It's counterintuitive, but, as with Arvind, for a shy person, sometimes the best position to be is in the front of the room. Remember Hillary Moglen, who hates networking events but excels at talking about her specific work in a room of people who will understand it? "I find opportunities to be in a thought-sharing position as opposed to just meeting people and having to explain myself to them," she says.

Find something to like. Journalist Claire Shipman says, "I dread the four hours leading up to a trip. But the minute I'm in the car headed toward the airport, I like the time to myself, and I like to get ready for my event. I try to focus on that. It's like when I'm looking at a new project. I try to remember the parts of the process that I enjoy, and remind myself I will get through it, even if there are some parts I don't love as much."

Showcase something authentic to you. Emily McKhann and Cooper Monroe founded a very successful social media agency called the Motherhood. For years, they made charming cloth bags just the size to hold business cards, and other goodies to hand out at conferences. I first got mine in 2007 and I still carry it in my purse today. They were so perfectly perfect for the brand and for Emily and Cooper: generous, beautiful, feminine. It was always a perfect and disarming way to begin or end what could be an awkward transaction.

Know what comes next. Are you attending the plenary session? Is there a dinner party the second night? The more you plan your schedule so you know you're hitting what you need to, the calmer you'll be (and the quicker you can exit).

Follow up. The magic of networking is that you can follow up from behind your screen. When I come home from an event, I put all the new business cards I have gathered in a safe place. I write down next steps for each; it could be everything from suggesting a phone call or coffee meeting to sending an article we discussed or a helpful introduction or link. Then, when I'm in a strong mood, I'll reach out via e-mail and suggest a next step.

It's also a good way to stop second-guessing what you said or didn't say, or beat yourself up for leaving early or feeling too shy to meet many people. A one-on-one conversation with someone new—regardless of who they are—is probably more valuable than any number of banal group conversations or short hellos, says Kate Gardiner.

Finally, give yourself a reward at the end of the day. You want to leave the event day with a positive memory, so you lower your internal stress response for planning the next one. If room service and a movie works for you, great. Don't judge yourself. Train yourself to push through the public time and then recharge.

Be Ruthlessly Strategic About Events: What's Worth It?

The conference and event industry is thriving; indeed, for many struggling news organizations and publishers, it's become a cash cow. You could attend a regular old conference to network every other day. And, increasingly, invite-only conferences on a ship in the Bahamas or in Utah at a ski resort seem invented purely to create FOMO and raise the value of exclusivity. But all that ego gratification—I'm cool enough to join the club!—is expensive, and all that glad-handing is time-consuming. How much of it is truly valuable to your career?

There may be some events you choose to attend in hopes of cultivating new business or relationships, and you will pay to attend those. If you have target clients, Google their brand name and "conference," or Google the name of a key executive at a target client and "conference." You're not stalking! You're conducting valuable reconnaissance. Even better, try to speak at the conference as well. If you're both speakers, you're more likely to feel confident and make a good connection. If not, try to find a smaller venue, or invite your target to speak or moderate something you're planning.

Simply being in the room for some invite-only events is worth it. You don't need the spotlight; I have never been invited even to attend a TED event, but former speakers have told me that giving a talk on the main stage requires Oscar-night levels of preparation. TED veteran Nilofer Merchant notes, "Relish the opportunity that not-speaking presents. TED attendees who have used it only as part of the professional get-ahead checklist are not beloved members of the community." So be sure, if you attend an invite-only event, these are communities you want to be part of for the long term.

A quick "Is it Worth It?" conference checklist:

❑ Will your superconnectors be there? That alone is a reason to attend.

❑ Will it serve your ego or drive biz dev? Arvind Rajan spent many uncomfortable hours at swanky tech gatherings until he realized, "It doesn't make a difference to my success or failure at work."

❑ Did it pay off before? Write down the new business contacts, or even contracts, from the past couple years of events and conferences you've attended. It will quickly become clear which were valuable and which were a waste of time. Then you can build your calendar.

❑ Is it a need-to-go event in your field? If so, make it count: book tons of meetings, chunk your time, and psych yourself up. This is where social media is incredibly helpful. Some events have a private Facebook group for attendees, or an "alumni" listserv that keeps connections growing throughout the years.

❑ Is there a chance to build your team? SheFinds founder Michelle Madhok looks at it from a holistic standpoint: "I'll go to an event because a decision maker is there, or if I can go with one of my staffers. If we're going to go and use our energy, we better get as much out of it."

❑ Will it pay off in the future? "It's just like in budgeting," says Amanda Clayman. "Review what happened, predict what's going to come up, and then come up with a plan for it."

❑ Last but not least: Does it pay? Kate Gardiner, veteran of many bro-heavy New York and Silicon Valley media conferences, believes if you are being paid to speak, consult, or add value, you will be more purposeful in a room. And you will be much less anxious because you will know your job.

The Power of Being Ambivalently Ambitious

When I sold this book and realized I was actually going to be a published author, I was thrilled and proud. But ten minutes later, I had an anxiety attack. I told my husband, "I'm going to have to get on lots of planes and hold lots of book events to promote it. I'm going to have to *ask* people to help me!"

I think perhaps out of all the moments in our eleven-year marriage, this was the one instance in which my husband truly thought I was insane. "So why the hell did you do it?" he asked, honestly flummoxed.

So why did I?

It was my goal to write a book for us hermits, introverts, and anxious people who struggle with success and do battle with our ambition.

But once I had the idea and set my mind to it, I needed a publisher to publish it. And every day of writing the book, my anticipatory anxiety has been high, thinking of how much I'm going to hate getting out there (getting on those flights won't be any easier . . .) and promoting the book. I dread its success as much as its failure.

If you have made it this far in the book, I know you can relate to this ambivalence. Your ambition and creative energy drive you and set you apart. And yet every time you need to push yourself outside your introvert or hermit comfort zone, you want to hide. And, because you're not going to magically cure your ambivalence or introverted nature, and as long as you retain your wonderful ambition, every day might present a new opportunity for conflict because *each step forward in your career will demand you leave you hermitage and push against your introversion*. And with each step forward, your Technicolor feelings will feel less like a burden and more like a resource.

The good news is, once you have tools and strategies to get out there, you'll be more resilient. Don't be afraid to push yourself, when it's worth it.

See you in the bathroom.

CONCLUSION

On my weekly podcast, I always ask my guests, "When is the last time you hid in the bathroom?"

The more extroverted think it's an amusing question. Their experiences are situational, like getting away from their whiny kids or surreptitiously checking their cell phones during a meeting.

The guests who struggle with shyness and introversion understand the question instinctively. Daily, their ambition clashes with their anxiety. A work presentation or speech at a conference becomes a minefield. Though they are great contributors and coworkers, they need their own space to get work done.

And yet most of us work in environments where we have to sneak into the lactation room or book a fake meeting just to get some alone time, or wait until we have a major life event like a baby in order to work from home on a regular basis. We hide in the bathroom if we're feeling emotional, and would more likely engage in a trust fall with our boss than admit that we have an anxiety disorder.

By now, you know that by tuning in, you can pay attention to the patterns in your own work life about what works and what doesn't, and figure out if it's possible to set up your life in a way that fits. If you're a powerful entrepreneur, it's easy. But what about the rest of us? Who said it's okay to ask to work from home without expecting a ding on career advancement? Most of us, myself included, can't ignore pushback from our managers, clients, and colleagues, no matter how subtle it may be.

There's a simple answer, but it's not easy: work needs to catch up with us.

In the twenty-first century, human capital is the most valuable resource in our economy. As we recognize neurological and emotional diversity in all its forms, workplace culture needs to begin to make room for the Technicolor range of emotion. Although so much has been done (rightly) to promote diversity at work, there's a giant hole in the understanding of how temperament and emotions play not just into our daily grind at the office, but into the very trajectory of success.

Think of all the talent companies lose because hermits need more control over their place, pace, and space. Think of all the potentially great entrepreneurs who feel discouraged from starting their businesses because "getting out there" is a trial. When one employee leaves a job, the typical cost of replacement is three months of salary. Think of the cost when a whole slice of the population struggles with the dominant workplace paradigm.

Recently, I've begun to think about the power of autonomy as it affects my own family. My eight-year-old son, Asa, has always had difficulty at school. It's hard for him to sit still. When he's passionate about a project, he gets obsessed. Small-group projects, he says, are the worst. (Wonder where he got all that?)

For three years, we changed his schools, hoping to find the right fit. Finally we did. In his current classroom, he has the ability to dialogue with his teachers when he needs a moment to manage his anxiety or is having trouble working in a group. He can take the space he needs, at the pace he needs.

School is changing to better fit the needs of students all along the temperament and neurological spectrum. It's my fondest wish that managers and HR professionals also begin to recognize the ambivalence and inner conflict that many insanely talented people feel. Because when they get the space they need, great employees have no reason to quit or feel miserable.

When I lived in Los Angeles, I often worked at the Santa Monica WeWork, the hippest coworking space I can imagine. Although the crowd made me feel old and extremely uncool, I loved experiencing the new and revolutionary optional office. People were only at WeWork because they wanted to be there. No one tracked their comings and goings, whether they were part of a four-person team or employed at a multinational corporation. Now the shared workplace is booming: in 2005, there was one coworking space in the United States. Today, there over seven thousand spaces globally, with thousands more added each year. It's not for everyone, but for introverts and hermits, a coworking space offers a delicious cocktail of freedom and structure.

Introversion, anxiety, and hiding in the bathroom are not weaknesses. They can, in fact, be the keys to your strength and success as a businessperson, whether it's using your sensitivity to attune to clients, your anxiety to be a better boss, or your need for space to forge new and interesting paths. They can help you attune to yourself, making your business life a more holistic part of your personal beliefs and goals. And, as a self-accepting hermit or introvert, you can show the business world how great things happen when teams are truly diverse and team members can be honest about who they truly are.

ACKNOWLEDGMENTS

To my editor Alieza Schvimer, thank you for seeing this book through, making it better, and always taking my anxious phone calls! Thanks to the wonderful team at HarperCollins: Lisa Sharkey, Lynn Grady, Michael Barrs and Kendra Newton, Lauren Janiec and Shelby Meizlik, Stephanie Vallejo, Jeanne Reina, and Paula Szafranski.

Thank you to the incredible Lizzie Skurnick: editor extraordinaire, fellow toddler mom, and wonderful creative partner.

I'm grateful to my wonderful agent, Lorin Rees, for both years of great conversations and friendship and also for assuring me always that the book proposal was "getting close." Thanks to Seth Schulman for helping get the book idea ready for the light of day.

To my wonderful husband, Nicco, for Saturdays, and to Jessie Nunez, who I truly depend on and who is a gift in our lives. We are blessed to have you as well as the incredible teachers who provide such a strong foundation for Asa, Tom, and JJ.

More thanks to:

To Christina Vuleta, Lilly Knoepp, and the team at *Forbes*, thank you for supporting the Hiding in the Bathroom podcast! To Molly Beck: you helped me start this all. The team at Podcast Garage in

Boston offer the very best place to podcast and think about all matters *Hiding in the Bathroom*.

To Susan Cain for writing *Quiet* and continuing the conversation about introversion at her wonderful website, QuietRev.com.

To my sisters in work and life: Julia LeStage, Rebecca Harley, Andrea Sparrey, Hillary Moglen, Amy Farley, Chrysula Winegar, Emily McKhann, Kristin Chalmers, Samantha Ettus, Camille Preston, Meighan Stone, Tanya Tarr, Susan McPherson, and Cali Yost, and of course my real sisters Georgia Aarons and Gabrielle Eisele who I love and treasure. And to the women of The Li.st for wisdom always.

To Christine Koh, what can I say? Every day you teach me so much and make me laugh.

To Jen Vento, my partner at work.

To Kaitlyn Dowling. I still miss you.

To Lisa Stone, for being the best role model.

To Dr. Carol Birnbaum, for everything.

To Donna Curry, who asked me to give the Women's Launchpad Keynote and changed my life.

To the smart people who lent their wisdom to the book: Amanda Clayman, Claire Shipman, Carrie Kerpen, Cari Sommer, Dr. Kim Leary, Kenny Lao, Morgan Shanahan, Naama Bloom, Christina Wallace, Sara Critchfield, Elan Morgan, Cheryl Contee, Mitra Kalita, Ana Flores, Anil Dash, Cal Newport, Anne Greenwood, Lauren Bacon, Alicia Lutes, Bea Arthur, Lane Wood, Courtney Nichols Gould, Nilofer Merchant, Jessica Jackley, Rhonesha Byng, Meredith Fineman, Gina Bianchini, Arvind Rajan, Dr. Hannah Riley Bowles, Talia Borodin, Kelsey Wirth, Aaron Sherinian, Steve Cunningham, Erica Keswin, Alicia Chevalier, Leah Ginsberg, Michael Ansara, Leah Russin, Kathryn Schotthoefer, Katie Orenstein, Maisie Pollard, Stephanie Goodell, Yalda Uhls, Reverend Claire Feingold Thoryn, Elisa Camahort Page, Tereza Nemessanyi, Stew Friedman, Dr. Ellen Hendriksen, Kate Gardiner, Juliette Kayyem,

Alan Dandron, Maryella Gockel, Lindy Huang Werges, Britt Bravo, and Clelia Peters.

And to my very first bosses, who taught me so much: Sarah Eaton, Betty Hudson, Nancy Evans (for introducing me to *Composing a Life* years ago) Selia Bellanca, and to my first clients Ellen Galinsky and Leslie Tullio, who took a chance.

Finally, a huge thank you to my children Asa, Tom, and Josephine, who dealt with way too many hours of mommy buried in her laptop. I love you so much.

NOTES

CHAPTER 1

1. H. Anderson, "Never Heard of FOMO? You're So Missing Out," *Observer*, April 16, 2011. https://en.wikipedia.org/wiki/Fear_of_missing_out.
2. Cal Newport, M.D., personal interview by Morra Aarons-Mele, *Hiding in the Bathroom* podcast episode, Forbes One Production, January 4, 2017.
3. J. E. Reich, "Chimamanda Ngozi Adichie Quietly Gave Birth, Refused to 'Perform Pregnancy,'" *Jezebel*, Gizmodo Media Group, July 5, 2016. http://jezebel.com/chimamanda-ngozi-adichie-quietly-gave-birth-refused-to-1783171806.
4. Y. Yamamiya, T. F. Cash, S. E. Melnyk, H. D. Posavac, and S. S. Posavac, "Women's Exposure to Thin-and-Beautiful Media Images: Body Image Effects of Media Ideal Internalization and Impact-Reduction Interventions," *Body Image* 2(1): 74–80. PMID: 18089176 DOI: 10.1016/j.bodyim.2004.11.001.
5. Ann Friedman, "Shine Theory: Why Powerful Women Make the Greatest Friends," *New York*, May 31, 2013. http://nymag.com/thecut/2013/05/shine-theory-how-to-stop-female-competition.html.

CHAPTER 2

1. Work+Life Fit is trademarked property of FlexStrategy Group/Work+Life Fit Inc. and is used with permission.
2. Vox Creative and Cadillac, "Where KIVA Founder Jessica Jackley Works and Finds Balance with Her Family," Vox Media, Inc., 2017. http://www.theverge.com/sponsored/8379807/jessica-jackley.

CHAPTER 3

1. Giovanni B. Cassano, M.D., Nicolò Baldini Rossi, M.D., and Stefano Pini, M.D., "Psychopharmacology of Anxiety Disorders," *Dialogues in Clinical Neuroscience* 4(3): 271–285, Sept. 2002. PMCID: PMC3181684.
2. Vanessa Coppard-Queensland, "Globally, 1 in 13 Suffers from Anxiety," *Fu-*

turity, Sept. 5, 2012.   http://www.futurity.org/globally-1-in-13-suffers-from
-anxiety/.

3. Thomas A. Richards, "What Is Social Anxiety?," *Social Anxiety Institute,*
2017. https://socialanxietyinstitute.org/what-is-social-anxiety.

4. Giovanni B. Cassano, M.D., Nicolò Baldini Rossi, M.D., and Stefano Pini,
M.D., "Psychopharmacology of Anxiety Disorders," *Dialogues in Clinical
Neuroscience* 4(3): 271–285, Sept. 2002. PMCID: PMC3181684.

5. A.D.A.M., Inc., "Anxiety In-Depth Report," *New York Times,* 2008. http://
www.nytimes.com/health/guides/symptoms/stress-and-anxiety/print.html.

6. Medco Health Solutions, Inc., "America's State of Mind," *Medco Health Solutions, Inc.* (n.d.).   http://apps.who.int/medicinedocs/documents/s19032en
/s19032en.pdf.

7. Ibid.

8. Postpartum Progress Inc., "Statistics," Postpartum Progress Inc., 2016.
http://postpartumprogress.org/the-facts-about-postpartum-depression/.

9. Anxiety and Depression Association of America, "Therapy," *ADAA,* 2010–
2016. https://www.adaa.org/finding-help/treatment/therapy.

10. Shian-Ling Keng, Moria J. Smoski, and Clive J. Robins, "Effects of Mindfulness on Psychological Health: A Review of Empirical Studies," May 13,
2013, *Clinical Psychology Review* (6): 1041–1056, Aug. 31, 2011. doi: 10.1016/j
.cpr.2011.04.006.

11. Y. Tibi-Elhanany and S. G.Shamay-Tsoory, "Social Cognition in Social Anxiety: First Evidence for Increased Empathic Abilities," *Israel Journal of Psy-
chiatry and Related Sciences* 48(2): 98–106, 2011. PMID: 22120444. https://
www.ncbi.nlm.nih.gov/pubmed/22120444.

12. Ellen Hendriksen, "The Differences Between Introversion and Social Anxiety," Quiet Revolution, 2017. http://www.quietrev.com/the-4-differences
-between-introversion-and-social-anxiety/.

CHAPTER 4

1. Global Workplace Analytics, "Latest Telecommuting Statistics," Global-
WorkPlaceAnalytics.com, 2016.   http://globalworkplaceanalytics.com/tel
ecommuting-statistics.

2. Laura Vanderkam, "Why and How Managers Should Help Workers Set
Boundaries, *Fortune,* April 8, 2015. http://fortune.com/2015/04/08/work-life-
setting-boundaries/.

3. KJ Dell'Antonia, "Am I Introverted or Just Rude?," *New York Times,* Sept. 24,
2016.   http://www.nytimes.com/2016/09/25/opinion/sunday/am-i-introverted
-or-just-rude.html.

4. Nicholas Epley and Juliana Schroeder, "Mistakenly Seeking Solitude," *Journal of Experimental Psychology: General* 143(5), Oct. 2014, 1980–1999. http://
dx.doi.org/10.1037/a0037323.

5. Eric Jaffe. "The Psychological Study of Smiling," Association for Psychological Science, Dec. 2010. http://www.psychologicalscience.org/index.php/pub
lications/observer/2010/December-10/the-psychological-study-of-smiling
.html.

6. Jessica Amortegui, "Why Finding Meaning at Work Is More Important

Than Feeling Happy," *Fast Company & Inc.*, June 24, 2014. https://www.fastcompany.com/3032126/how-to-find-meaning-during-your-pursuit-of-happiness-at-work.

7. Nicholas Epley and Juliana Schroeder, "Mistakenly Seeking Solitude," *Journal of Experimental Psychology: General* 143(5), Oct. 2014, 1980–1999. http://dx.doi.org/10.1037/a0037323.

8. Susan Dominus, "Is Giving the Secret to Getting Ahead?," *New York Times*, March 27, 2013. http://www.nytimes.com/2013/03/31/magazine/is-giving-the-secret-to-getting-ahead.html.

CHAPTER 5

1. Ryan Westwood, "What Traits Do We Need to Succeed as Entrepreneurs?," *Forbes*, Sept. 4, 2015. http://www.forbes.com/sites/ryanwestwood/2015/09/04/what-traits-Do-we-Need-to-succeed-as-entrepreneurs/#60401e127f8f.

2. Krista Tippett, "James Doty—the Magic Shop of the Brain," *On Being*, Feb. 11, 2016. https://www.onbeing.org/programs/james-doty-the-magic-shop-of-the-brain/.

CHAPTER 6

1. Darlene Lancer, "What Are Personal Boundaries? How Do I Get Some?," *Psych Central*. https://psychcentral.com/lib/what-are-personal-boundaries-how-do-i-get-some/.

CHAPTER 8

1. Cal Newport, "Quit Social Media. Your Career May Depend on It," *New York Times*, Nov. 19, 2016. http://www.nytimes.com/2016/11/20/jobs/quit-social-media-your-career-may-depend-on-it.html.

2. Crystal Martin, "An App to Help Black Women with Hair Care," *New York Times*, Dec. 29, 2016, p. D5. http://www.nytimes.com/2016/12/26/fashion/black-hair-care-app-swivel.html.

3. Maeve Duggan, "Demographics of Social Media Users," *Pew Research Center, Washington, D.C.*, Aug. 19, 2015. http://www.pewinternet.org/2015/08/19/the-demographics-of-social-media-users/.

4. Georgina Pearce, "100 Women 2016: How Women Are Winning Online," *BBC News*, December 8, 2016. http://www.bbc.com/news/world-37255004. Lisa Witter and Lisa Chen, "The She Spot: Why Women Are the Market for Changing the World—and How to Reach Them," San Francisco: Berrett-Koehler Publishers, June 1, 2008.

CHAPTER 9

1. Jess Hempel, "A Unicorn Is the Last Thing This Web 2.0 Survivor Wants," *Wired Business*, Condé Nast, Feb. 29, 2016. https://www.wired.com/2016/02/unicorn-last-thing-web-2-0-survivor-wants/.

2. Donna Maria Coles Johnson, "7 Ways to Avoid Handmade Business Burnout," *Handmade Business, Small Business Trends LLC.*, Aug. 4, 2016. https://smallbiztrends.com/2016/08/how-to-avoid-burnout-handmade-business.html.

CHAPTER 10

1. Maryella Gockel, EY Global Flexibility Leader, *Personal Interview* by Morra Aarons-Mele, Nov. 9, 2016.

2. Jim Harter, Sangeeta Agrawal, and Susan Sorenson, "Most U.S. Workers See Upside to Staying Connected to Work," *Gallup*, April 30, 2014. http://www.gallup.com/poll/168794/workers-upside-staying-connected-work.aspx.

3. Sara Holoubek, "I'll Be Online Later," LinkedIn Corporation, Oct. 10, 2016. https://www.linkedin.com/pulse/ill-online-later-sara-holoubek.

4. Jody Thompson and Cali Ressler, "3 Ways to Change Toxic Tendencies at Work," *Management Innovation eXchange*, Nov. 20, 2013. http://www.managementexchange.com/blog/3-ways-change-toxic-tendencies-work.

5. Phil Montero, "For Sun Microsystems, Open Work Is Working," *Anywhere Office*, Sept. 12, 2008. http://theanywhereoffice.com/mobile-work/for-sun-microsystems-open-work-is-working.htm.

6. Sara Sutton Fell, "Office, Schmoffice: How 3 Big-Name Companies Succeed with Remote Working," *Entrepreneur Media, Inc,* March 7, 2016. https://www.entrepreneur.com/article/270585.

7. Katheryn Reynolds-Lewis, "How Men Flex," *Working Mother, Bonnier Corporation Company,* Oct. 18, 2016. http://www.workingmother.com/content/how-men-flex.

8. Jessica Stillman, "Red Flags That New Job Will Give You No Work-Life Balance," *Baltimore Sun,* Oct. 28, 2016. http://www.baltimoresun.com/business/success/inc/tca-red-flags-that-new-job-will-give-you-no-work-life-balance-20161028-story.html.

9. Jenna Goudreau, "The Happiest Jobs for Working Moms," *Forbes,* May 6, 2011. http://www.forbes.com/sites/jennagoudreau/2011/05/06/the-happiest-jobs-for-working-moms/#7a09747d25d1.

10. Med Reps, "Love It or Leave It: Medical Sales Job Satisfaction Study," featured in On the Job, *MedReps,* Oct. 4, 2013. https://www.medreps.com/medical-sales-careers/love-it-or-leave-it-medical-sales-job-satisfaction-study/.

11. George Musser, "The Origin of Cubicles and the Open-Plan Office," *Scientific American,* Aug. 17, 2009. https://www.scientificamerican.com/article/the-origin-of-cubicles-an/.

12. Vinesh G. Oommen, Mike Knowles, and Isabella Zhao, "Should Health Service Managers Embrace Open Plan Work Environments? A Review," *Asia Pacific Journal of Health Management* 3(2): 37–43.

13. Nanette Fondas, "How Women and Men Use Flexible Work Policies Differently," *Atlantic,* July 19, 2013. http://www.theatlantic.com/sexes/archive/2013/07/how-women-and-men-use-flexible-work-policies-differently/277954/.

14. Pamela Stone and Lisa Ackerly-Hernandez, "The All-or-Nothing Workplace: Flexibility Stigma and 'Opting Out' Among Professional-Managerial Women," *Journal of Social Issues* 69: 235–256, June 12, 2013. doi:10.1111/josi.12013.

CHAPTER 11

1. Hannah Riley Bowles and Kathleen L. McGinn, "When Does Gender Matter in Negotiation?," *John F. Kennedy School of Government Harvard University Faculty*

Research Working Papers Series RWP02–036, Sept. 2002). https://research.hks .harvard.edu/publications/getFile.aspx?Id=51.

2. Katie Orenstein, "Own Your Own Expertise," http://www.theopedproject .org/. Used with permission.

CHAPTER 12

1. Natalie Reynolds, "Deal or No Deal? Five Common Mistakes People Make When Negotiating Deals," *Guardian News and Media Limited,* April 28, 2014. https://www.theguardian.com/women-in-leadership/2014/apr/28/five-com mon-mistakes-made-by-negotiators.

2. Tanya Tarr, "Negotiate This!" negotiate-this.com, Jan. 17, 2017.

3. Linda Babcock and Sara Laschever, "Women Don't Ask: Negotiation and the Gender Divide," Princeton, NJ: Princeton University Press, 2003.

4. Olga Khazan, "Women Know When Negotiating Isn't Worth It," *Atlantic,* Jan. 6, 2017. https://www.theatlantic.com/business/archive/2017/01/women -negotiating/512174/.

5. Beth Fisher-Yoshida, "Climate Change and the Need for Collaboration," in P. T. Coleman, M. Deutsch, and E. C. Marcus, eds., *The Handbook of Conflict Resolution: Theory and Practice.* San Francisco: Jossey-Bass, *2014.* https://beth fisheryoshida.wordpress.com/tag/deutschs-crude-law-of-social-relations/.

CHAPTER 13

1. Wayne E. Baker, *Achieving Success Through Social Capital.* New York: John Wiley & Sons, Inc., 2000.

2. Ibid.

3. Ibid., p. 20.

4. Wayne E. Baker, *Achieving Success Through Social Capital,* New York: John Wiley & Sons, 2000, p. 20.

5. Christopher E. Beaudoin, "Explaining the Relationship Between Internet Use and Interpersonal Trust: Taking into Account Motivation and Information Overload," *Journal of Computer-Mediated Communication Association* 13, 2008, 550–568. doi:10.1111/j.1083–6101.2008.00410.x.

CHAPTER 14

1. Stephanie Pappas, "Why You Should Smile at Strangers," *Live Science— PURCH,* May 25, 2012. http://www.livescience.com/20578-social-connec tion-smile-strangers.html.

ABOUT THE AUTHOR

MORRA AARONS-MELE is the founder of the award-winning social impact agency Women Online, hosts the *Forbes* podcast *Hiding in the Bathroom,* and created the influencer network the Mission List. She was founding political director of BlogHer.com, and has written for the *Harvard Business Review,* the Huffington Post, MomsRising, the *Wall Street Journal,* the *New York Times,* and the *Guardian.* She has lectured at the Yale Women's Campaign School, the Harvard Kennedy School, and at the World Economic Forum for Young Global Leaders. Aarons-Mele is a graduate of Brown University and the Harvard Kennedy School, and lives in her pajamas in Boston, Massachusetts.